# Navigating Neurodiversity:

## My Journey as a Twice Exceptional Adult

John Truitt

Deborah Gennarelli, M.Ed.

**Gifted**
UNLIMITED

Edited by: William Beuscher
Interior design: The Printed Page
Cover design: Kelly Crimi

Published by
Gifted Unlimited, LLC
12340 U.S. Highway 42, No. 453
Goshen, KY 40026
www.giftedunlimitedllc.com

© 2024 by John Truitt and Deborah Gennarelli

ISBN: 978-1-953360-380

At the time of this book's publication, all facts and figures cited are the most current available. All telephone numbers, addresses, and website URLs are accurate and active; all publications, organizations, websites, and other resources exist as described in this book; and all have been verified as of the time this book went to press. The author(s) and Gifted Unlimited make no warranty or guarantee concerning the information and materials given out by organizations or content found at websites, and we are not responsible for any changes that occur after this book's publication. If you find an error or believe that a resource listed here is not as described, please contact Gifted Unlimited.

# Dedication

*This book is dedicated to all diagnosed and undiagnosed twice-exceptional people.*

*It is our sincere hope that it helps you with your journey.*

# Acknowledgments

We would like to express our sincere appreciation to our publisher Molly Isaacs-McLeod and Gifted Unlimited, LLC for seeing the importance of sharing the story of a twice-exceptional adult like John. There are many books on the market today about gifted and 2e children, but not many are about twice-exceptional adults.

John would like to thank:

- ○ His wife and friend Ashley Truitt for her unwavering love, kindness, and immediate acceptance of his diagnosis.
- ○ Pierce and Fowler Knight. The former for his lifelong friendship and brotherhood. The latter for her resolute support and understanding. She has become a sister to me.
- ○ His four parents-dad Southworth, Joyce, his mother, and father.
- ○ His brother Bryan for always being there and being a great brother and friend.
- ○ Marvin, Judy, and Marc Knight. Without them he would never have made it this far.
- ○ Deb Gennarelli because without her compassion, dedication, and encouragement, this book would have never been written.
- ○ Dr. Stuart Robinson for showing him the pathway to happiness.
- ○ His Mamaw and Papaw Grantham. He wishes they were here to witness the completion of this book.

- Nic, Matt, Rosy, Capeci, Lobo, Chief, and my brothers from Bravo Company 4/87 25th Infantry (light) for over 30 years of friendship and helping him get through his recent and hardest times.

- Gus and Brian for their friendship, helping to keep him stable, and for all the damn good times.

- Brandon for being there and opening his home when it was needed most.

- Bill Mimms for his friendship, comradery, and fun times.

- Scott Mackinaw for his commitment to our foundation.

- Emily, Emilia, and his kids at Heron School. His experiences there have truly been lifesaving.

- His ever-faithful canine companion Cassidy. She never leaves his side.

- And his many friends and advocates and supporters throughout the years.

◇◇◇

Deb would like to thank:

- All the educators, parents, and individuals who are advocates for 2e students. With their support, this special group of children can thrive in schools and at home.

- Brian B., Bryan S., Gus, Matt, Nick, Pierce, Fowler, Emily Neihaus, Dr. Stuart Robinson, John's parents, and Ashley Truitt for their time to speak with her about their relationships with John. They are *all* truly beautiful people.

- Her family Bob, Nicole, Noah, and Milo. Their love and encouragement made writing another book a joy.

- John for allowing her to support his dream of helping other twice-exceptional people. She found his intelligence, kindness, and honesty a pleasure to experience during the writing process. Everything John provides for those he works with and supports is not only informative but enlightening. Deb is delighted she has made a life-long friend.

# Contents

# Foreword

In the many years I have practiced as a licensed psychologist, it still troubles me that the general public views autistic individuals as different 'bad' instead of different 'good'. Much of this perception comes from seeing overexaggerated characters on television or in movies that project a stereotype of what a neurodiverse person is like. This is unfortunate because no two people are alike, and this is certainly true of people with developmental or learning differences.

I specialize in diagnosing and treating adults with autism, ADHD, dyslexia, and other learning differences and the anxiety that accompanies these conditions. I provide neuropsychological testing, coaching, counseling, and therapy to my patients so they not only can cope, but they can "own" their challenges and be *proud* of their differences. As a therapist, I also work closely with patients' primary care or family physicians, neurologists, and psychiatrists to improve the quality of care provided. I know a cognitive deficit can be frustrating, sad, and unfair. But trying to live a life without ever recognizing one's passion would be downright tragic!

I am excited *Navigating Neurodiversity: My Journey as a Twice Exceptional Adult* has been published because there are few books available today about twice exceptional adults. John Truitt's exceptional story, including being diagnosed 2e later in life, and Deborah Gennarelli's background as a gifted/2e specialist and author of another book on twice-exceptional boys, will help readers understand that every individual should be allowed to reach their fullest potential, regardless of developmental or learning differences. We don't tell people in wheelchairs to "try harder" to walk, or people who can't see to "try harder" to see. If someone has poor vision, we don't consider them lazy if they try harder, but they still can't see, and we certainly don't consider them stupid: we give them glasses. So why are we telling neurodiverse people to "try harder" to stop procrastinating, "try harder" to stay focused, "try harder" to be on time, "try harder" to not get anxious, and "try harder" to not worry so much about being perfect. The list can go on and on. With a broad-based approach to testing, diagnosing, therapy, counseling, and coaching, an adult can return to college or work with proper accommodations, a new level of confidence, and self-esteem.

I met John Truitt several years ago after his marriage counselor thought he might be 'on the spectrum' or autistic. Until this time in his life—he was forty-five years old—

John was told he was like everyone else. However, every minor setback he experienced reminded him he was different.

Neurotypicals have a strong need to conform. This need is so strong that a large portion of the American public have a fear of being different. Neurodiverse individuals respond by *masking* or pretending to be 'normal'. This usually results in failed attempts to 'fit in' which is why so many neurodiverse adults develop the belief that they are 'different-bad', or experience rejection sensitive dysphoria (RSD). John, however, is the exception. Unlike other neurodiverse individuals, he has developed the self-esteem that comes with accepting that he is 'different-good'. John is dedicated to passing on this gift of self-acceptance to other 2es, including individuals on the spectrum, with ADHD, or with other learning differences.

Note: More about masking will be addressed Chapter 1.

After several days of thorough testing, John was identified as gifted with autism and dyslexia. He discovered that his slow processing speed was the catalyst for many of his issues. Individuals like John learn that their superior language processing skills can rapidly deteriorate when confronted with a stressful situation. They lose the ability to process what someone else is saying as fast as they are saying it; they cannot formulate a response fast enough to keep up. Over time, they become conflict avoidant. They may even be prone to anticipate confrontations. They may get defensive or even confrontational themselves, even though the neurotypical that started the conversation wasn't being confrontational in the first place. This self-fulfilling prophecy can be considered *autistic paranoia*. John finds that overcoming his autistic paranoia takes hyper-focusing and overconcentrating. By the end of a day of conversing with neurotypical colleagues, co-workers, supervisors, vendors, advisors, students, faculty, and others, he is usually too exhausted to enjoy life. Attending a family wedding over a weekend will often require taking a Monday off to recover.

Through therapy, counseling, and coaching, John learned many things that helped with his communication. He realized he was mixing up emotions because he couldn't recognize them. Is that person angry, or anxious, or sad? He would assume a person's emotion was one thing when it was something else entirely. This led to reacting to an individual inappropriately. John would over-rely on verbal communication since he couldn't figure out non-verbal communication.

Many adults on the spectrum consider their advanced intelligence one of their few positive features. They often believe that to ask an individual how they feel, e.g., if they are angry or anxious, places them at risk of being perceived as 'stupid' (because they are focused on intellect and uncomfortable with emotional communication). Therefore, they don't ask. They guess instead and end up being wrong more often than not.

'Chit chat' is another 'fitting in' challenge. John will tell you how frustrating it is to attempt to participate in 'small talk'. One of John's major strengths is his cognitive inflexibility, committed to thorough examination of an idea at hand. This cognitive talent allows him to develop intense interests and use inductive reasoning to find creative solutions to complex problems. It also causes him to resist changing a subject during a conversation if he is still interested in the topic or if he has more information to contribute. The feeling he experiences is similar to how we feel when someone plays a song on a piano but stops before playing the last note. Neurotypicals, on the other hand, are usually cognitive-flexible. They don't need as much information about a topic before moving on to the next. They relate time during a conversation to 'fitting in' and even to intimacy: the longer the conversation, the closer they feel to each other. Communicating information is often of secondary importance, but not to John. For John, information always comes first: why else would people talk to each other? This is one more challenge John experiences on a daily basis, minute-to-minute, hour-to- hour, day-to-day, week-to-week, year-to-year, continuously throughout his life.

Many patients get evaluated but are not convinced they are autistic. It is helpful to bring together two or more 2e individuals in a joint session, as I did with John, and allow them to speak with one another. After a short time, they realize they are not alone. Other patients, especially older adults in their 40's and older, *embrace* a late diagnosis. They are relieved and even elated to finally have an explanation for why they have felt different their entire life. This is how John felt after his diagnosis and why, on his own now, he has provided support for many 2e people. His efforts to help them see themselves as different 'good' and not different 'bad' has offered life-changing relief for many neuro-diverse people.

Deborah Gennarelli has advocated for 2e children and their families for over thirty years. Her extensive background as a gifted education specialist has put her in the position to help smart students with learning differences see that their strengths are greater than their challenges. Her book *Twice-Exceptional Boys: A Roadmap to Getting it Right* emphasizes how we must get to know and plan for the whole child. When schools and families focus on areas of strength, and not just learning differences, the child is more likely to succeed.

In *Navigating Neurodiversity: My Journey as a Twice-Exceptional Adult*, John and Deborah help readers see the immense strengths that neurodiverse people possess. Some of these include attention to detail, sustained concentration, high quality work, excellent long-term memory with a recall for details, tolerance of repetition and routine, strong logic and analytical skills, and the ability to think 'outside the box'. I discovered early in my meetings with John that he, like Thomas Jefferson and Henry Ford, is always seeing things that can be improved which others have missed.

John, Deborah, and I are a team when it comes to our shared philosophy that every individual deserves a happy and satisfying life. We want others to see John's life as an example that can help one comfortably understand and accept who they are. There may be resistance along their journey, and one may lose a few battles. However, winning the war is what counts.

Stuart N. Robinson, Ph.D.
Licensed Psychologist
Dallas, Texas

# Preface

My journey understanding the world while being twice-exceptional (gifted with one or more learning differences) began when I was 45 years old. After fifteen years of marriage to an intelligent, beautiful, and kind woman, I found myself in counseling with her. Most of our relationship (while we were often successful and had some amazing times) had been an 'ongoing skirmish', and we were both at the end of our tether. After three months of couples therapy and little progress, our counselor expressed that she suspected I was likely 'on the spectrum'- a condition called autism spectrum disorder or ASD.

Quickly my wife and I sought the advice from an expert who dealt specifically with high-functioning adults on the spectrum. While there was no immediate 'magic' after a battery of tests and a great deal of discussion with my doctor, my wife and I had at least a road map to guide us through the first steps of understanding each other. It has now been six years since my diagnosis. While our marriage is not perfect, we now know that we speak two different languages, and it takes time to listen to one another. We no longer argue and the most difficult challenge we face is my occasional meltdown due to overstimulation and anxiety.

This is by no means the beginning of my story. I was born in a small town in Texas in 1972. My father was a dentist who specialized in maxilla-facial orthopedics, orthodontics and

TMD (temporomandibular joint disorder), and my mother was an elementary school teacher with a master's degree in early childhood development. They divorced when I was very young, and both remarried. My stepparents were integral in raising me.

My experiences growing up are not typical of those on the spectrum. I walked and talked (in complete sentences) by the time I was a year old. I never crawled, never spoke 'baby talk', and I could read by the age of three. I socialized well and I was never bullied at school. I scored remarkably high on achievement tests (except calculating math), and I participated in honors classes. I was never considered for special education, which in my opinion would have been an inappropriate label and would have destroyed my confidence.

Nonetheless, there were early indications that I was on the spectrum. Overstimulation, adverse reactions to bright lights, and high-pitched or repetitive sounds (like a smoke alarm going off, or someone chewing gum with their mouth open) all affected my day-to-day life. I could never wear a shirt with a tag or socks with a line across the toe. I had meltdowns that looked like tantrums. I would get in trouble at home, but never at school.

Although I was popular in high school (participated in wrestling, played in a rock band, and dated), there were always some underlying social matters that festered and eventually led to fractured relationships. As an adult, I can develop friendships, but it is often difficult for me to read facial expressions and body language. This often leads to conflict, and I risk losing a new friend or social group.

Neurodiverse individuals have challenges making friends because a large percentage of neurotypicals' communication is nonverbal. As I become better friends with someone or get closer to a partner, it is more difficult for me to understand them and communicate. The people who have known me the longest, and are true friends, know I am not argumentative, difficult, or a bad person. They accommodate me without either of us knowing.

As I have come to learn, *when you meet one person on the spectrum, you have met one person on the spectrum.* We are as individually unique as every neurotypical. There is no 'look' to Asperger's (which I understand is not a relevant term today). But it is the best descriptor for me. It is very offensive when someone says, "You don't look like you are on the spectrum". When I hear this, I respond, "What exactly does autism look like?"; but I would like to say, "Well, you don't look ignorant like a moron, but I guess we are both wrong". I don't want to offend anyone, and I realize that the individual is uninformed about the subject matter.

In addition to autism spectrum disorder, I have been diagnosed with dyslexia (a learning difference that affects reading, spelling, and writing), and dyscalculia (a learning difference that affects calculating math), which led to additional diagnoses. I experience generalized anxiety disorder (feeling guilty over not performing to my self-imposed, overly high standards), obsessive-compulsive disorder (OCD: a mental health disorder characterized by repetitive actions that seem impossible to stop), insomnia, and depression. All of these, coupled with giftedness, can make my life very challenging.

Several years ago, with my wife's help, I began a non-profit organization called On the Spectrum Foundation (www.onthespectrumfoundation.org), which is dedicated to the identification and advocacy of teens and adults who are on the spectrum, as well as those with accompanying conditions such as dyslexia and other learning differences, combined with giftedness: this is termed 'twice exceptional (2e)'. Our goal is to empower people on the autism spectrum and increase awareness of the neurodiverse population's many strengths and talents, and how they can improve society for everybody.

I felt compelled to write about my story as a twice-exceptional adult for several reasons. First, I thought my head was going to explode if I didn't write this book. I knew I had a lot to share that would help others like me. Then I realized that there are few resources available about twice-exceptional adults, especially those on the autism spectrum. I believe it is important to raise awareness that many of us do not seek a cure or want to be 'fixed'. My real goal is to help people understand our limitations and appreciate our strengths. Finally, I would like to help 2e children and teens. I would like to shine a light on how to correctly identify giftedness and learning differences while a child is in school. When I was diagnosed at 45 years old, my entire life shifted for the better. I can now understand how to help myself and explain to others how to support me. If we help twice-exceptional children and teens understand their strengths and limitations and give them the proper support in school and at home, they will learn how to advocate for themselves and lead a more satisfying life.

As I thought about writing this book, I knew I would need help from a professional who understands twice-exceptional individuals. I met Deborah Gennarelli through LinkedIn. She is a former gifted education specialist, now a gifted consultant with her company Smart Strategies. After working with many 2e boys in her teaching career, she wrote *Twice- Exceptional Boys: A Roadmap to Getting it Right* (2022). Deborah discovered that due to lack of proper identification and early planning in the boys' lives, school suddenly became very challenging for them. I knew from her experience working with younger versions of myself that I could trust her to support me as I explained that twice-exceptional individuals are 'different good', not 'different bad'.

This book has three parts. The first part is an introduction. It includes important background information for those who do not know about neurodiversity and autism spectrum disorder (difference). It is still true today that too many healthcare professionals, teachers, and others in the public consider autism as a severe mental illness, falsely illustrated with the image of a 4-year-old wearing a helmet, holding their head while screaming uncontrollably, or as a quirky 'weirdo' character like Sheldon Cooper from the television show *Big Bang Theory*. To help change this perception, readers will learn the history of ASD, general characteristics of Asperger's syndrome, neurodiversity, the differences in boys and girls, the genetics behind autism, and some relevant statistics. The introduction also includes information about important distinctions to be made; classic autism compared to Asperger's; autism compared to giftedness; levels of severity in ASD; the comparison of children to adults with autism spectrum disorder (difference). Finally, this section explains the importance of an appropriate medical diagnosis. By understanding my misdiagnosis—bipolar at 19 years old, and then the correct diagnosis as gifted with autism spectrum disorder (difference) at age 45, others can take the steps to be correctly identified and supported.

Deborah and I are aware of the dynamics of autism, and we prefer modes of acceptance and understanding, rather than seeing a problem which needs a cure. We respect everyone's opinions and unique situations, but we distinctly choose positive dynamics and terminology.

The second part of the book is about my life. I share stories about my family history, schooling, time serving in the military, jobs, and relationships. I feel it is important to communicate how I manage differences like dyslexia, dyscalculia, OCD, insomnia, anxiety, and depression in my everyday life. Although 2e individuals are unique, Deborah and I want the world to focus on strengths, and not dismiss individuals for their limitations. It is our desire that readers will find inspiration as I reflect on the ups and downs of my unique life, explaining how one can create a personal learning curve after diagnosis, and to find happiness and inner fulfillment.

Finally, the third part of the book is called, 'What I know for sure'. This popular phrase, made famous by Oprah Winfrey, has helped many individuals realize they can keep moving forward in their lives regardless of the circumstances. This section begins with a chapter that includes helpful tips for neurotypicals working and living with twice-exceptional adults. It can be challenging living and/or working with someone like me; but gaining a better understanding helps everyone. Readers will also find strategies to help 2e adults feel more fulfilled.

The last part of section three includes a chapter that will help families of 2e children find the right school fit for their child. Deborah's experience as a gifted specialist, working with many 2e students, has enabled her to know what works and what does not work in schools for this special population. She guides parents to ask the right questions of school staff, so mistakes are not made, and a child is not potentially harmed.

One should not assume that the suggestions and strategies given here will work for every 2e person and every type of school. Each individual must determine what works for them, what works for the student at school, and what works for the adult in their workplace. Dr. Temple Grandin is a well-known professor of animal science at Colorado State University, and prominent speaker on both autism and animal behavior, and she signifies with the title of her book: *Different...Not Less* (2021), that we should learn to be comfortable with ourselves. With acceptance and patience, my family, friends, co-workers, and I have all risen to the challenge to better understand what it means to be twice-exceptional.

It is our hope that this book will guide the reader to understand that recognizing the unique differences in people is instrumental to everyone's success at school, work, and home. My experiences as a child and an adult offer perspective to parents of twice exceptional children and other neurotypicals who have spoken only to doctors about autism. My stories fill in the missing pieces that will help readers understand what was beneficial and what was harmful even before my 2e diagnosis. I know that if one can 'weather the storms' that often come with being twice- exceptional or living with someone who is twice-exceptional, the outcomes can be awe-inspiring!

# PART 1:
# Introduction

*"Watch out, you might get what you're after"*
~Talking Heads

# What is Neurodiversity?

Throughout this book you will see the terms *neurotypical*, *neurodiverse* and *neurodiversity*. It is important to know what they mean, and how society uses them to describe people.

The word neurodiversity refers to the diversity of all people, but it is often used in the context of autism spectrum disorder (ASD). The neurodiversity movement emerged during the 1990's, aiming to increase the acceptance and inclusion of all people while embracing neurological differences.[1] Before that, in 1977, Australian sociologist Judy Singer, also autistic, coined the term neurodiversity to promote equality and inclusion of 'neurological minorities'.[2]

When speaking and writing about neurodiversity, words matter. Neurodiversity advocates encourage inclusive nonjudgmental language. While many disability advocacy organizations prefer person-first language like 'a person with autism', or 'a person with Down Syndrome', some in the autistic community prefer identity-first language such as 'an autistic person'. When one uses first person language, they are saying that there is more to a person than their autism diagnosis. When one uses identify first, the individual shows there is no shame in being autistic. This is often seen as a symbol of pride amongst those in the autism community. Rather than making assumptions, it is best to ask directly about a person's preferred language and how they want to be addressed.[3]

Though 'neurodiversity' was coined in reference to people on the autism spectrum, it has broadened to include additional ways that brains can function. Under the umbrella of neurodiversity there are two subcategories: neurotypical and neurodivergent. Neurotypical describes people who have standard or typical brain processing and behaviors. Being neurotypical often means one does not have to think about how their brain functions or how it manifests in your behaviors because you function in a way that so many other people do.[4] Unlike neurotypical people, neurodivergent people become aware that their brains work differently. They have one or more ways in which their brain functions outside the 'typical way'.[5] These neurodivergent people may thus be diagnosed with autism, ADHD, OCD, dyspraxia, dyslexia, dyscalculia, Tourette's, and even giftedness.

In the past these conditions were treated as problems. But with improved understanding of neurodiversity, we now have better and more appropriate ways of identifying and handling such differences. Neurodiversity advocacy focuses on embracing and celebrating neurodiverse brains, instead of trying to 'fix' them and make them neurotypical. The qualities and traits that neurodivergence creates are not problems, they are unique skills: they are widely varied, and include everything from high perception to strong abilities with computer systems to enhanced creativity.[6]

The acceptance of neurodiversity allows us to appreciate how each of us functions differently. Instead of labelling unique functioning as 'right' or 'wrong, we rather embrace the differences and a broadened sense of creativity and cooperation.[7]

# Chapter 1

# What is Autism Spectrum Disorder?

*"I'm dancing barefoot, heading for a spin-here I go*
*and I don't know why-I spin so ceaselessly."*
~Patti Smith

Autism spectrum disorder (difference) can sometimes go undiagnosed until adulthood, as with me. My diagnosis as gifted with autism did not occur until I was 45 years old. I went to work trying to understand more about myself and all the things that make me different from neurotypicals. I started with trying to understand autism spectrum disorder, or as I prefer to call it, autism spectrum *'difference'*.

## Definition

Today autistic people go to college, work, marry, and raise families. Because of this, school and work environments are more diverse. More and more people are interested in learning about autism, so it is important to start with a definition.

According to the American Psychiatric Association's *Diagnostic and Statistical Manual of Mental Health Disorders* 5th edition (DSM-5), autism spectrum disorder (ASD) is a neurodevelopmental disorder/difference characterized by impaired social communication skills, restrictive and repetitive patterns of behavior, and interests with unusual sensory responses.[8] Individuals with ASD might behave, communicate, interact, and learn in ways that are different from most other people. There is often nothing about how they look or seem that sets them apart from others.[9] Autism is not defined as a single disease, condition, ailment, affliction, or malady, but rather as many related disorders-differences.[10] The autism spectrum is very broad, ranging from socially awkward but otherwise brilliant workers in Silicon Valley, to individuals who will always have to live in a supervised living situation.[11]

## History

Medical professionals have been observing and trying to understand autism for years. In the 1930's, Austrian American physician Leo Kanner and Austrian pediatrician Johann 'Hans' Asperger both focused their research on what is now known as autism spectrum disorder. Leo Kanner borrowed the term 'autism' from Swiss psychiatrist Paul Eugene Bleuler, who coined the term. It comes from the Greek 'autos-', meaning 'self', because those on the spectrum seem the happiest in isolation.[12] Unlike Paul Bleuler, who thought autism was part of the mental disorder schizophrenia, Leo Kanner focused on understanding it in terms of social deficiencies.[13] He defined autism as a hinderance to someone's ability to bond with others. Kanner also felt that this difference appeared very early in life, and he noticed a tendency toward autism in some families.

Hans Asperger had many of the same ideas as Leo Kanner, but he emphasized that the children he observed often displayed marked intelligence.[14] Asperger was excited because the children he studied could describe their interests in detail; they did not display cognitive impairment. Many years later, Asperger's syndrome, a higher-functioning form of autism, was named after him.

Decades have passed since Kanner and Asperger explored autism spectrum disorder. Since their work, scientists and medical practitioners have studied the unique signs and symptoms that individuals diagnosed with ASD can exhibit. It has been established that there is a broad range of signs, symptoms, prognoses, treatments, and outcomes.[15] For this reason, the *Diagnostic Statistical Manual of Mental Disorders* (DSM-5th edition) was updated in 2013, and the term autism was changed to autism spectrum disorder, and Asperger's syndrome was no longer a separate condition.

## Signs and Symptoms

Since mid-2020, there has been a spike in Google searches for the term "neurodivergent." There has also been curiosity about adult autism.[16] The graph from Google Trends clearly shows continued interest in these topics.[17]

*Figure 1.1 Google related searches about neurodiversity*

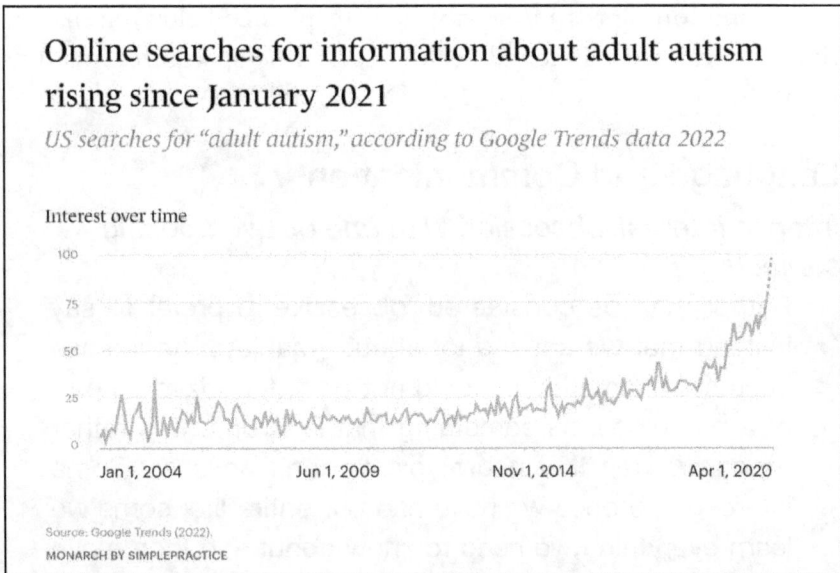

**Online searches for information about adult autism rising since January 2021**

*US searches for "adult autism," according to Google Trends data 2022*

Interest over time

Source: Google Trends (2022).
MONARCH BY SIMPLEPRACTICE

Some of the most popular questions searched are:

- ⭘ What are some of the signs of autism?
- ⭘ Is autism a disability?
- ⭘ What causes autism?
- ⭘ Is autism curable?
- ⭘ Is autism increasing?
- ⭘ Is autism caused by vaccines?

○ Why do people with autism 'stim'? (Stimming refers to self-stimulating behaviors. It is discussed later in this chapter.)

○ Do people with autism have empathy?

Autism is neurological in nature, affecting the brain in four major areas of functioning: language/communication, social skills, sensory systems, and behavior,[18] and so there are specific signs and symptoms to look for to determine if someone may be on the spectrum. (A 'sign' is defined as anything a physician might notice in a patient. A 'symptom' is defined as something the patient notices without the intervention of a medical provider.) The severity of symptoms can vary among individuals, which means autism can look different from person to person.[19] If you feel you or a loved one exhibits any of the more common signs and/or symptoms (explained below), it may be time to speak with a mental health expert who specializes in adults with ASD.

## Language and Communication

### Intense interest/obsession with one or two specific subjects

Rather than be considered 'obsessive', I prefer to say instead that we know a lot about a subject. An intense interest in something should not be categorized as part of a pathology, as something that is wrong. It is rather a positive trait that neurotypicals don't possess. Some interests are ones we have had our entire life; some we learn everything we need to know about and then move onto the next. My areas of interest have always been history (particularly military history), business, music, and medicine. History was special to my dad, and our trips to war museums sparked an early interest in me. After twenty years focused on the Civil War, I shifted to Egyptian, Greek, and Roman history.

When neurodiverse people with ASD begin talking, we tend to lead or dominate the conversation and may appear as a 'know it all'. This leads to social deficits or difficulties.

Unless neurotypicals truly understand us, they may feel we are egocentric and label us as narcissistic or self-centered. This makes it difficult to make and keep friends.

Figures of speech and sarcasm can be especially tricky to detect because the speaker says something different than what they mean. Because we think literally, conversational phrases such as 'my back is against the wall' or 'keep an ear to the ground' are quite puzzling and evoke incongruous pictures in our mind's eye: I see someone with their back literally against a wall or with their ear literally to the ground. I understand the meanings, but I still see the same images—and sometimes laugh! As for sarcasm, one could end up befriending people who are bullies. For example, if someone thinks I am acting bizarre, they may say, "Is it time for your medication?" Covert bullying can include negative joking at someone else's expense. These types of toxic comments are hallmarks of a bully. Our concreteness of thought makes us appear different, and it is perhaps this component that also makes us appear to lack empathy, specifically cognitive empathy.[20]

### *Inability for prosody*

Prosody is the ability to understand the patterns of stress and intonation in a language. Some neurodiverse individuals lack prosody, and they find it difficult to understand what is being communicated. It can lead to a myriad of social communication issues, ranging from embarrassing blunders to accusations of verbal assault. Some neurodiverse people also speak in 'boring' monotones, called 'flat voice', which can be misinterpreted as a lack of interest, lack of intelligence, lack of humor, or lack of emotional response.[21]

As with many of the signs and symptoms of autism, there are some of us who don't have a problem understanding patterns of stress and intonation in language. For example, while working in one of my businesses, I wrote and voiced all the radio and television commercials. I am also asked to speak to groups on occasion: I do not have a flat voice. This dichotomy actually makes me like everyone else: I am good at some things and poor at others.

### Limited facial expressions

If someone has limited facial expressions, it makes it difficult for others to interpret their thoughts and feelings.[22] Autistic and non-autistic people produce facial expressions quite different from 'the norm', so our faces may be essentially speaking a different language. Thus, people can struggle to read each other's expressions, which can lead to less successful social interactions.[23] In addition, our moods are not reflected in our body language, which can be very confusing to a neurotypical. For example, if you and I were speaking, you might see my face as 'flat' and my body language signaling disapproval, when in fact I am indeed happy and excited about our conversation.

## Social Skills

### Missed non-verbal cues

It is estimated that 60%-65% of the way humans communicate with others is through nonverbal behaviors.[24] Neurotypical people organically learn non-verbal cues during childhood, puberty, and adulthood, but neurodiverse people often fail to develop understanding of non-verbal cues. Some examples of such social cues are posture, angling of the body, mirroring (copying a person's body movement), touching (depends on the situation), fidgeting (playing with an object, moving in a chair), facial expression of emotions, proxemics (how close one person is standing to another person), and hand gesturing (talking with one's hands). Hand gestures are challenging because they are not universal: a particular hand gesture which is accepted in America may be inappropriate in another country.[25]

Visiting Europe as a child, I observed two cultures that gesticulate often. Italian and French people point, wave, shrug, and nod to get attention. I grew up learning and expressing myself this way too, which has been a great advantage for me when I communicate with others.

### *Difficulty with Interpersonal Relations*

Those on the spectrum have difficulty interpreting social cues and nuances. We are limited in being able to attribute mental states to others, which is a failure at what is called *Theory of Mind*.[26] Behavior generally results from the interplay of thoughts, intentions, and emotions, and this can be quite different from the reality seen by the neurodivergent.[27] Those on the spectrum often misread social situations because Theory of Mind has not been as fully integrated as it has been with neurotypicals. This can lead others to think we do not possess empathy.

I have often misread social situations that affected relationships. Some examples: I thought people were interested in what I had to say, but then realized that I was the lone voice in a one-sided conversation; I misread a former co-worker's sarcastic sense of humor and face gestures, and so I was not sure of their intent; I was single and dating, I could not read whether a date was ready to leave a place together and get romantic, or just didn't want to give me her phone number. Dating was tough.

People on the spectrum are often thought to lack empathy, however, we can be very empathetic. One must recognize there are three types of empathy: cognitive (related to *Theory of Mind* skills and limitations on executive function), emotional, and compassionate. While it is true that we often have issues with cognitive empathy, once we comprehend what the other person is thinking, we often become very emotional. Then we act to help with compassionate empathy. Think about an empath; they are an emotional sponge. They have a deep connection to the people and events around them.[28] (Personally, I am very much an empath.) One of the reasons why autistic people are seen as lacking emotional empathy is that they don't generally express their empathy in the expected way, with body language, gestures, and statements such as "I'm sorry" or "I understand". An autistic person might express empathy by offering a solution to a problem, or by sharing a similar experience.[29] Also, in studies, autistic people show less cognitive empathy or ability to take the perspective of others than neurotypicals. It is possible that black and white thinking tends to frame things as right or wrong so a different perspective might be dismissed.[30]

Another reason for difficulty with interpersonal relations is poor executive function. This 'management system of the brain' consists of a set of cognitive skills that are needed for self-control and managing behaviors. Many experts believe the human mind contains eight different executive functions; one is emotional regulation.[31] People on the spectrum often have difficulty self-regulating their emotions. Behaviors such as meltdowns, running away from a situation, aggression toward others, abusing oneself, inability to stay calm or process logical information, are all possible and will require help. Personally, the three topics that can still 'wind me up' emotionally are fairness and justice, animal cruelty, and gaslighting. But having learned how to regulate, I stay focused and busy working on something important. I find that having a positive distraction allows me to stop ruminating, relax, and then excel.

*Table 1.1: Eight key executive functions*[32]

| Executive Function | Cognitive Process/ Mental Skills |
|---|---|
| 1. Impulse Control | 1. Think before acting. |
| 2. Emotional Control | 2. Keep feelings in check. |
| 3. Flexible Thinking | 3. Adjust behavior to unexpected changes. |
| 4. Working Memory | 4. Keep key information in mind while using it. |
| 5. Self-Monitoring | 5. Self-awareness to how one is doing in the moment. |
| 6. Planning and Prioritizing | 6. To set and meet goals. |
| 7. Task Iniation | 7. Take action to get started on tasks. |
| 8. Organization | 8. Keep track of things physically and mentally. |

## Sensory Systems:

Children and adults on the autism spectrum may have a different sensory system. This is referred to as sensory integration disorder (SID). Sensory integration is an innate neurobiological process. But people with SID find it difficult to process and respond to sensory information from the environment. One or more senses can be either over-reactive or under-reactive to stimulation.[33] It is thought that this is caused by sensory receptors in the nervous system malfunctioning. Common stimuli like light, noise, and textures may be perceived as too bright, too loud, or too uncomfortable. Because the sensory input with SID is not integrated or organized appropriately in the brain, a varying degree of problems in development, information processing, and behavior may result.[34]

Sensory integration focuses on three basic aspects of sensing: tactile (nerves under the skin send messages to the brain); vestibular (structures in the inner ear detect movement of the head); and proprioceptive (components of muscles, joints and tendons that provide a person with awareness of body position). These awarenesses begin to form at birth and develop into adulthood as one learns to interact with their environment. A person can be hyper-sensitive in one area, like hearing, and hypo-sensitive in another, like touch. Complicating matters even further, in some individuals the sensory sensitivities can change on a day-to-day basis, especially when the person is tired or stressed.[35]

### Dysfunction in the Tactile System[36]

A dysfunctional tactile system may lead to a misperception of touch and/or pain (hyper- or hypo-sensitive) and may lead to self-imposed isolation, general irritability, distractibility, and hyperactivity. Dysfunction in the tactile system can be seen when an individual:

- Withdraws from being touched.
- Refuses to eat certain textured foods.
- Refuses to wear certain types of clothing.
- Complaints about having one's face or hair washed.
- Avoids getting one's hands dirty.
- Uses one's fingertips rather than the whole hand to manipulate objects.

As I was growing up, I could not tolerate tags in shirts and clothing. I had to wear socks that had seams across the top of the foot instead of the end of the stock. I HATED to be tickled or surprised when someone would come up behind me and say "boo"! As an adult, I have great difficulty with bright lights: I began wearing sunglasses outside at twelve years old. Repetitive high- pitched sounds (babies crying, fire alarms) just kill me. These can increase my anxiety and move me to a meltdown.

### Dysfunction in the Vestibular System

The vestibular system is responsible for our sense of balance and spatial orientation. Vestibular *dysfunction*, then, is a disturbance of the body's balance system. When one experiences this, it can be seen as over-responsiveness or under-responsiveness, which can lead to injury from falling, a reduced quality of life, and general discomfort. What to watch for:

○ **Over**-*responsiveness to vestibular stimulation*: One is fearful of ordinary movement activities like playing on swings or slides, climbing stairs, or walking on uneven surfaces. Individuals can appear clumsy. Sensitivity to bright lights, certain sounds, smells, textures, and some tastes can make them overwhelming.

○ **Under**-*responsiveness to vestibular stimulation:* One seeks very intense sensory experiences like jumping and spinning; they may have difficulty recognizing sensations like hunger and pain; they are attracted to loud noises, bright colors or anything that stimulates their senses.

### Dysfunction in the Proprioceptive System:

Proprioception is guided by receptors in the body (skin, muscles, joints) that connect with the brain through the nervous system, so that even without sight a person knows what their body is doing. Vision plays a key role in the ability to sense one's body in space, but it is not necessary for a person to understand body ownership.[37]

Dysfunction in the proprioceptive system occurs when the connections between the brain and other sensory receptor systems in the body break. Most autistic people have some sort of motor difficulty, ranging from an atypical gait while walking to problems with handwriting. However, it is not considered a core trait of autism because this dysfunction can occur in other conditions like Down Syndrome, Cerebral Palsy, and ADHD.[38]

(I don't like watching sports. But I enjoy playing the ones I can. I wrestled in high school, and when I was a kid, I played 'front-yard football' as a linebacker and a running back, but I never caught or threw the ball due to a lack of hand-eye coordination.)

What to watch for:

- ○ Clumsiness
- ○ Tendency to fall
- ○ A lack of body position in space
- ○ Odd body posturing
- ○ Difficulty manipulating small objects, like buttons or snaps
- ○ Eating in a sloppy manner
- ○ Resistance to new motor movement activities
- ○ Need to rest head on desk while working

# Behaviors

## *Stimming*

Many people tap a pen on a table, shake their leg while seated in a meeting, or doodle on paper. These are considered fidgeting behaviors. But when people on the spectrum do this in ways that are less socially acceptable—like hand flapping, rocking back and forth, or repeating sounds or phrases—it is called 'stimming',[39] which is short for 'self-stimulation'. It is a way to regulate stress and emotion or help with sensory processing. The DSM-5 includes stimming as a diagnostic criterion for autism.

> As a child, when I was overstimulated or sick, I would self-sooth by taking deep breaths and slowly letting them out, making a funny 'Ommmm' sound. It worked well. Now, I often rub my hands along the tops of my thighs under the table, say in a business meeting situation. I constantly 'crack my knuckles' too. When I am talking on the phone, I pace in circles or squares during the entire conversation. When I am alone or painting, I do a funny dance/performance thing while listening to music. Finally, driving is a 'macro' stim for me. I can drive hours or days at a time just listening to music or looking outside the car. It helps me think clearly about large topics or problems. Stimming overall helps me with anxiety. By doing these activities, I relax and calm down.

In the ancient Indo-European language of India (Sanskrit), the sound 'Om' or 'Aum' represents Pranava, an original word of power, and is considered an unlimited or eternal sound which represents Absolute Reality. Maybe I was more in touch with Jung's *Theory of Synchronicity* than I knew at the time I self-soothed as a child.

Stimming is not bad behavior, but it is often viewed as hyperactivity or a discipline problem. Punishing or judging an autistic child or adult for stimming can make the situation much worse. Stimming helps autistic individuals manage their behavior. But when stims are disruptive to others like jumping or pacing in school or dangerous (causing injury), they need to be modified. Aggressive behaviors like head-banging, hand biting, self-scratching, and ear clapping are examples of stimming behaviors that require professional intervention to determine the best way to manage them.

### Masking

Masking is the act of camouflaging the way one acts in a social setting. Neurotypical people do it from time to time. For example, they put on a happy face at the grocery store or at the post office. After a brief interaction with someone at these places, they can return to being their authentic self. However, for autistics, masking can become a way of life. The desire to fit in and the pressure to be seen as neurotypical can drive autistic individuals to hide who they really are all the time. They may see it as social survival. They may not feel valued unless they suppress those behaviors that are typically and negatively associated with ASD.[40]

Masking varies depending on moods and behavioral demands and will be different depending on where the individual is at the time, and how comfortable they feel with their surroundings. Here are some examples:[41]

○ *People pleasing:* Often seen as the one in a friendship doing acts of service or giving things away.

○ *Mimicking social behaviors and non-verbal cues:* Attempts to sound and look like those around them, constantly watching others during social interactions, with intense and forced eye contact.

○ *Spending lots of time creating social scripts:* Rehearses conversations, insists on rigid responses to questions, gets overly upset when a conversation doesn't go 'their way'.

○ *Hiding or minimizing interests:* Destroys items they've cherished, refuses to talk about interests they've had in the past.

○ *Suppressing stims:* Replaces usual stims—flapping, spinning in circles, jumping, rocking, etc.—with private behaviors, like self-harm during times of sensory overload; replaces a 'traditional stim' with more 'typical nervous habits' such as chewing fingernails or tapping a pencil.

○ *Pushing through intense sensory discomfort:* Attends a loud concert because a friend invited you to go.

Why do individuals mask? There are a variety of reasons:

○ To feel safe and avoid stigma.
○ To avoid mistreatment or bullying.
○ To succeed at work.
○ To attract a romantic partner.
○ To make friends and other social connections.
○ To fit in or feel a sense of belonging.

It is important to understand the effects of autism masking. While masking may have certain benefits, there are significant costs. Time spent learning neurotypical behaviors, so as to fit in with *other* people's norms, is time not invested in one's unique and unusual personal development. Further, the effort to mimic neurotypical interactions can quickly lead to social overload[42]. Here are some of the effects of regular masking:[43]

○ *Stress and anxiety:* Research shows that stress and anxiety were higher in people who routinely masked autistic traits, compared to those who masked less often.[44]

○ *Depression:* Research also shows that that those who reported masking their autistic traits had symptoms of depression and felt unaccepted by people in their social sphere.[45]

○ *Exhaustion:* Masking consumes huge amounts of energy. Research indicates that women who used masking to satisfy neurotypical standards said they felt exhausted by the constant effort.[46] (This is equally true for men.)

○ *Delayed identification of autism:* People can be so successful at masking that their autism, that it isn't identified until they are much older, can lead to mental health issues because they don't get the support or understanding they need. This is what happened in my case.

○ *Loss of identity:* People who mask their identity, interests, and traits can end up feeling that they no longer know who they really are. Some have said masking feels like self-betrayal; others have said masking makes them feel they're deceiving other people.

### Routines

In general, people on the spectrum live for routine. When these routines change or they are modified, it causes anxiety, which can be extreme. This can impact relationships at school, home, and the workplace. It can cause the person to wonder, "What do I do next now that the routine is changed?" We often enjoy rote tasks because there is a beginning, middle, and end—a clear sense of predictability. Things go much better when the autistic person is involved in the decision making, in the management of the routine.[47] If tasks are assigned by a neurotypical teacher, parent, or boss, they will be perceived as 'busy work' (chores unrelated to their autistic perspective) and rarely will the child or adult execute these tasks. Behavioral outbursts like anger, tantrums or self-injury can occur.

Routines for autistic individuals can sometimes be useful, such as using them as a coping strategy to enable daily functioning. The world can be chaotic, unpredictable, overwhelming, loud, and exhausting. Maintaining a consistent routine or keeping items organized can help life feel more secure and predictable.[48] Routines help the ASD person to deal with depression, anxiety, and uncertainty that can confront us in our daily lives. Routines bring calm and self-regulation to an otherwise anxious mind.[49] Structure and activities serve to remind one that life is not a one-way street and that there is more to it than just thinking about oneself.[50] It means having a purpose in life.

## Sleeping Problems

*Figure 1.2: Sleeping Problems*

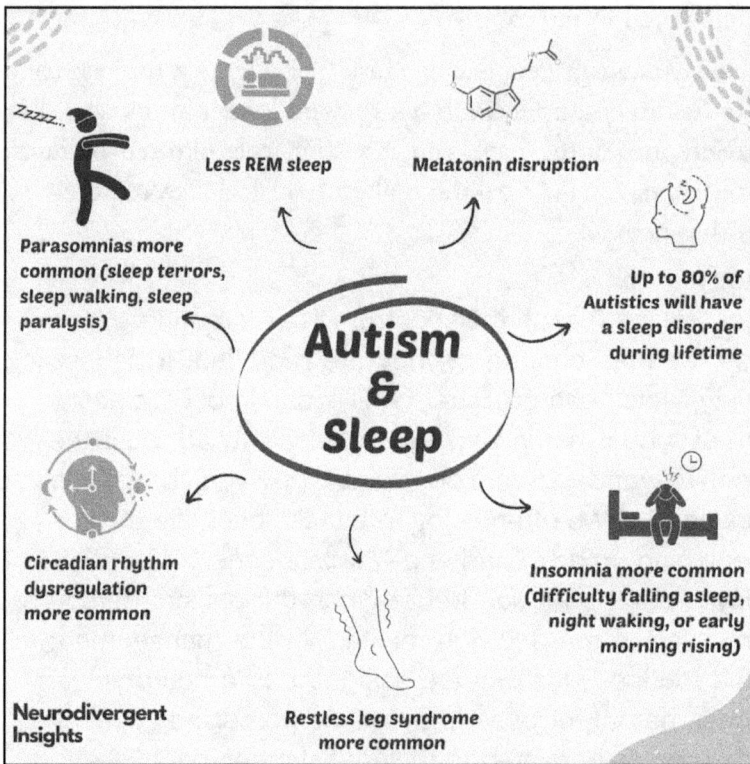

Less REM sleep

Melatonin disruption

Parasomnias more common (sleep terrors, sleep walking, sleep paralysis)

Up to 80% of Autistics will have a sleep disorder during lifetime

**Autism & Sleep**

Circadian rhythm dysregulation more common

Insomnia more common (difficulty falling asleep, night waking, or early morning rising)

Neurodivergent Insights

Restless leg syndrome more common

Sleep problems occur often among people with ASD (See diagram).[51] They take an average of 11 minutes longer to fall asleep than neuro-typical people.[52] Many wake up frequently during the night as well as wake early. Some children cry at bedtime, find it difficult to wind down, and are unable to sleep alone. Rapid eye movement (REM) in sleep is critical for learning and retaining memories: most neurotypical people spend about 23% of their night's rest in REM, whereas autistic people spend only 15% of their sleep in REM.[53]

Autistic individuals are more likely to have a mutation in genes regulating melatonin, a hormone in our body that plays a role in sleep. This results in a 'flat melatonin curve',[54] which means one's body often does not feel tired or send the same level of tired cues at night. When an individual does fall asleep, they are more likely than neurotypicals to experience *parasomnias* (conditions of sleep disruption where one appears awake but is not) like waking but not being able to move, sleepwalking, and night terrors.[55]

Autistic people can have sleeping difficulties due to other conditions as well: gastrointestinal problems (i.e., cramps from constipation), ADHD, anxiety, sensory sensitivities to light, sound, and/or touch, and medications that affect sleep (ADHD meds can cause insomnia). Lack of sleep can worsen certain features of autism, increasing repetitive behaviors, sensory sensitivities and executive function struggles.

> Although sleeping has been a lifelong issue for me, neuroscience studies show that no two brains are alike, each with a distinctive 'signature', like a fingerprint.[56] Some autistic people may not experience sleep problems at all, and those that do may not experience them in the same way as another person. It is important to note that sleep problems affect between 50% and 80% of children with autism, and about 50% of adolescents with autism; but nearly 80% of adults with ASD experience sleep disturbances.[57] When sleeping behavior is a severe problem, a doctor's guidance is required for proper treatment. This can improve the quality of an individual's life.[58]

## Males versus Females[59]

Are there differences between autistic boys and girls? This question is a common one. Research shows that males are diagnosed more often than girls (4:1) and this is consistent around the globe regardless of racial, social, ethnic and community differences.[60] Although research continues to explore this difference between autism in boys and girls, there are other facts to consider:

○ Boys get referred for diagnostic and treatment services earlier in development than girls.

○ Some girls are diagnosed later—in middle childhood, adolescence, or even young adulthood—while other girls may be missed and will never be appropriately supported.[61]

○ Girls seem to do better at imitating those around them, making it more difficult for teachers, parents, doctors, and others to recognize their differences.

○ Ratios of diagnosis are affected because females learn to 'mask' behaviors that draw peoples' attention away from them, so many females go undiagnosed and untreated. (Men, me included, can be as adept at masking as women, which additionally complicates the dynamic.) It is also possible that women with ASD have repetitive behavior tendencies and interests that aren't seen as unusual, like neatly organizing dishes.[62]

○ Boys and girls may show signs and symptoms of autism in different ways.[63]

*Table 1.2: Signs and symptoms of autism in boys versus girls*

| Boys | Girls |
|------|-------|
| Boys tend to have very repetitive behaviors and limited areas of play. | Girls are less repetitive and have broader areas of play. |
| Boys' social communication issues become challenging very early in their lives. | Girls are more likely to be able to respond to non-verbal communication such as pointing or "gaze following." They are also somewhat more focused, less prone to distraction. |
| Boys tend to engage in disruptive behavior to gain objects. | Girls may be able to manage the social demands of early childhood but run into difficulties entering early adolescence. |
| Boys may talk about a special interest a lot which interferes with conversations with others. | Girls are more likely to suffer from anxiety and/or depression. |
| Boys are less likely to control their behavior, or less inclined to try and fit in. | Girls are less likely to behave aggressively and more likely to be passive or withdrawn. |

Traditional thought views girls and boys with autism quite differently based on their signs and symptoms. But we feel it is not as simple as thinking along gender lines. For example, I exhibit some of the traits listed above attributed to girls. I mask (or used to) very well, have anxiety/depression, and had zero issues with social demands until adolescence. We must consider the whole individual when constructing a medical diagnosis. If we focus only on gender, we may miss the opportunity for early treatment. Furthermore, to categorize women as against men when we speak about autism is biased, which is true with many medical diagnoses. We hope that future research will help clarify the role of gender in the diagnosis for autism spectrum disorder.

# Monitoring/Screening/Diagnosis/Professionals

It is important to monitor, screen, evaluate, and diagnose autistic children as early as possible, so that they receive the services and support they need to reach their potential.

### Developmental Monitoring

The Centers for Disease Control and Prevention (CDC) defines 'developmental monitoring' as '…an active, ongoing process of watching a child grow and encouraging conversations between parents and providers about a child's skills and abilities.'[64] The CDC's *Learn the Signs, Act Early* program has developed free materials, including CDC's *Milestones Tracker* app,[65] to help caregivers monitor a child's development. It can help to determine if there is evidence for concern, and if more screening is needed.[66] The CDC also provides a 'brief checklist of milestones'[67] to see how your child is developing. If you notice that there is trouble with your child's progress, speak with your pediatrician. Be sure to let them know of any family history of ASD, learning disorders (differences), or ADHD. They may want to begin developmental screening.

### Developmental Screening

Developmental screening takes a closer look at your child's development. The American Academy of Pediatrics (AAP) recommends all children be screened specifically for ASD during regular 'well-child visits' at eighteen and twenty-four months of age.[68] Screening questions and checklists are based on research that compares you child to children of the same age, and asks questions about language, movement, thinking skills, behavior, and emotions.[69] The doctor may also ask the parent or caregiver to complete a questionnaire as part of the process.

Note: Many autistic adults were never screened as children. Some of them are self-diagnosed later in life. Because any person could answer 'yes' to some or all the following questions doesn't mean the individual is autistic. Many neurotypicals could answer 'yes' to these as well. It is always best to speak with one's doctor before diagnosing oneself with any disorder.

Here are ten questions you can ask yourself before the medical screening:[70]

1. Do you get confused as to whether someone is joking or not?
2. Did you learn to speak or walk late?
3. Is it hard for you to handle bright lights or loud noise?
4. Did you struggle with temper tantrums as a child?
5. Do you often notice small details that others seem to miss?
6. Do you find small talk difficult and exhausting?
7. Do you find social situations confusing?
8. Do you have an overwhelming passion for one specific subject?
9. Do changes in your routine upset you?
10. Do you have habits that people say are inappropriate for your age?

### Developmental Diagnosis

Monitoring and screening tools are both important parts of the journey to determine if a child may be autistic; but the information collected from them should not be considered a diagnosis. A formal evaluation is usually done by a trained specialist, like developmental pediatrician, child psychologist, speech-language pathologist, occupational therapist, etc. It involves observation, structured testing, and engages the parents and caregivers with questions or a questionnaire. The results will highlight your child's strengths and challenges and can indicate whether they meet criteria for a developmental diagnosis.[71]

### Formal Diagnosis/Professionals

Many clinicians, teachers, and counselors have the experience to recognize the signs and characteristics of someone on the spectrum. A formal diagnosis, however, needs to come from a licensed professional with a doctoral and/or medical degree. They will determine the level of ASD and the accommodation needed. The patient's medical team should include a developmental pediatrician, child neurologist, child psychiatrist, or child psychologist.

It is important to note that not all psychologists are equipped to treat ASD. Always ask a professional about their field of expertise before arranging an appointment. Pediatric neurologists can make a formal diagnosis, but their expertise is in children, and they are not necessarily equipped to help an ASD child with upcoming teen and adult needs.

A growing interest in the transition into adolescence and adulthood has occurred because more children are being diagnosed as on the spectrum. New challenges arise as a child grows up, including finishing high school, getting a job, and living as an adult, perhaps on their own. The CDC funds a program called Autism and Developmental Disabilities Monitoring Network (ADDM). It collects data to better understand the number and characteristics of children with ASD and other developmental differences in the United States.[72] Recently collected data is providing valuable information for transition planning in special education services, and potential service needs after high school.

> Note: I had extensive testing before I was diagnosed as 'twice exceptional', completed by a licensed psychologist who specializes in diagnosing, counseling, and coaching adults with Asperger's/Autism, dyslexia, and other learning differences. Later in this book I will provide more details about my experience being diagnosed.

## Heredity/Genetics

Humans have always had the desire to determine the cause of their medical disorders. Parkinson's Disease, Cerebral Palsy, Alzheimer's Disease, and Multiple Sclerosis are just a few life-changing conditions, about which years of research and millions of dollars have been spent to find the causes and cures. Autism is a disorder (difference) that researchers have studied for some time, but it does not have a cure. Many of us do not seek a 'cure' because we are not damaged, we are different and misunderstood.

According to Sir Simon Baron-Cohen, the Director of the Autism Research Center at The University of Cambridge, "Genetics plays a large role in autism. Knowing more about which genes influence it could allow a better understanding of the condition."[73] Doctors today refer individuals for genetic counseling and testing to determine if a child has autism. (Genetic testing looks for causes of ASD, but it cannot be used to diagnose it.[74]) Children born to parents with autism have an increased rate of developing the disorder. My mother and father are both on the spectrum, so it is no wonder I am as well. My mother is self-diagnosed, while my father is very obviously on the spectrum, but neither formally nor self- diagnosed. I mentioned it to him, and he did not deny it nor take offense. If autism is suspected, medical professionals can take a careful family health history, including older family members who have or had signs of ASD, even if they weren't diagnosed.

Specific genetic tests assist medical specialists when determining ASD. The most ordered test is chromosomal microarray (CMA), which examines chromosomes to see if there are extra or missing parts that could cause autism. CMA finds a genetic cause in 5%-14% of people with ASD.[75] If CMA and genetic testing do not find a reason for ASD, a whole exome sequencing is considered. 'Exome' refers to the *part* of the whole genome (an individual's genetic 'map') which is involved with building proteins. Whole exome sequencing can find a cause in 8%-20% of people with ASD.[76]

In addition to learning about one's family history to determine if autism is prevalent, there are other medical issues that can lead to a prognosis of autism spectrum disorder. First, Fragile X syndrome is a disorder that leads to intellectual issues; about one in three individuals with it are also diagnosed with autism.[77] Next, Rett syndrome is a rare neurological disorder that causes physical and developmental delays. Researchers think this could have a high autism overlap.[78] Finally, tuberous sclerosis is a medical condition that leads to the growth of benign brain tumors. Somewhere between 25-50% of children with this condition develop autism.[79] Important research must continue to further understand the role of genetics and other medical conditions in the development of autism, so that the lives of challenged individuals are changed for the better. Early detection of autism allows for interventions that target symptoms of disability or distress, for example language delays and learning difficulties.[80]

In addition to genetic studies, it is vital to address the *myth* that vaccines cause autism: *this has been unequivocally proven false*: the doctor who published the original study citing vaccines as a cause lost his license for falsifying data.[81] The CDC has funded nine relevant studies, all of which found no link between the vaccine ingredient thimerosal and autism. While autism is not likely caused by a disease or other external factors, it is true that environmental factors can exacerbate symptoms, like bright lights or loud noises in a grocery store (or classroom),[82] leading to overstimulation and perhaps a meltdown.

Although it is unknown why autism rates have been increasing in recent years, the scientific community is very interested in uncovering all the determining factors. Working to find innovative diagnostic methods will help detect this neurotype much earlier; early diagnosis and treatments lead to better long-term outcomes for autistic people.[83]

## Data/Statistics

As mentioned earlier, The Autism and Developmental Disabilities Monitoring (ADDM) Network collects data to better understand the number and characteristics of children with autism living in the United States. Their goals are:[84]

- ○ Obtain as complete a count as possible of the number of 4-year-old and 8-year-old children with ASD in each ADDM Network area and identify changes in that count over time.

- ○ Provide information about early identification of children with ASD, including ages of evaluation and diagnosis.

- ○ Describe health and service needs of adolescents with ASD.

○ Provide information on the characteristics of children with ASD, including sex, race/ethnicity, and co-occurring conditions like developmental delays, motor difficulties, and attention deficit disorder.

○ Determine whether ASD is more common in some groups of children (for example, among boys versus girls), and if those differences are changing over time.

○ Understand the impact of ASD and related conditions upon children, families, and communities in the United States.

The ADDM's 2021 Community Report on Autism[85] shows the rates of autism since 2000. Some important facts to consider are:

○ About one in 44 children has been identified with autism spectrum disorder (ASD) according to estimates from CDC's Autism and Developmental Disabilities Monitoring (ADDM) Network.

○ ASD is reported to occur in all racial, ethnic, and socioeconomic groups.

○ ASD is more than four times more common among boys than girls.

○ About one in six (17%) children aged 3 to 17 were diagnosed with a developmental disability, as reported by parents, during a study period of 2009-2017. These included autism, attention-deficit/hyperactivity disorder, blindness, cerebral palsy.

In addition to this report's important information, the CDC acknowledges that knowing how many children with autism is just part of the picture. Understanding more about the characteristics of children with ASD, such as the age of diagnosis, is also important.[86] Key findings indicate that more children are being identified with ASD at an earlier age. (See graph.[87]) This may indicate greater awareness of ASD among families, healthcare providers, and educators, which leads to earlier evaluation and identification of children with ASD.

*Figure 1.3 Earlier age identification of ASD*

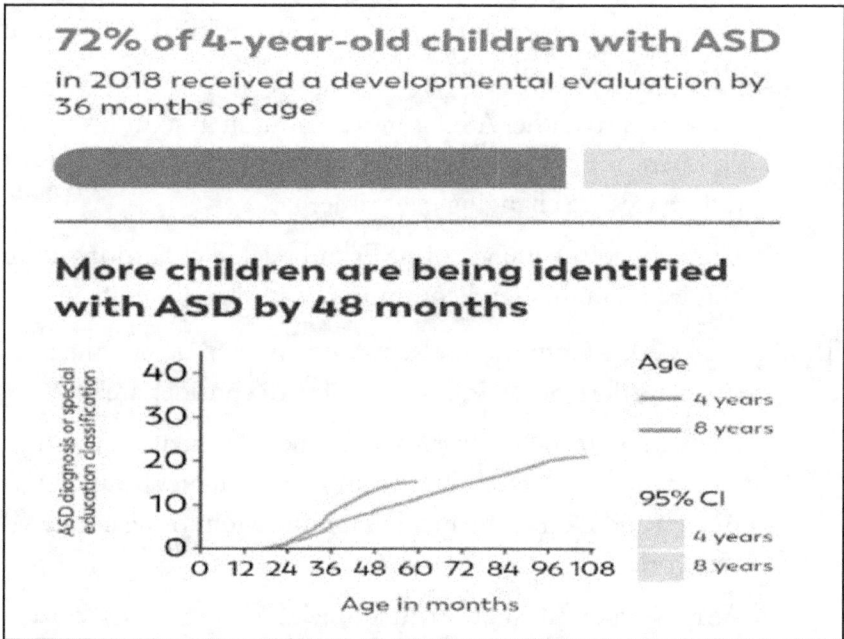

**72% of 4-year-old children with ASD**
in 2018 received a developmental evaluation by
36 months of age

**More children are being identified
with ASD by 48 months**

Age
— 4 years
— 8 years

95% CI
4 years
8 years

ASD diagnosis or special
education classification

40
30
20
10
0

0  12  24  36  48  60  72  84  96 108
Age in months

Finally, the ADDM Network's information provides other data to use in several important areas, further advancing initiatives that help ASD children:[88]

○ *The federal government can use this information* to: Guide research on ASD and inform and promote early identification efforts using the CDC's '*Learn the Signs. Act Early*' tools to track and celebrate a child's developmental milestones from two months to five years old.[89]

○ *Policy makers and community leaders can use this information to:* 1) Promote awareness of ASD and bring communities together to address the growing needs of families with ASD. 2) Develop policies which promote early identification and equal access to services and support so that all children get the help they need. 3) Serve as the basis for the creation of a task force or commission focused on the coordination of ASD activities in local communities.

○ *Service providers, such as healthcare organizations and school systems, can use this information to*: 1) Promote early identification efforts to lower the age when children are first evaluated for developmental concerns, diagnosed with ASD, and enrolled in community-based support systems. 2) Plan for resource and service needs. 3) Target outreach to under-identified groups, such as Hispanic children.

○ *Researchers can use this information to*: 1) Document the need for accelerated ASD research. 2) Guide future research projects. 3) Examine more closely why and how ASD affects children differently by sex, race/ethnicity, intellectual ability, and community. 4) Support the creation of ASD research groups in local communities.

CHAPTER 2:
# Important Differences to Understand

*"I'm a walking contradiction-a victim of catch 22"*
~Green Day

As I speak publicly about being a twice-exceptional adult, there are always questions I am asked that I find important to address here. These questions are generally from parents of 2e children, educators who work with 2e children, and people who have self-diagnosed or suspect they have ASD. Comparing the similarities and differences of the following can provide greater understanding.

## Asperger's versus Autism

In this section, we will sometimes use the now dated term 'Asperger's' as a descriptor for explanatory purposes. I personally feel this term best describes me. However, I no longer use it in conversation, and I categorically loathe the labels 'high functioning' and 'low functioning' because they discriminate against all people on the spectrum. Those considered high functioning, like me, may face disbelief or inadequate support for their challenges.[90] (I am very intelligent, function moderately well in social situations, and have mid-low functioning when it comes to structure and emotional regulation.) Conversely, those considered low functioning may experience low expectations that limit their growth and development opportunities. This individual could have a genius IQ and simply not be able to fully express themselves and showcase their superior abilities. When labels are attached to a person, inappropriate judgments are likely to be made.

### Is there a difference between Asperger's syndrome and classic autism?

I like people to realize that it is confusing to distinguish Asperger's and autism. As I mentioned in Chapter 1, the term autism was changed to autism spectrum disorder (ASD) in 2013, when the *Diagnostic Statistical Manual of Mental Disorders* was updated. Asperger's syndrome was no longer considered a standalone diagnosis, and instead was included in ASD. The phrase 'being on the spectrum' clarifies the fact that not all people diagnosed as autistic exhibit or experience the same signs and symptoms to the same degree. (Like me, many people diagnosed with Asperger's still identify with the term. But I now use the terms 'neurodiverse' and 'twice-exceptional' in conversation and presentations to avoid terminological vagueness and unfairness.)

Although clinicians today do not differentiate between Asperger's syndrome and classic autism, I nonetheless feel the need to explicate. They are both complex disorders (differences) of brain development that are characterized by social and communication difficulties. Both classic autism and Asperger's syndrome can affect a person's behavior, social interactions, and relationships. Individuals diagnosed with either Asperger's or ASD may require support for specific behaviors, which might include medication for anxiety or obsessive-compulsive disorder (OCD), speech or language therapy, and dietary modifications. Psychological therapies may also be required for both Asperger's and ASD.

These can include the following:[91]

○ *Cognitive behavioral therapy*: This helps address conditions like anxiety, depression, and other psychological challenges facing someone with Asperger's.

○ *Social skills training*: This can help someone with Asperger's understand social and conversation cues and help them to interact with others more effectively.

○ *Physical or occupational therapy*: This can help to improve motor skills in people with Asperger's that have problems with coordination.

○ *Family therapy*: This can help parents or family members of someone with Asperger's learn how to interact with them in a positive way that promotes things like good social and living skills.

The differences between Asperger's and classic autism are generally distinguished by the severity of signs and symptoms. Individuals with Asperger's tend to have milder symptoms. One example concerns language delays. 'Aspies' (an affectionate name for those with Asperger's) may be only mildly affected, and they frequently have good language and cognitive skills (I spoke in complete sentences by the time I was one.) Aspies may not understand the subtleties of language, such as humor or irony, or the give and take of conversations, but we have average-to above-average intelligence and excel in specific areas of interest. We have a 'specialist' mind when compared to neurotypicals. Others on the spectrum may struggle with speech and may speak late. To the untrained observer, a child with Asperger's may seem like a neurotypical child behaving differently.[92] This is true of Aspie adults as well. They may seem like neurotypical adults, just with some behavior 'quirks'.

Another key difference is that Aspies prefer to move along with society. We want to fit in and interact with others. We can be socially awkward, not understand conventional social rules, or show lack of cognitive empathy. But we try to improve at these things because we want to live a more fulfilling life. Individuals with classic autism frequently seem uninterested in others. They usually prefer to stay isolated from society.

Finally, Aspies fall prey to depression and anxiety because they are aware of their differences, as compared to those who are classically autistic. Those with classic autism are mostly unbothered by or unconnected to what is happening in their social lives, and as a result their daily lives need to be micromanaged to maintain stability. A person with Asperger's might start to sense being different from others and notice the difficulty in forming relation-ships or taking part in social events,[93] but they can form loving relationships: I have been married for over twenty years, and I have close friendships with people I have met at different times in my life, and some of these have lasted for thirty-five years or more.

My answer to the question, "Is there a difference between classic autism and Asperger's?", is that it is a condition of extremes. Unlike individuals with classic autism, individ-uals with Asperger's can live a very successful life. Aspies can be employed, have relationships, and accomplish amazing things. Steve Jobs, founder and former CEO of Apple, is an example of a person suspected to have been autistic who used his differences to his advantage. (Other celebrated 2e people, and my successful business career, will be addressed in Chapter 5.)

## Levels of Severity of ASD

### Are there levels of severity with ASD?

There are different levels of severity in people with ASD. Many people with autism share similar symptoms, but the degree to which they experience them varies.[94] According to the DSM-5, doctors categorize autism into three levels of functioning for social communication, and for restricted, repetitive and/or sensory behaviors, or degree of interests. (Note: Although there are many signs of autism, ASD is not the only reason a person might behave a certain way. Only a professional well-versed in autism should assess an individual.) Dividing ASD into three levels helps providers prescribe the most effective therapies for each patient's needs. Therapies help people with ASD make the most of their strengths and improve in areas in which they are deficient.[95]

### Difficulties in social communication

To be diagnosed with ASD, children must have difficulties and/or differences from what's typical in social communication. Signs may include:[96]

- Rarely using language to communicate.
- Not speaking at all.
- Rarely responding when spoken to.
- Not sharing interests or achievements with parents.
- Rarely using or understanding gestures, like pointing or waving.
- Using only limited facial expressions to communicate.
- Not showing an interest in friends or having difficulties making friends.
- Rarely engaging in imaginative play.

Some individuals, however, are not diagnosed with autism as a child because they do *not* demonstrate any of the above differences. I was one of these children, and this will be addressed in Chapter 4.

### Difficulties in restricted, repetitive and/or sensory behaviors

To be diagnosed with autism spectrum disorder, children must have difficulties and/or differences from what's typical, and these are seen in restricted, repetitive and/or sensory behaviors or interests. Signs in this area may include:[97]

- Lining up toys in a particular way repeatedly.
- Frequently flicking switches or spinning objects.

○ Speaking repetitively.

○ Having very narrow or intense interests.

○ Needing things to always happen in the same way.

○ Having trouble with schedule changes or changing quickly from one activity to another.

○ Showing signs of sensory sensitivity: becoming distressed by everyday sounds like hand dryers, not liking the feel of clothes labels, or licking or sniffing objects.

## Levels of support

A diagnosis will indicate support levels for each area of communication and behavior. Individuals might have different support levels for their social communication skills, as compared to their restricted, repetitive and/or sensory behaviors, or they might have the same support level for both.

The mildest type of ASD is *Level One*. It requires some support, and it is often referred to as 'high-functioning autism'. Children and adults at this level have a more difficult time communicating with their peers. They may also have difficulty interpreting social cues and body language. *Level One* adults will find it challenging to initiate or maintain a conversation with others; they have trouble moving from one task to another or trying something new; organization and planning can be more difficult to accomplish. Both children and adults prefer to follow a rigid behavioral pattern, and so changing environments or situations can be very uncomfortable.

*Level Two* requires more substantial support. People at this level have more obvious verbal and interpersonal communication issues. They speak in short, simple sentences, or struggle with nonverbal communication, and can have difficulty understanding others. Children and adults can exhibit repetitive behaviors, like pacing back and forth, that can cause problems with functioning in certain situations. They can also experience significant distress if they face changes, like a new school, or the birth of a sibling.

*Level Three* is the most severe form of ASD. Problems are similar to levels one and two, but they are more severe. Individuals experience trouble speaking clearly or may be nonverbal, seldom initiate interactions with others, and when they do it is usually awkward. Individual response usually requires very direct social approaches from others.[98] In addition, Level Three individuals face extreme difficulty in changing daily routines. They follow repetitive behavior patterns, like flipping objects, to the degree that it affects their ability to function. They experience a high level of distress if a situation requires them to alter their focus or task.[99]

Although levels of severity are assigned at the time of diagnosis, they can change as the person grows and develops. Symptoms can become more or less severe.[100] It is also important to note that a person may function well in one environment, but need significant support in another, like school or social events.

> No two people are alike: I 'classify' on two different levels. Overall, I am socially on Level One: I can function well with others in groups settings, like business meetings. I can also communicate well one-on-one. But for some social traits I require substantial support, which puts me on Level Two. Sometimes I have one-sided conversations, and I mirror poorly. I need support from my wife when it comes to balancing our bank account. She also makes sure I am on track each day. I can 'spin out' or meltdown over changes in routine. It would be extremely difficult for me to live alone. Recently, my wife went out of town and, unbeknownst to me, she arranged for friends to come by and check on me twice a week.
>
> It is quite true that one may function perfectly well in one environment but need significant support in another. When I travel to speaking engagements and my wife does not accompany me, I must plan extensively. This is to make sure I can manage all the details of environments like airports, hotels, or a university setting where I may be

speaking. Regardless of *accommodations,* it is still very stressful for me to travel alone to a meeting or an event. There are too many moving pieces, and this always creates anxiety.

Note: The word 'accommodation(s)' will be used frequently throughout the book. Accommodations in school help students learn the same material as their peers, which allows them to meet the same expectations. For example, a student with dyslexia will be accommodated with an audio version of a book being studied. Accommodations about employment relate to three areas and seek to:[101] 1) ensure equal opportunity in the application process; 2) enable a qualified individual with a disability (difference) to perform the essential functions of a job; and 3) make it possible for an employee with a disability (difference) to enjoy equal benefits and privileges of employment. Accommodations should not be viewed as 'special treatment'. Examples of reasonable accommodations include changing how tests are administered, job restructuring, part-time or modified work schedules, acquiring or modifying equipment, special training materials or policies, and the provision of qualified readers or interpreters.[102]

# Synesthesia

### Can someone really experience music as colors in their mind's eye?

Absolutely: it is called synesthesia. It is a neurological condition in which stimulation of one sensory or cognitive pathway leads to automatic, involuntary experiences in a second sensory or cognitive pathway. People who experience this are called 'synesthetes'.[103] People are usually born with it or develop it early in childhood.

According to a new study, many people on the spectrum have synesthesia.[104] Researchers believe people with this difference have a high level of interconnectedness between parts of the brain concerned with sensory stimuli. Sounds are louder, colors are brighter, and touch can be a disturbing intrusion.[105] Cognitive neuroscientist Simon Baron-Cohen, who led this study, said "Their experience is somewhere in between, neither imaginary nor external, an extra layer in the mind."[106] Synesthetes realize their perceptions are in their mind, not part of objects in the outside world.

There are many types of synesthesia because there are many possible combinations of different senses. Some of the most well-known are:[107]

- ○ *Auditory-tactile*: A sound prompts specific bodily sensations. (Example: pain in your hands when you hear a whistle.)

- ○ *Chromesthesia:* This is sometimes called 'colored hearing'. A certain sound triggers color. (Example: One sees green at the sound of a bird.)

- ○ *Grapheme-color synesthesia:* A person sees colors associated with letters of the alphabet. (Example: Colors may affect how a person 'sees' an entire word: the word could be one color to match the first letter's color, or each letter may maintain its own color.)

- ○ *Lexical-gustatory synesthesia:* A person may experience an unrelated taste when hearing a certain word. (Example: hearing 'spring' may cause the taste of lemons.)

- ○ *Mirror-touch synesthesia*: One can feel a sensation when they see another person experience it. (Example: One feels someone else pricking their finger or getting a hug.)

- ○ *Number-form synesthesia*: Instead of seeing numbers in a physical plane, one sees a mental map of numbers that they can navigate.

- ○ *Ordinal-linguistic synesthesia:* A person attributes personality traits and/or genders to numbers, letters, or colors. (Example: an angry number, or a feminine color.)

- ○ *Spatial-sequence synesthesia*: A person can see sequences either in their mind's eye or in their actual vision, making it easier to memorize mathematical facts and historical dates.

Synesthetes feel they have value added to their life.[108] One does not have a dominant side of the brain. Both sides can harmonize as one pursues their passion. Some successful artists who experience synesthesia are singer/songwriter Pharrell Williams, singer/songwriter/actress Mary J. Blige, and singer/pianist/songwriter Billy Joel. Artist Vincent Van Gogh was also suspected to have had synesthesia. It seems clear that these famous individuals' creativity and art benefited greatly from synesthesia.

### *Duke Ellington: jazz musician and orchestra leader*

In *Sweet Man: The Real Duke Ellington*, author Don George recounts Ellington's comments on how his synesthesia impacted his music. He said, "I hear a note by one of the fellows in the band and it's one color. I hear the same note played by someone else and it's a different color. When I hear sustained musical tones, I see just about the same colors, but I also see them in textures. If Harry Carney is playing his instrument, D is dark blue burlap. If Johnny Hodges is playing his instrument, G becomes light blue satin."[109]

> Personally, I see my grapheme (unit of language structure) and spatial sequence synesthesia as total gifts. I honestly believed everyone thought the way I did until I learned about this difference. I love having it. It gives me a unique perspective on a lot of things. For example, days and seasons are on an oval clock in my head. December 10th is roughly 11:15 on the clock. Days of the week are associated with colors. In my mind's eye, Monday is light yellow, Wednesday is orange, Friday is dark blue, and Sunday is red. I see time, events, and dates in a timeline. Playing trivia games are unfair to my opponents because I usually get the history, literature and music questions correct due to my spatial sequence synesthesia. If people understood this difference better, I think everyone would want it too!

# Gifted versus Autism Spectrum Disorder (2e)

### *Do giftedness and ASD share commonalities?*

The answer to this question is not as clear-cut as others. Giftedness and autism do share some qualities, but it becomes difficult to understand these similarities because the DMS-5 continues to adjust its diagnostic criteria for ASD, and there is no universal definition for giftedness.[110] Schools will often use the National Association for Gifted Children's definition of giftedness to identify children for gifted programs.[111]

*"Students with gifts and talents perform, or have the capability to perform, at higher levels compared to others of the same age, experience, and environment in one or more domains. They require modification(s) to their educational experience(s) to learn and realize their potential."* Student with gifts and talents:

○ Come from all racial, ethnic, and cultural populations, as well as all economic strata.

○ Require sufficient access to appropriate learning opportunities to realize their potential.

○ Can have learning and processing disorders (differences) that require specialized intervention and accommodation.

○ Need support and guidance to develop socially and emotionally as well as in their areas of talent.

Seventy percent of autistic people have intellectual difficulty, which means they have an IQ lower than 70%.[112] The remaining 30% of autistic people have intelligence ranges from average to gifted.[113] Dr. Edward Amend, clinical psychologist, whose work focuses on the social, emotional, psychological, and educational needs of gifted, talented, and twice-exceptional youth and their families, cocreated the *Giftedness-Asperger's Disorder Checklist* (GADC).[114] Dr. Amend said, "This clinically developed instrument was designed as a tool to help guide parents, educators, and clinicians toward possible interventions and to help them begin to determine whether an unsuitable, inflexible, or unreceptive education environment is contributing to the child's unusual or inappropriate behavior."[115] The behavior descriptors and characteristics in the GADC are intended to help differentiate between giftedness and Asperger's. The pre-referral checklist includes areas of memory, attention, speech, language, social and emotional behaviors, and motor skills. (The GADC should never be used as a substitute for formal and comprehensive evaluation when further information is necessary to determine the causes of behaviors.)

In the well-respected book *Misdiagnosis and Dual Diagnoses of Gifted Children and Adults (2016),* co-author Dr. James Webb, who also founder of the advocacy group, Supporting the Emotional Needs of the Gifted (SENG), describes three key parameters to help accurately differentiate between giftedness, ASD, and the 2e individual with both:[116]

1.  Examine the child's behaviors when the child is with others who share his/her intellectual passion. True Aspie kids lack cognitive empathy, and they will continue to demonstrate social ineptness with a wider range of peers. They may talk over others and act like little professors even when others are not interested.

2.  Examine the child's perception and insight regarding how others see him and his behaviors. Gifted kids typically have good intellectual insight into social situations, and they will know how others see them. Children with ASD do not. This ability to recognize other's perceptions and feelings (Theory of Mind) is frequently absent in Aspies.

3.  Giftedness and ASD differ in their level of asynchronous development. Asynchronous development is a term used to describe the mismatch between the cognitive, emotional, and physical development of gifted individuals.[117] For the gifted with ASD, asynchrony can be observed as an extreme skills range, from well below chronological age to well above chronological age, out of synch with their emotional or physical development. An example is a twice exceptional twelve-year-old who is taking college classes but is socially delayed. They may refuse to bathe; or they may hug their college age peers as a young child would hug other young children.

### Gifted Alone

In addition to the behaviors and descriptors included in the *Gifted-Asperger's Disorder Checklist*, it is important to point out some additional observations about those who are gifted without Asperger's syndrome. First, it is not uncommon for gifted children and adults to enjoy being with people but also feel that socializing can be exhausting. Gifted individuals will frequently retreat into alone time until they feel refreshed. They also avoid superficial social relationships, which they find banal and uninteresting.[118] Sensitivity could be a concern as well: worrying about how to live up to how others see them or how they see themselves can cause anxiety. Increased sensitivity can make gifted children and adults reluctant to take risks, particularly if they think they might be evaluated negatively.[119] If the person is also a perfectionist, they may avoid taking any risks at all.

Gifted children and adults without Asperger's may show anxiety in specific but not all situations. In interpersonal situations with others who share the individual's interest, there will be adequate conversational reciprocity, cognitive empathy, and a strong capacity to engage in abstract thinking, and less anxiety.[120] Gifted children and adults can also feel continually evaluated by others, even bullied; they can be repeatedly teased, taunted, and possibly ridiculed for their gifted characteristics. Such negative judgment may cause the child or adult to avoid interpersonal relationships.

### Asperger's Alone

Just as there are characteristics that describe only gifted individuals, there are a few behaviors which concern those with just Asperger's syndrome. Although people with Asperger's often show significant unevenness in their abilities, they may score quite highly on intelligence or achievement tests and do especially well with verbal tasks and tests that rely highly on memory.[121] But the level of impairment in a person with Asperger's goes well beyond the occasional social awkwardness of a quirky gifted individual: Dr. James Webb wrote "The words 'severe', 'sustained' and 'significant' should be applied for ASD."[122]

### Both Gifted with Asperger's Syndrome

Both giftedness and Asperger's are considered developmental conditions that result from brain-based differences.[123] Individuals with both conditions share intellectual excitability and sensory differences. They are also typically concerned with fairness and justice, although for Aspies this is less emotional and more an extension of logic.[124] Highly gifted children and adults are not always well-adjusted high achievers. They can be intense and over excitable, leading to sensory and executive function issues, much like in students with ASD.[125] Both groups are absorbed in one or more special interests, and enjoy learning vast amounts of information about that interest.

Similarities between those who are gifted and those with Asperger's are particularly important for school personnel to be aware of. Both groups have excellent memory and verbal fluency; they may talk a lot with many questions. Both groups adapt poorly to change and will resist attempts to redirect their attention. Hypersensitivity to stimuli like noise, lights, smells, textures, and flavors is common. Both are considered quirky by parents and teachers. Gifted kids may be perceived that way only at times, whereas Asperger's kids will *almost always* be seen that way. Parents of children who are both gifted and autistic feel they cannot get the benefits of either label, preventing access to advanced learning opportunities or 'scaffolding' in school when their child needs extra support[126]. (Scaffolding gives students the support they need by breaking learning into achievable sizes while they progress toward understanding and independence.) Whether your child is gifted, autistic, or both, it is extremely important to advocate for them by establishing a full learning profile with a trained professional who has worked with both gifted and autistic children.

### Twice-Exceptional

The term twice-exceptional has been around for some time. It is generally used to describe a group of gifted children who experience one or more coexisting differences, including medical, physical, sensory, cognitive, communicative, behavioral, or social-emotional challenges. The National Twice-Exceptional Community of Practice (2eCoP) defines 2e as:

*"Twice- exceptional (2e) individuals evidence exceptional ability and disability, which results in a unique set of circumstances. Their exceptional ability may dominate, hiding their disability; their disability may dominate, hiding their exceptional ability; each may mask the other so that neither is recognized or addressed."[127]*

Since 2e individuals often experience more than one difference, people wonder why the term is not 'multi-exceptional'. This is because in the term 2e, the '2' stands for two things: 1) exceptional challenges and 2) exceptional strengths, which are on opposite ends of the learning spectrum. Individuals can be gifted, and also have challenges such as autism, dyslexia, ADHD, dyspraxia, and/or obsessive-compulsive disorder. It is also important to recognize that giftedness is not limited to intellectual potential but instead can refer to extraordinary capabilities in creative thinking, specific academic areas, psychomotor functioning, or visual/performing arts.[128]

The Belin-Blank Center for Gifted and Talented Development at the University of Iowa developed a packet of information for professionals who work with gifted and talented students who have ASD. In *The Paradox of Giftedness and Autism* (2008), the authors state, "If the disability is not addressed, the gift may never fully develop, and if the gift is not addressed, it may generate anxiety that could exacerbate some of the unusual behaviors associated with ASD. Therefore, a multifaceted approach is necessary so that both strengths and areas for growth are identified and accommodations are put in place."[129]

### Intelligence Tests

It is important to note that not all intelligence tests are the same. There are different tests for a variety of situations, such as identifying children and adults for gifted programs, or evaluating future employees. Tests will attempt to assess *abstract thinking* (thinking laterally and from a unique perspective), *spatial reasoning* (understanding and visualizing 2D & 3D patterns and shapes), *verbal ability* (how a person uses words), *logical and critical reasoning* (logical inference/drawing sensible conclusions), *visual reasoning* (creating the mental image of an object to find a conclusion), and *problem solving* (using available data and information to deal with a problem).

First published in 1955 by psychologist David Wechsler, The Wechsler Intelligence Test is the most frequently used exam to understand whether a person is gifted, and to determine an individual's strengths and weaknesses. It has been updated many times since. Wechsler believed that intelligence was made up of a number of mental abilities, rather than a single general intelligence factor.[130] His full-scale IQ scores are comprised of measures of verbal comprehension, working memory, perceptional reasoning, and processing speed. The components of the exam are appropriate for a wide range of ages.[131]

○ Wechsler Pre-School and Primary Scale of Intelligence-WPPSI (3-7 years old)

○ Wechsler Intelligence Scale for Children-WISC-V (7-16 years old)

○ Wechsler Adult Intelligence Scale-WAIS (16 years old and above)

*Figure 2.1 Full scale IQ score components*

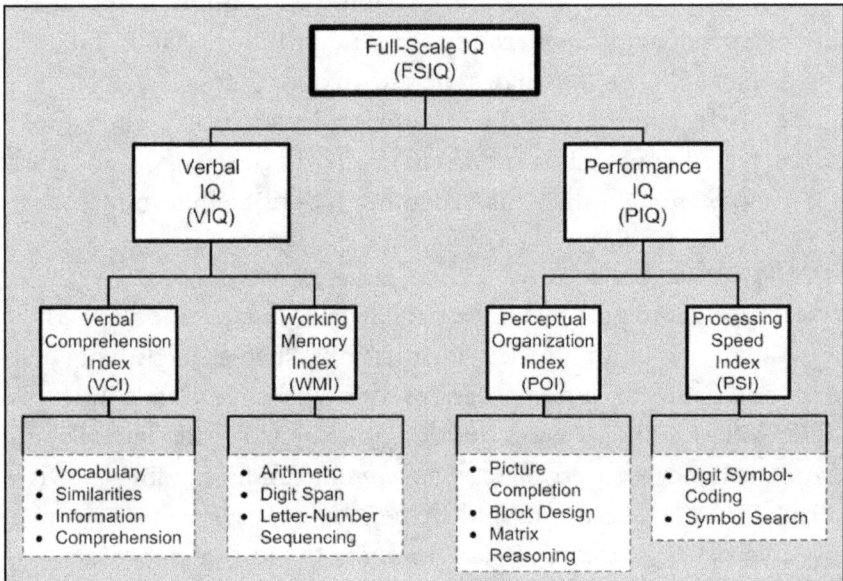

Schools, employers, and individuals must realize that "intelligence quotient" tests measure only one part of a person. They don't measure *practical* intelligence (knowing how to make things work), nor do they measure *creativity* and *curiosity*.[132] Furthermore, it is crucial to use the appropriate test when individuals are suspected of a learning difference. For example, The *Raven's Progressive Matrices* (RPM)[133] test is entirely visual: the test taker does not have to answer written questions because the measurement of intelligence is not dependent on reading comprehension. This test eliminates challenging variables such as native language, age, and possible reading disability.[134] It is important to note that autistic individuals tend to score higher on the RPM test than on the Wechsler Adult Intelligence Test (WAIS-IV) because they often have difficulty on tasks that need to be solved verbally.[135]

While intelligence tests claim to be culture-fair, none of the IQ tests created thus far are completely unbiased; some are clearly biased in favor of neurotypical individuals.[136] By measuring only one specific part of intelligence, some tests erroneously identify twice-exceptional individuals as having a cognitive deficit. When testing 2e children for gifted programming purposes, it is important to understand that one test component's score, like processing speed, could be significantly lower than the other exam scores. This scenario would require further measures to determine the child's strengths and weaknesses and possible giftedness.

While intelligence testing serves a purpose, we often try to fit cognition into a box, and this disvalues cognitive diversity. It is important that we do not cause an individual to be negatively impacted just because their unique intelligence isn't identified in a test. Well-known animal behaviorist Dr. Temple Grandin's autism allows her to see the world in pictures, but we do not consider her to be cognitively deficient. Her inner thoughts are entirely devoid of language: she thinks in extremely detailed movies.[137] Imagine groups of brilliant thinkers, like Dr. Grandin, Alan Turin, Henry Ford, and Albert Einstein who solved problems from a very different expanded perspective. If not for these neurodiverse individuals, and others like them, who would solve many of our world problems today?

## *Importance of Proper Diagnosis*

When a doctor gives you the wrong medical diagnosis, you are also prescribed a set of interventions that don't help. This happens far too often when attempts are made to diagnose twice-exceptional individuals. Think about the effects of these situations. A well-meaning but often uninformed—or more likely ill-informed—clinician, applies the Asperger's label to anyone who is socially awkward, who has difficulties reading interpersonal cues, or simply seems aloof in social situations.[138] This is not an appropriate label for simple awkwardness. Or consider when a teacher or employer interprets a person's executive function difficulties as laziness, sensory sensitivities as pickiness, or difficulty with eye contact as disrespect.[139] The student is punished, or the employee is fired. Or imagine a child who exhibits asynchronous development, in which their judgement lags relative to their insight and intellect. They are eight years old, but often act much younger, as though they are five years old, and so is diagnosed with oppositional defiant disorder instead of as gifted. The dangers of such misdiagnosis indicate the importance of a professional diagnosis by people who have specialized training in ASD assessment and a thorough understanding of giftedness.[140]

With an accurate diagnosis, an individual can realize that their difficulty relating to same-age peers is because they are *gifted*. Their preference for older relationships to fulfill the need to take deeper dives into topics of interest now makes sense. This same individual who struggles with interpreting facial expressions, expressing emotions and engaging in tasks with reciprocity does not in fact have oppositional defiant disorder, but instead has *Asperger's syndrome*. With correct diagnoses, the needs of the 2e child or 2e adult become the guidelines for interventions. As emphasized in *The Paradox of Giftedness and Autism*, "Evaluation of gifts and talents, as well as ASD, is a complex process, and requires a comprehensive assessment that is tailored to the student's specific presenting issues."[141]

# Myths versus Truths

Myths are widely held, but such false beliefs and ideas are harmful when actions and decisions are based on them. Neurotypical individuals can perpetuate stereotypes of neurodiverse people and cause damage without even knowing it. Specific groups of people, like gifted, autistic, and twice-exceptional, are unfortunately judged on myths from television shows, books, and just plain misinformation. In her book *Twice-Exceptional Boys: A Roadmap to Getting it Right*, Deborah Gennarelli says of her work with gifted students, "I observed too many instances when the myths surrounding the 'smart kid' permeated the decisions adults made, and the child suffered as a result. To correctly understand and manage giftedness in school, we must eliminate the myths and deal with the reality of what gifted children need to reach their potential."[142] This applies to all groups of people who have been held back because of stereotypes or myths. When we hold onto ideas that are not true, individuals of all ages experience challenges to their full potential. What do you mistakenly believe about those who are gifted, autistic, and twice-exceptional?

### Gifted Adults

In her book *Journey into Your Rainforest Mind, A Field Guide for Gifted Adults and Teens* (2019), licensed psychotherapist Paula Prober compares gifted adults and teens to a rainforest. From her introduction: "The rainforest-mind analogy is a way to describe a type of giftedness. If people are compared to ecosystems, then people as meadows, deserts, and oceans are all valuable and beautiful. One is not better than another. It is just that the rainforest ecosystem is most complex, and it is being destroyed every day. We might compare this to our gifted individuals who are suffering when we misunderstand and misdiagnose them."[143] Prober's analogy of gifted individuals to a rainforest is powerful. It certainly motivates us to ask, "How could gifted adults be under stress?"

Many adults are not aware they are gifted because of a lack of information, or stigma, or misconceptions about giftedness. If they are parents of gifted children, they often fail to recognize their own giftedness. If they were identified as gifted children and not told what it means to be gifted, they feel they have outgrown their 'giftedness'. Many gifted adults observe that society seems to disapprove of the term 'gifted' because it is interpreted as 'better than', when it just means 'different'. When these adults become acquainted with the identifying characteristics of giftedness and their meanings, their once-clouded experiences become clear.

According to clinical psychologist and founder of The Gifted Resource Center of New England Dr. Deirdre Lovecky, five specific traits in gifted adults can produce potential interpersonal (communication between people) and intrapersonal (self-communication) conflict. They are:[144]

○ *Divergency*: preference for unusual, original, and creative responses; people with this trait are high achievers, task committed, self-starters, and highly independent, experience great satisfaction in developing new ideas, and find it hard to support ideas they deem foolish. Writers, artists, composers, and philosophers may be divergent thinkers. Adults may find it difficult to maintain their identity in the face of pressure to conform.

○ *Excitability*: high energy level, emotional reactivity, high nervous system arousal, do many things well, take risks, enjoy challenges. Inventors and entrepreneurs may have this gifted trait. Adults may find it difficult to self-regulate. Boredom and the need for stimulation can produce a habit of constant activity.

○ *Sensitivity*: depth of feeling that results in a sense of identification with others; they think with their feelings. Poets, Peace Corp workers, and religious workers may have this trait. Adults form deep attachments and are concerned about doing the right thing.

○ *Perceptivity*: ability to view several aspects of a situation simultaneously; quickly see the core of an issue. Philosophers, creative writers, and poets may be highly perceptive. They often experience fear of closeness or intimacy.

○ *Entelechy*: bring deep feelings to a relationship. Teachers, therapists, and physicians most likely have this trait. It may be difficult for adults to find ways to nurture themselves through others without giving away all their personal resources.

Misconceptions about gifted adults can sometimes be corrected, but if they are too deeply embedded in one's beliefs and they become difficult to change. When this happens, the gifted adult can find themselves seriously judged and often rejected. Some common myths are:[145]

○ They are nerds.
○ They are socially inept.
○ They were exceptional students.
○ They have attained a high level of formal education.
○ They are book smart.
○ They are physically awkward.
○ They excel at everything uniformly.
○ They have exceptional careers.
○ They can get ahead because of their intelligence.
○ They cannot be successful with practical things because they are too intelligent.

To correct the misconceptions about gifted adults, we must understand that there are characteristics this group possess that set them apart from other adults. These don't make the individuals better, just different. Dr. Patricia Turner, a psychologist who works specifically with gifted adults in her practice in Canada, stated, "I find that gifted adults readily say they are different from the norm. But after some exploration they say they did not know that these differences are 'normal' for the gifted."[146] Some of these differences are:[147]

○ *Gifted adults are unusually bright.* This intelligence can be observed through extensive vocabularies (a specialized/technical vocabulary may be difficult to spot), remarkable abilities with numbers, long attention spans, and/or ability to learn new things rapidly.

○ *Gifted minds are always on.* They tend to be imaginative and original, curious, and ingenious, visionaries, have high degrees of energy, and/or love ardent discussions.

○ *Gifted adults see the big picture.* They are empathetic, perceptive, and insightful, able to connect seemingly unrelated ideas, and/or aware of things others are not.

○ *Gifted adults are outliers.* They are often described as non-conforming, quirky and eccentric, and/or a perfectionist with high standards.

○ *Gifted adults are their worst critics.* They can be introverted and need periods of contemplation, and they are their own worst critic.

○ *Gifted adults are highly sensitive.* These can include sensitivities to light, sound, smell, and/or touch.

○ *Gifted adults need constant intellectual stimulation.* To be happy, they must be challenged. They are flexible and adaptable in their thinking, tolerant of ambiguity and complexity, and thrive on challenges.

○ *Gifted adults are often self-starters.* They tend to have a high degree of energy, are independent and self-disciplined, have a wide range of interests, and strong moral convictions.

○ *Gifted adults can be perceived negatively at times.* They can often be described as driven and intense, threatening, and intimidating, and/or prone to question authority.

○ *Gifted adults can face additional challenges in the workplace.* They can find themselves under-stimulated, less motivated by rewards and praise, unable to comprehend why ideas are not acted upon, and have frequent career changes.

○ *Gifted adults are prone to burnout.* This is because they are unable to switch off their thinking, work themselves to exhaustion, and/or work to the exclusion of other activities.

Gifted adults, like gifted children, should be able to feel comfortable in their own skin. They live with traits that don't always make life simple, and don't guarantee that they are headed for great success. Being gifted affects not only the cognitive and academic aspects of individuals, but also their emotional, social, and spiritual well-being.[148] Eliminating the myths and focusing on the truths about giftedness is a step in the right direction for this group of people to find satisfaction in their lives.

### Adults with Asperger's

We tend to put people into categories, and thus stereotypes are formed. We are all familiar with this, regarding races, cultures, genders, and even disabled people. Stereotypes can cause harm when they guide decisions about employment, housing, relationships, and educational opportunities. Gender stereotyping affects women's paths to leadership in a variety of ways, including limits on income, promotions, and more respected status in the workplace. Women also face double standards when applying for leadership roles: they are supposed to exhibit certain 'male' traits, but also remain feminine.[149]

When a person is defined only by the stereotype attached to them, their real individuality will be hidden behind that *label*. Being judged by features or traits that 'fit' the criteria for a stereotype is unfortunate. Imagine never getting a chance to tell your own story, to show others your uniqueness. This is how myths and stereotypes rob an individual of themselves. It is important to remember that when we begin to interact with open minds and without stereotyping judgments to people who are different from us, our experience of the 'other' person expands.

The disabled community has long experienced limiting stereotypes that have severe repercussions. They affect how others see them and how they see themselves. People with differences are often thought of as helpless members of society and are lumped into a group as 'all the same', regardless of the type of difference they have. The mysterious nature of Asperger's has led to several misconceptions about it, as well as misunderstandings about the individuals who have it.[150]

When people think of autism spectrum disorder, they are likely guided by their limited stereotype of what they think it is. Perhaps they know someone who is on the spectrum, and erroneously assume that every individual with ASD is like the one they know. Some people's reference point for understanding ASD is merely a stereotype in movies or television. The 1988 Academy Award-winning movie *Rain Man* unfortunately created the misconception that everyone with autism is an autistic savant or has serious mental disabilities along with their extraordinary talent.

One of the strongest reasons for writing this book is to dispel the many myths that exist about Asperger's syndrome and the people who have been diagnosed with it. Sadly, it takes time to change stereotypes, but we must try. Stereotypes and myths prevent us from accepting differences in others. Here are a few of the more common myths and stereotypes I feel it important to discuss.

I am often asked if ASD is a mental disorder or disability. ASD is a brain *difference* that may or may not be accompanied by difficulties. Some people struggle to hold jobs, while others are very successful.[151] This concerns the myth that Asperger's always correlates to superior intelligence. Being on the spectrum doesn't automatically make one a musical, mathematical, or artistic genius.[152] Individuals can be perceived as being highly intelligent because they talk about a special interest for hours and appear to know everything about it. Some Asperger's individuals have average intelligence while most have above average intelligence, and a small group are considered geniuses. Their *difference* is not a disorder or a disability.

Next, the myth that individuals with ASD don't go to college can be dispelled. An increasing number of people with autism attend college for a bachelor's, a master's, and even a doctoral degree. Some universities have programs designed specifically for students with ASD. Some 2e students complete college independently, while others will need some support.[153] Alternately, many of us do not go to college or finish a university program for a myriad of individual reasons. In my case, I began college, but I found the subject matter uninteresting with no practical application.

Another inaccurate description of people with Asperger's is that we are emotionless, unempathetic, and can be rude. Although deficits in regulating emotions leads to incongruent or awkward expression,[154] this does not mean people with ASD do not have emotions or do not care deeply about other's feelings. The truth is that many people with Asperger's have difficulty interpreting the facial expressions and emotions of others and our facial expressions and body language may not reflect our actual emotions. We can also seem detached because we are overstimulated or overwhelmed. Often, we are interpreted as being impolite, which is the result of not being able to hear the tone or manner of speech as others do.[155] We may sound very formal when speaking, but this is a difference of expression, not a lack of emotion. I can honestly say that my compassionate empathy (connection with the lives and feelings of others) has enabled me to do some amazing things for people, like starting the non-profit organization *On the Spectrum Foundation*.

It is untrue that adults with Asperger's cannot form romantic relationships. Though many have trouble initiating romantic relationships and have difficulty knowing what to do in a relationship, Aspies can and do 'date', and sometimes get married and have children. It is important for us to find a partner who can understand our differences and the idiosyncrasies that come with it. I have been married to an amazing woman for over twenty years. We are both motivated to keep learning about each other and maintain an emotional connection.

Finally, too many neurotypicals think there is a cure for autism, but autism is not a disease. Being on the spectrum is an integral part of who people are. It is not 'treatable' with medications, because hypersensitivity, unusual speech tones, intense obsessions, and clumsiness in body movements are not sicknesses, but rather signs of physical differences and heightened awarenesses. It is nonetheless true that certain medications can help manage severe Asperger symptoms or related conditions like anxiety. Other treatments like cognitive behavioral therapy, speech therapy, and vocational therapy can help with difficulties.

It is stressful to live with the discrimination that accompanies stereotypes. People with differences may feel discouraged, nervous, or frustrated because of it. Perceived discrimination has serious health consequences: it leads to heightened stress responses and less healthy habits.[156] Some people cope by distancing themselves from part of their identity. Someone with autism might say, "But I'm very high functioning" to avoid the stereotype of being on the spectrum. Individuals may avoid situations or withdraw from groups altogether when they feel they will be faced with the threat of a stereotype. This 'self-censoring' is harmful (in this case a result of fear) because one with ASD could think, "No one can stereotype me if they cannot see me." Who wants to go through life invisible? Stereotypes hurt both individuals and society, because society is at its best when everyone is supported and included.

# Chapter 3:
# The Need for an Appropriate Medical Diagnosis

*"When it keeps on raining, levee's goin' to break.*
*When the levee breaks, I'll have no place to stay."*
~ Joe & Memphis Minnie/Led Zeplin

As I reflect on the life I have lived thus far, I know I have been very fortunate. I have traveled to some amazing places in the world, explored some incredible career opportunities, and met some fascinating people. But throughout this journey I couldn't figure out why things continually got more difficult as I tried to live my best life. Misreading people's nonverbal communication, experiencing extreme overstimulation in certain environments, accused of not being empathetic, losing my cool with others way too often, and challenges with reading out loud and math calculation never made sense to my family, friends, or me. But on August 18, 2018, the 'fog was lifted'. I received the results from an appropriate medical diagnosis. I am gifted with autism spectrum disorder, also known as *twice- exceptional* (2e).

I have often wondered how my life would have changed had I been diagnosed with these differences in early childhood. Could interventions and accommodations have helped me struggle less from teen to adulthood? Regardless of these queries, I prefer to look ahead and not back. I want to keep improving my life.

Since my important diagnosis, I'm determined to help others like me. First, I encourage anyone to get an appropriate medical diagnosis if learning and behavioral differences are making life challenging and unhappy. With the right diagnosis, an adult can begin to understand past challenges, identify personal strengths, and find the right help.[157] For children, a prompt diagnosis is important for early intervention. With the help of some amazing people, I started a non-profit organization called *On the Spectrum Foundation*. We are dedicated to the identification of, and advocacy for, teens and adults on the spectrum, as well as people with accompanying conditions such as dyslexia, other learning differences, and twice-exceptionality. Finally, along with my foundation partners, we want to empower adults with ASD to live their best life and increase awareness of how ASD's strengths and talents improve society for everyone.

Recently I had an in-depth conversation with my parents about my childhood. I discovered there was little awareness (by teachers or parents) of the various learning differences, including autism, during the 70's and 80's when I attended elementary and middle school. Because of this lack of awareness, that every child is unique and their learning differences equally so, too many children then and now were and are misdiagnosed or not diagnosed at all. Fortunately, in 1975 the United States passed the Education for All Handicapped Children Act[158] to ensure that all children, regardless of differences, should have access to free public-school education. This government act brought federal funds into schools to help them create special education for children who did not learn the same way as general education students. In 1990, the act became law, and the name was changed to the Individuals with Disabilities Education Act (IDEA).[159]

## Individuals with Disabilities Education Act

The Individuals with Disabilities Education Act protects the rights of children with disabilities and gives parents a voice in their child's education. It requires schools to identify students who require special education programs and services. A learning disability is recognized as:

*'...a disorder in one or more of the basic psychological processes involved in understanding or in using language, spoken, or written, that may manifest itself in the imperfect ability to listen, speak, read, write, spell, or to do mathematical calculations.'* [160]

Not every child with learning and attention issues is eligible for special education services under IDEA. First, a child must be found to have at least one of the thirteen kinds of disabilities (differences), including:[161]

○ *Autism:* A developmental disability that mainly affects social and communication skills and can also impact behavior.

○ *Deaf-blindness:* Severe loss of both hearing and eyesight.

○ *Hearing impairment/deafness:* A hearing loss not covered by the definition of deafness.

○ *Visual impairment, including blindness:* If eyewear can correct a vision problem, it doesn't qualify.

○ *Emotional disturbance:* Anxiety disorder, schizophrenia, bipolar disorder, obsessive- compulsive disorder, depression.

○ *Intellectual disability:* Individuals have below-average intellectual ability. They may have poor communication, self-care, and social skills; an example is Down syndrome.

○ *Orthopedic impairment:* This relates to the lack of function or ability in one's body; an example is cerebral palsy.

○ *Other health impairment:* This includes ADHD which impacts attention and executive function.

○ *Specific learning disability:* This includes dyslexia, dyscalculia, and dysgraphia among others.

○ *Speech or language impairment:* A common example is stuttering. Included in this impairment are trouble pronouncing words or making sounds with the voice, and language problems that make it hard for children to understand words or express themselves.

○ *Traumatic brain injury:* This is caused by some accident or physical force.

○ *Multiple disabilities:* This individual has more than one condition covered by IDEA, creating educational needs that can't be met by a program designed for one disability.

Family members begin to detect learning and behavioral differences in their children as they grow up. It usually comes about when parents compare siblings, neighborhood children and classmates. They may ask, "When did your child crawl?", "When did they walk?", "When did they talk?" These questions are part of casual conversations to check if their child is meeting developmental milestones for a given age. But in my case, I was not compared to anyone, not even my brother. My parents considered me very bright and active. They had no concerns that I was different from any other child and recognized that I was intellectually (though not emotionally) mature far beyond my age. Even when a pediatrician commented at a doctor's appointment that I was 'hyperactive', my mother thought it was perfectly normal for her son to be *overly* active. And when I began school, there were apparently no indications or 'flags' that I was different from my peers, other than that I read significantly above grade level, and my vocabulary was like that of a 'little professor'. These were signs of early giftedness that no one understood at the time.

As I think back now from adulthood, I realize my father and mother are both undiagnosed on the spectrum. They each have learning differences as well. But because they felt they were living 'neurotypical' lives, any behaviors I displayed growing up seemed normal to them. And in school, teachers liked me. They knew I was smart and accepted my 'quirks'. I was friendly with them and my classmates. Teachers helped me when I had trouble writing, spelling, reading aloud, or doing math calculations. They also complimented me on my overall intellectual ability, including the ability to speak publicly, convey complicated observations, and read well above my same-age peers. They never said to my parents that they were concerned about any type of learning difference. I truly fit the category of a '2e' student, where my giftedness masked my differences. Furthermore, *no one* imagined I was on the spectrum: why would they? Asperger's syndrome was not highlighted until 1994, by which time I was already out of school.

## Troubling Misdiagnosis

As I made my way through elementary, middle, and high school, signs of learning differences slowly began to appear. In middle school I noticed difficulties with organization, following through on multistep routines, and needing extra time to process. However, when it came to larger project-type assignments, I always had a friend or partner who could accommodate my areas of need, as well as allow my strengths to shine through. For example, I hated to write, but I loved to speak. So my project partner always did the written elements of a project, and I presented it to the class. By high school, when assignments had longer deadlines to remember, my attention span was challenged: I either did them quickly and turned them in early, or asked forgiveness when I turned them in late. Because I could learn material quickly, I never had to study for tests. These few examples from my school years illustrate how I should have been provided with early interventions and accommodations for areas of need *and* areas of strengths. I never received either. I have been told by many clinicians and educators that *if* I had been diagnosed and accommodated early in school, I likely would have graduated high school early and started college level coursework before I was eighteen years old.

Relationships for me were starting to be more tenuous as well. Expectations for me to read body language became challenging. In high school, when boys and girls started to date, I often misread the facial cues and other body language of a girl I was interested in. When this happened, the girl would get mad at me because my responses were not what she expected. It became an upsetting circle of misunderstanding that I could never figure out. In addition, I sometimes got into verbal altercations with teachers because I was perceived as 'too smart for my own good' or misread a teacher's body language and said something that was inappropriate. Teachers who received my remarks as inappropriate were the ones who taught out of a teacher's manual, instead of truly knowing their subject matter (or their students). I lost respect for them early.

After graduating from high school, I attended university for a little over a year. I knew I was not prepared for college *life*, but I enrolled anyway. After all, both of my parents had gone to college and finished with advanced degrees. (My mother earned a master's degree and my father a medical degree.) At 18 years old, I knew in the back of my mind that I needed structure, accommodations to support my learning needs, and coping skills to navigate relationship dilemmas. I didn't worry too much though because I thought, "I'm exceptionally smart. I can make it through like I did in high school". Beyond all that, at that point in my life I just wanted to socialize in a fraternity like I had seen in the 1978 comedy movie *Animal House*.

Unfortunately, I was wrong to believe only intelligence is necessary for success! Dorm life, fraternity events, socializing in bars where people are drinking and listening to loud music, and advanced academic expectations were all taking their toll on me. I made it through the first year and a half of college, but then I withdrew. The emotional reaction from this enormous change triggered a mini breakdown that landed me in a hospital. After several days there, I left with a 'diagnosis' of bipolar disorder.

My family, friends, and I knew this diagnosis could not be correct. No one in my family was bipolar, and I did not exhibit any of the major symptoms, i.e., particularly long periods of mania or mood swings. But *no thorough evaluation* that considered autism, giftedness or other differences was undertaken, and the medical staff simply prescribed lithium and sent me home. (Lithium is a pharmaceutical mood stabilizer and the first line of therapy for bipolar disorder.) The side effects of this drug were horrible: I became extremely lethargic, nauseated, my hands shook, and I gained weight. After a month, I decided to stop taking the drug. I began a very clean lifestyle that included a good diet, not drinking, and working out a lot with an old buddy from high school. I began to feel much better.

### Comparison of Bipolar Disorder to Autism Spectrum Disorder

I understand now why in 1991 the medical staff who saw me in the hospital would think I was bipolar. In 1994, Asperger's syndrome was still its own category in the Diagnostic and Statistical Manual of Mental Disorders-4. In 2013, the DSM-5 combined all subcategories of autism into a single diagnosis. It became clear that bipolar disorder and autism spectrum disorder *share* some similar behavior differences.

Overlap includes:[162]

- ○ Elevated or depressed mood.
- ○ Intense irritability.
- ○ Aggression.
- ○ Excessive talking.
- ○ Distractibility.
- ○ A tendency to 'get in trouble' or do risky things.
- ○ Repetitive activities or behaviors, such as pacing.
- ○ Sleep disturbances.
- ○ Being accident prone.
- ○ Racing thoughts or trouble organizing thoughts.

One of the main reasons I realized bipolar disorder was the wrong diagnosis is that people with this disorder can spend weeks to months in hysteria or depression. I can get very focused and creative, and I can experience depression, but not for weeks or months at a time. In addition, individuals with bipolar disorder have neutral periods in between opposing mood episodes or alternate between these periods in a process called 'rapid cycling'.[163] To properly determine whether someone has ASD, bipolar disorder, or both, a doctor will assess when symptoms occur, how long they last, their severity, and when they make sense in context. For example, talking too much or easily losing focus is occasionally normal for most people, especially people on the spectrum. But someone who suddenly has high energy, acts inappropriately, and goes for days on end without sleep may be experiencing a 'manic' episode.[164]

Medical diagnoses are rarely clear cut, especially when symptoms of one difference can overlap into another. Aware now that autism and bipolar disorder share some behavior differences, I am nonetheless alarmed that after only a few days in a hospital, my family was told I was bipolar. To avoid this mistake, it is important to recognize legitimate symptoms of bipolar disorder so as not to confuse it with autism. The following may help one understand if they or a loved one may be experiencing bipolar disorder. Individuals and their families should speak with a licensed medical professional, like a psychiatrist, to seek an appropriate diagnosis.

## *Categories of Bipolar Disorder*[165]

*Bipolar I-* symptoms of a manic episode include:

○ Acting unusually happy, upbeat, and wired for long periods.
○ Increased energy and agitation.
○ Exaggerated sense of self-and inflated self-esteem.
○ Sleep disturbances- reduced need for sleep.
○ Being easily distracted.
○ Feeling as if you can do anything.
○ Engage in risky behaviors like impulsive sex, gambling with life savings, and experiencing large spending sprees.
○ Low appetite.

*Bipolar II-*symptoms of a depressive episode include:

○ Acting or feeling down or depressed, sad, hopeless.
○ Loss of interest in normal activities
○ Sudden and dramatic changes in appetite.
○ Withdraw from family and friends.
○ Unexpected weight loss or weight gain.
○ Fatigue, loss of energy, frequent sleeping.
○ An inability to focus or concentrate.
○ Thinking about death, suicide or attempting suicide.

Finally, cyclothymia (cyclothymic disorder) is a rare mood disorder that could be confused with autism because some of the symptoms overlap. Cyclothymia causes emotional ups and downs, but they're not as extreme as those in bipolar I or II disorder. The highs include symptoms of an elevated mood (hypomanic symptoms). The lows consist of mild or moderate depressive symptoms. One can typically function in their daily life, though not always well. The unpredictable nature of mood shifts may significantly disrupt one's life because they never know how they are going to feel. Some symptoms to be aware of with cyclothymia are:[166]

*Table 3.1 Cyclothymia symptoms*

| Hypomanic Symptoms | Depressive Symptoms |
|---|---|
| Exaggerated feeling of happiness | Feeling sad, hopeless, empty |
| Extreme optimism | Tearfulness |
| Inflated self-esteem | Irritability, especially in children and teens |
| Talking more than usual | Loss of interest in enjoyable activities |
| Poor judgment | Changes in weight |
| Racing thoughts | Feelings of worthlessness or guilt |
| Irritable or agitated behaviors | Sleep problems |
| Excessive physical activity | Restlessness |
| Increased drive to perform or achieve goals | Fatigue or feeling slowed down |
| Decreased need for sleep | Problems concentrating |
| Tendency to be easily distracted | Thinking of death or suicide |

# Reasons for Children and Adults Receiving So Many Diagnoses

Differentiating characteristics that can indicate more than one condition is difficult, and challenges clinicians when seeking a correct diagnosis. An individual with one diagnosed difference could have another one that has not been diagnosed. It is all too common for teachers, parents or doctors to be thrown off track, causing misdiagnosis or in some cases overdiagnosis. For example, a student has obsessive-compulsive disorder (OCD), but is mis-labeled as autistic, gifted or both; a student is diagnosed with ADHD but their overexcitability is never considered to be part of giftedness. In *Misdiagnosis and Dual Diagnoses*, the authors suggest three main reasons why this happens to gifted individuals:[167]

1. *The tendency in recent decades to over-diagnose and to label quirks as though they were disorders.* Socialization of children is highly valued in schools as well as for adults in most work situations. However, it is important to realize that quirks are not the same as mental disorders.

2. *There is a lack of knowledge among professionals about common characteristics, resulting in typical gifted behaviors being mistaken for one or more disorders.* Professionals such as psychiatrists, psychologists, and pediatricians, as well as school counselors and teachers, receive little training that allows them to distinguish between behaviors derived from giftedness as compared to behaviors that arise from diagnosable behavior disorders.

3. *There are disorders, such as existential depression or anorexia nervosa, that are more likely to occur among certain groups of gifted children and adults, and diagnoses of these disorders are, thus, accurate. Yet how many of these disorders are the result of interaction between temperament and environment?* Health care professionals could provide more appropriate treatment if they incorporated into their planning more understanding of the person's mental functioning within the person's environment, whether the environment is home, school, or workplace.

## Dual Diagnoses or Twice-Exceptional

Dual diagnosis, or twice exceptionality, is a term I was not familiar with before my diagnosis in 2018. Now I realize the importance of understanding it. A 2e person can have obvious gifts and talents, but their difference remains hidden. They can seem to have one or more differences, but their special intelligence is unobserved or hidden by prejudice. Some children with both giftedness and learning differences are seen as neurotypical students, and so both giftedness and disability are unobserved. Now that I understand 2e better, I know I fit perfectly into the first group. As a child, I could simply absorb school material quickly by listening and watching most of the time, which meant that my learning challenges, like dyslexia and dyscalculia, were not recognized until I was much older.

Unfortunately, individuals who have differences like cerebral palsy, vision or hearing issues, and autism, are too often *not* recognized as twice exceptional. Their *abilities* are overlooked because their *dis*-ability (difference) is pronounced. Another reason gifted individuals with learning differences are undiagnosed is that they do not know how to describe their own shortcomings. They may inadvertently hide a sense of their own weakness because they can't express it, thereby preventing educators or therapists from ascertaining the real issues. So both groups of 2e individuals are challenged to find the best accommodations for their special needs, and this has serious implications with regard to education, jobs, and treatment plans.

## The Right Diagnosis

As I mentioned earlier, the 'fog was lifted' in my life on August 18, 2018. I finally received a formal medical diagnosis at 45 years old. As I explain the information I received that day, it will be eye-opening to see how I was able to manage (and often mismanage) college, military experience, my business career, and relationships—including marriage all these years. It also provides a very important lesson, that getting the *correct* medical diagnosis is life-changing! It has been for me.

My wife is one of the most amazing people I have ever met. I was drawn to her because she is not only beautiful, but she is very smart, elegant, worldly, and caring. We have been married for 20 years, but around the midpoint of our marriage things started falling apart. We were 'speaking' different languages; emotions were high; our marriage was not going to make it if we did not get help.

For three months we visited a marriage therapist. During one of our appointments the therapist said, "John, I think you are *on the spectrum*". These words came as a shock to my wife and me, much like a doctor telling someone they have cancer. But even so, it made a lot of sense. We immediately knew our next step was to see an expert in clinical psychology and neuropsychology. A good friend from college named Jeff, who has an autistic daughter, reached out to his network, and good fortune led us to Dr. Stuart Robinson of *Live More Simply, Inc.,* in Dallas. Dr. Robinson specializes in diagnosing ADHD, dyslexia, and other learning differences and anxieties in adults. Our experience with him made all the difference in finding answers to questions I had held for years!

Before *Live More Simply* was started, Dr. Robinson had well-established business credentials. He started and managed a national consumer research and market planning firm. His business background provided an instant connection between patient and doctor; our special interests and abilities in business created a common platform for us to understand each other. The fact that Dr. Robinson specializes in diagnosing and treating adults with autism spectrum disorder also increased my confidence. He emphasizes a broad-based, complete approach to testing, diagnosing, counseling, coaching, and therapy. His goal is to help people return to college or work with proper accommodations and with a new level of confidence and self-esteem.

## Tests, Checklists, and Rating Scales

When I met Dr. Robinson for the first time, I requested an evaluation of neuropsychological and neurocognitive aptitude, and achievement strengths and weaknesses. Having a background in medicine, I was aware that getting help is 95% diagnosis and 5% treatment. So, I took every test available to give Dr. Robinson as much data as possible. As I prepared for the three days of testing, I was clear about two things. First, I had been successful completing my business objectives and career goals up to this point, but I was only able to do this by being highly motivated, over-concentrated, and hyper-focused. This way of living gave me a life of moderate to severe anxiety on an hourly basis. Second, until my marriage began to unravel, I was reluctant to seek help. Working with Dr. Robinson led me to realize that seeking the proper diagnosis would head me in a direction where I could achieve my true potential in my marriage, business, and social life.

When an individual requests a general psychological assessment, it generally includes the following:[168]

○ *Cognitive evaluation*: assesses intelligence.

○ *Psychoeducational evaluation*: assesses intelligence in academic areas like reading and math.

○ *Neuropsychological evaluation*: assesses brain-based strengths and weaknesses across many functional domains, including general intelligence, executive function, language, visual spatial abilities, learning and memory, social problem-solving abilities, fine motor skills, and perhaps also one's current emotional state.

During my evaluation, Dr. Robinson administered these tests, checklists, and rating scales.

○ Wechsler Adult Intelligence Scale-Fourth Edition (WAIS-IV)[169]
○ Scholastic Abilities Test for Adults-1991 (SATA)
○ Nelson-Denny Reading Test- 1993
○ Scan -3A-Auditory Processing Test for Adults including measures of phonologic and symbolic processing
○ Grooved Pegboard Test[170]

○ IVA-AE2 Test for both visual and auditory attention and response control functioning
○ NeuroPsych Questionnaire (NPQ) LF-207
○ Tests and Measures of Test-Taking Validity
○ MMPI-2 test of personality and clinical traits, conditions, and behavioral tendencies
○ Australian Scale for Asperger Syndrome-Adult version[171]

It is important to emphasize that there is no statistically valid or reliable test for autism in adults. However, neuro-psychological tests identify several relevant cognitive psychological profiles. It is also very important to study the answers to questionnaires completed by the patient, family members, and spouse. They can contribute as much or more than test results in establishing the validity of a diagnosis.

When I completed the battery of tests, Dr. Robinson offered his findings and recommendations in a fifty-six-page report. First, I was diagnosed with the following:

○ *Autism Spectrum Disorder-Level 2.* (Requiring substantial support.)

• Without accompanying intellectual impairment
• With processing deficits when processing conversations and language or visual information.

○ *Central Auditory Processing Disorder* with deficits processing auditory information.

○ *Mixed Receptive-Expressive Communication Disorder* with deficits listening and processing conversations.

○ *Specific Developmental Disorders* of scholastic skills with visual processing deficits.

○ *Specific Reading Disorder (Dyslexia)* with slow reading rate to obtain comprehension.

○ *Mathematics Disorder (Dyscalculia)* with deficits calculating but *strengths in applied math.*

My problems processing visual information, text, auditory information, conversations, language, and non-verbal social information caused me to fear performing poorly on everyday tasks. As I mentioned earlier in this book, I attempted to manage my deficits by hyper-focusing and over-concentrating. This led to excessive fatigue, as well as to Directed Attention Fatigue (DAF or *zoning out*), irritability, stress, and moderate to severe anxiety. These symptoms worsened my ability to pay attention and process information, so the cycle repeated.

Over time, these challenges led to chronic worry, social avoidance, and difficulties sleeping. The anxiety and sleep symptoms were prominent, and justified additional diagnoses, which included:

○ *Over Situational Type Phobia-Performance Anxiety.*

○ *Generalized Anxiety Disorder.* Worrying about being perceived as having limited skills and abilities and feeling guilty for performing to self-imposed overly high standards.

○ *Obsessive Compulsive Disorder.* Obsessing and perseverating over details and catastrophizing about failures.

○ *Insomnia.*

○ *Depression.* Major, Recurrent, Moderate.

Some people with autism may reject a professional evaluation and diagnosis as not personally meaningful, because they don't feel a formal affirmation would further their understanding of autism or its relation to themselves.[172] But a formal diagnosis is the key to services that are only available to people who have been formally diagnosed by a licensed psychologist or psychiatrist.

Formal diagnostic testing takes time and is expensive: my complete battery of tests took three days and cost $3,000. But I don't think anyone would hesitate to proceed with any other type of major medical testing just because it took time to complete and was costly. Living a healthy and productive life is what matters. For too long, I had been challenged by academic deficits that contributed to day-to-day anxiety, poor executive function skills that caused stress, and challenges performing personal tasks and marital responsibilities. For self-protection, I fended off the outside world, rather than modify myself to fit better in with my surroundings. Now I know I don't have to live this way any longer. Accepting Dr. Robinson's conclusion that my autism is an 'umbrella' diagnosis which includes my other conditions along with autism, and that I do not have bipolar or personality disorders, finally afforded me great relief.

I understand that my test results indicate the need for accommodations due to legitimate neuropsychological and psychological conditions, and not due to weakness in character. My diagnosis taught me that my difference/disability is pervasive, in that it limits my access to many and varied major life activities (and to think that these conditions have challenged me since childhood!). So I was happy to immediately take advantage of all the accommodations presented by Dr. Robinson. If I had not, it would be like an individual with eyesight issues not wearing their glasses. It is important to take advantage of professional accommodations to fully realize the desired benefits.

## Accommodations

Living life can be exhausting for me. Unlike other people who also have high intelligence but do not have any deficits or academic learning differences or disorders and can remain calm and in control throughout their day, I can be in a chronic state of moderate to high stress and vigilance almost constantly. Learning that I am neurodiverse helps me address some of the accumulated costs of being so often misunderstood. These costs are emotional, social, financial, and educational.[173] Below are my accommodations, which I follow to *thrive* instead of just *survive*.

## Accommodation Examples

### Severe anxiety during conversations

○ Have important conversations in a private room as opposed to a public area.

○ Allocate extra time and avoid rushing through a conversation.

○ Allow breaks when communication starts to deteriorate.

○ Become familiar with new buildings, rooms, or other locations at least one or two days before a meeting.

○ Arrange to choose seating in a conference room or staff meeting.

### Dyslexia

○ Use listening software/technology (on phone, laptop) for 'reading' text such as emails, text messages, internet articles, books, etc.

○ *Read along* while listening to audible books.

○ Ask people to send messages in larger or bold print.

○ Use a line guide or ruler, or colored transparent overlays to keep place while reading.

○ Use symbols or pictures where appropriate.

○ Color-coding whenever possible.

### Dyscalculia

○ Use a calculator (including a talking calculator) at all times.

○ Keep scratch paper handy at all times.

### Processing deficits

○ Text or announce reminders like location of the conference room, time remaining during a conference or discussion, when breaks are planned, necessary materials to put away or keep out during conferences.

○ Schedule a limited number of important conferences or discussions per day.

○ Allow extended time/flexibility. For example, break a discussion into two sections giving the opportunity to read in preparation for each part.

○ Have a proctor announce time intervals or set alarm on watch/phone/laptop for intervals before during, and at the end of each important discussion.

○ Maintain a written task list or have others provide you with the tasks they need you to complete in a written to-do list format.

### *Auditory, conversation, language, or visual processing deficits*

○ To reduce auditory distractions:

- Use noise canceling headset or earplugs.
- Use a white noise machine.
- Relocate workspace away from audible distractions.
- Redesign workspace to minimize audible distractions.

○ To reduce visual distractions due to anxiety, stress, and overstimulation:

- Redesign workspace to minimize visual distractions.
- Relocate workspace away from visual distractions.

### *Difficulty with getting or staying organized; prioritizing tasks and activities*

○ Develop color-code systems for files, projects, or activities.

○ Use charts to organize activities and assignments.

○ Use coaches who understand the disability to help create and maintain daily, monthly, and yearly schedules, or higher a personal assistant.

○ Use a coach to help develop personal organization skills or hire a personal assistant.

○ When possible, start new projects (home/personal) when previous project is completed.

○ When required to work in a group, each person should be held accountable for a specific portion of the project.

### Social skills

○ Have someone define appropriate behavior for each social situation.

○ Develop a simple, but appropriate, code of conduct for dealing with people.
- Rules for tardiness or leaving early.
- Rules for engaging in debate or discussion.
- Rules for good citizenship.

○ Take lessons in sensitivity training.

○ Ask friends to demonstrate and model appropriate social skills.

○ Adjust method of communication to best suit my needs.

# Different Trajectory

When I think about being *misdiagnosed* as bipolar at 19 years old, and the idea of being on a medication that was not right for me, I become deeply disturbed. Diagnostic errors lead to negative health outcomes, psychological distress, and financial cost. When misdiagnosis happens, one or more steps go wrong as a result. In my case, medical staff assumed that since I had an emotional meltdown after leaving college, I must be bipolar. No personal or family history or other pertinent information was collected while I was in the hospital. Their attitude was to 'fix me' by prescribing a mood stabilizer and then send me back home. I have since learned that this is unfortunately quite common, especially in adults.

Medical diagnosis involves a comprehensive look to identify the origin of a symptom or behavior, as opposed to simply attempting to manage or treat the symptom.[174] It is important to note that high intelligence should be considered as a symptom. In *Misdiagnosis and Dual Diagnoses of Gifted Children and Adults*, Dr. Webb et al. state that if the DSM-5 recognizes that mental capacity affects diagnostic implications at the base of the intellectual spectrum, it is important to acknowledge the significance of higher intelligence levels and the role they should play in the diagnostic process as well.[175] Medical professionals must evaluate the *whole* brain to arrive at an accurate diagnosis.

> If I had only thought to tell medical staff that I felt guilty about not finishing school, I believe the entire trajectory of my experience would have changed. I knew, due to my high intelligence, that I was more than capable of excelling at a university level and beyond. But because there were no academic interventions for my learning differences (which had not been diagnosed yet, including autism) and my perfectionism (giftedness), college life got the best of me. I recommend that younger 2e individuals learn to understand gifted behaviors, and realize that they can coexist with, or mask, other personally significant behavioral dynamics, or problems.[176] With such knowledge, outcomes can be remarkably better.

For those seeking more information about psychologists and counselors who work with gifted children and adults, consider the following:

- ○ *Navigating Guidance & Counseling for Gifted Children* (2021) at: https://www.davidsongifted.org/gifted-blog/finding-a-therapist-for-your-gifted-child/

- ○ *Finding a Mental Health Professional* (Peters, M., & Niles K., 2018) at: http://www.nagc.org

- ○ *Psychologists Familiar with Testing for Gifted and Exceptionally Gifted* (n.d.) at: https://www.hoagiesgifted.org/psychologists.htm

- ○ *Supporting the Emotional Needs of the Gifted* at https://www.sengifted.org/

- ○ *Hoagies' Gifted Education Page (Educators, Psychologists, Counselors)* at: https://www.hoagiesgifted.org/educators.htm

○ *2E Newsletter: Health and Wellness* (n.d.) at: https://www.2enews.com/category/health-wellness/

○ *The Gifted Resource Center of New England* (Deidre V. Lovecky, Ph.D.) at: http://www.grcne.com/

○ *Your Rainforest Mind (Paula Prober) at:* https://rainforestmind.com/

○ See state gifted associations.

○ See state chapters of American Psychological Associations.

# PART II:
# My 2E Life

*"Oh my God, it's a mirage, I'm tellin' y'all, it's a sabotage"*
~Beastie Boys

# Spectrum of Extremes

*It is important for readers to note that the following is an abridged 'PG' version of an 'R' rated life.*

*It is not a resume or vitae. It is just a view.*

As I begin to take you on a journey of my twice-exceptional life, it is important to understand that I see it as a 'spectrum of extremes'. I am not only gifted, and on the spectrum, but my life experiences have been ones of duality. For example, during my childhood, I traveled around the world part of each year with one parent and lived the rest of the year with my other parent in a small Texas town, roaming around on my grandparents' farm. I attended public schools as well as a prestigious private school. I had a career as an army medic and then I was the CEO of a medical device company. I have lived in large cities in Australia and the United Kingdom and small towns in the United States. I have experienced earning lots of money within the profit-oriented corporate world, and I have lived modestly working for my non-profit organization that helps people like me. I have worked in large boardrooms in big cities, and I have created beautiful pieces of abstract art in a small art studio in Durango, Colorado. I am thankful for every twist and turn that has led me to this time in my life.

It seems these extremes should have created competing forces that would cause havoc in my life, but it is just the opposite. Like being twice- exceptional, the spectrum of experience in my life has served to create a playground where I have had the opportunity to experience, learn and grow. Every experience has allowed me the opportunity to let my strengths shine. It is my hope that when you finish this section of the book, your eyes will be opened to all the possibilities for twice-exceptional people, particularly those with autism spectrum disorder/difference.

# Chapter 4:
# Early Life

*"I am, I am I said I'm not myself,
but I'm not dead and I'm not for sale."*
~Stone Temple Pilots

Some very important events occurred in the year 1972. It was the start of the Watergate scandal in Washington, D.C.; NASA's space shuttle program was launched; eleven Israeli athletes were killed during the Munich Olympics; the Equal Rights Amendment passed the United States Senate; and I was born on September 13th.

Gainesville, Texas was an idealistic town when I was born and raised there. People did not lock their doors, kids rode bikes everywhere, and we had a one-screen movie theater in town. The population was around 14,000. As I mentioned earlier, my father was a dentist who specialized in maxillo-facial orthopedics and TMD, and my mother was an elementary school teacher with a master's degree in early childhood development. I remember having some supportive adults around as a child growing up in Texas, especially my maternal grandparents.

My neighborhood was also a wonderful place to be raised. All the families watched out for each other's children. The idiom 'it takes a village to raise a child' describes how the families, home environment, schools, and town connected to impact me in a most positive way. Our next-door neighbor had a son six weeks younger than me, and our mothers raised us together. Pierce became my best friend, although he felt more like a brother. We did everything together except sports. Pierce has been a constant influence throughout my life and is still a dear friend to this day.

My family reminds me that during the first years of life, I achieved many of the developmental milestones quite early. For example, I began to eat adult food early with a palate very diverse for someone so young. I was not interested in crawling as an infant and began to walk and talk at 8 months old. I was social with everyone, not just family members. My mother and father read to me early and often and we loved rocking in the chair in my bedroom. I was certainly one of those kids who didn't start to show symptoms of autism until later in my childhood: it was quite the opposite.

Unfortunately, when I was 8 months old, my parents divorced. I am told the custody battle was ugly. It became very personal, and my father's sister even testified against him. The town even took sides in our family's conflict since my dad and grandfather were well-known dentists. Both of my parents remarried soon after, and it was determined that until I started elementary school, I would spend every Wednesday and every other weekend with my father and his new wife. They lived in a popular lake community outside of Gainesville. Because I was so young when I started commuting between two homes, it felt normal to have four parents instead of two. I also had much older stepsiblings, my stepmother's children from a previous marriage.

## Parenting Styles

Gifted children, and those with learning differences, are happiest when their parents accept their uniqueness and support their interests. Parents must be the trusted allies in a world that may not understand their child.[177] But parents must also impose limits and discipline while allowing a degree of autonomy that supports the child's level of maturity. Some parents have one specific approach to parenting while others have a combination of styles. Regardless, a child wants to feel loved and nurtured. They want to feel as though their parents have their best interest at heart.

> Growing up, I was given lots of freedom to explore my environment. My parents knew I was smart and interested in many things. They felt that putting constraints on me would diminish my love for investigating my world. I would often say, "You are not the boss of me!", because I thought I was a 'little adult' and could do pretty much what I wanted. As I began traveling back and forth between two homes and four parents, I became confused about what was expected of me, because of the very different approaches of each parent attempting to raise me.
>
> My mother, father, and stepparents' styles of parenting[178] (and in some cases non-parenting) strongly influenced me as I grew up. First, my mother is on the spectrum, with obsessive compulsive disorder and dyscalculia (self-diagnosed). She could be described as a *bold* parent. There was always something for me to improve upon in her eyes. I remember my clothes always had to be arranged in a certain way in my closet. When I began doing chores around the house, they had to be done in a certain way to please her. She often said, "Try harder". When she punished me for misbehaving, I had to sit in my rocking chair in my room for a specific period. This was not too bad because I loved that rocking chair. However, I constantly asked, "Can I come out of my room now?", because it was very difficult for me to sit still.

My stepfather was the exact opposite. His parenting style was *permissive*. He preferred to avoid confrontations with my mother and me. He was extremely patient with my very high level of energy. My mom said he had the patience of Job from the Bible. He was the equalizer and peace-keeper in our house. If my mother got angry with me, my stepfather would not intervene until later. He would 'track back' around to me and explain in a calm manner what I had done wrong.

My stepmother could be described as an authoritative (as opposed to authoritarian) parent. She was responsive to her own children and to me. She was willing to listen to my questions. She provided direct feedback—whether good or bad, and adequate support while she was married to my dad. She set her 'goal posts' of expectations for her children and never wavered. She also kept my father in check when he got overly frustrated with me. My step-mother and I spent lots of time together, especially when we traveled, since my father was always working. On our many overseas and domestic trips, she would prepare a fun 'academic itinerary'. We visited many museums and well-known places all over Europe and the United States. These 'hands on', out-of-the-classroom experiences had an incredible positive impact. Overall, my stepmother and I got along very well.

I saved my father to describe last because he is a very interesting man, to say the least. As I mentioned earlier, he is on the spectrum and dyslexic (undiagnosed). His parenting style (which was never apparent to me as I grew up) can best be described as a combination of uninvolved and dismissive, authoritarian, *and* overambi-tious. Sounds crazy right? How can these three types of parenting be rolled into one person? I will explain. First, my father was an *uninvolved* parent: he put all his time and energy into his dental practice. Then in 1978, he developed a dental diagnostic and treatment protocol that was both unique and highly successful. He founded The Clinical Foundation of Orthopedics, Orthodontics and TMD (Temporomandibular Joint Disorder, a group of more than 30 conditions that cause pain and dysfunction in the jaw joint and muscles that control jaw movement). He practiced this form of specialized dentistry for over forty years, and he also helped other doctors around the world to elevate their practices to more advanced levels. As a child I received little guidance, discipline, or nurturing from him. He was never abusive; he simply was emotionally absent. Any achievements I made were largely dismissed. Most needs or desires beyond basic food, clothing and shelter were taken care of by my stepmother when I was at their house.

My father was also *authoritarian*. He was domineering in nature. He placed high expectations on me with little responsiveness. I experienced a need to control me rather than nurture me. If I made mistakes, his feedback was often negative comments, sarcasm, and passive-aggressive behavior. As I got older, my decisions and interests were based on what he deemed important. For example, those on the spectrum have a strong area of interest about a particular topic; but I felt like I had no choice but to learn *his* interests. I very much enjoyed them, nonetheless. One of my dad's areas of interest is World War II history, as well as model trains, SCUBA diving, and collecting bear statues. When I began to travel around the world with him to symposia, he took me to the same museums repeatedly to learn about WWII, art, natural history, and other intriguing subjects. For this, I thank him. We visited the London Museum of Natural History at least a dozen times, and I feel like I could earn an advanced degree in world history for all the knowledge he helped me gain about this topic.

Just for some additional insight into my father, it is important to know he was married five times. The first wife, of course, was my mother. The second wife helped raise me. The third wife was a cool Australia lady who was closer to my age than his. She was more like a big sister to me. His fourth wife, my half-sister's mother, I never got to know. His current, and fifth wife, was an orthodontist from Guadalajara. They have been married almost 25 years. I initially never gave her a chance because I thought, 'here we go again-number five.' However, after my father and I reconnected six years ago, my wife and I have gotten to know her well and we enjoy spending time with her. We appreciate similar activities, passions, and a love for animals-especially dogs.

Finally, *overambitious* parents may overschedule their child and expect exceptional performance in a variety of activities. My father learned from his father to be extremely ambitious and competitive, which partially explains why he went into the same profession as my grandfather, and then went on to develop his specialized clinical foundation. My father infused in me his fierce need to perform to perfection. As I got older, he felt he had to compete with me—and not in a good way. His actions always indicated that 'I needed to be a real man', which included his strange and outdated concept of the very different roles men and women should play in society. To this day I experience stress from the need to feel perfect. I like to compete in business, but not to the extent of hurting others. I have many memories of meltdowns in my childhood and teenage years. It is important to remember that neither my mother, father, nor I knew we were on the spectrum.

Overambitious parents can also schedule their kid's life with one activity after another. Such overscheduling can make a child prone to anxiety. From the time I was 3 years old, I began traveling to Europe and other continents with my father and stepmother on his business trips. These trips were priceless in terms of the education I received, and we traveled often. By the time I was 9 years old, I had flown to Europe by myself. I stayed with some family friends in France for a month and then flew back to America alone. By ten years old, I had been to Europe a dozen times, and by the age of fifteen, I had traveled to roughly forty American states and flown around the world for the first time.

Today, my father and I have a much better relationship. He has told me that he is proud of my accomplishments and I in turn appreciate everything that he has achieved in his career. Most of my career has revolved around maxillofacial orthopedics and dental sleep medicine. I became an expert in the former due to the many hours I spent listening to his lectures and visual presentations.

When I was 4 years old, I was thrilled to become a big brother to Bryan. As he got older, I showed him around the neighborhood and helped take care of him. We have been described as opposites by those who know us well: I am an extrovert and sociable, and my brother is an introvert and generally prefers the same group of friends. My parents told me that as my little brother grew up, they worried he wasn't learning to talk. Then they realized I was doing all the talking for him. I always included my brother when I played with neighborhood friends, and they were happy to have him as part of our group. My brother is not on the spectrum, but he does consider himself obsessive compulsive.

When most children from divorced homes begin their routine of visiting each parent, the ex-spouses usually have conversations about the child's school progress, extracurricular activity schedules and such—but not mine. My parents were passive-aggressive to each other after their divorce, and I felt it deeply. Too often I was told that I reminded my mother of my father, and vice versa. Ultimately, I felt their anger, and I was left to emotionally fend for myself much of the time. This meant I could make my own decisions about when and where I wanted to go. In high school, I decided what classes to take without any input from my parents, and I figured out which college to attend-mind you I hadn't really thought about much until March of my senior year. I felt alone, especially when it came to making big decisions in my life. Apparently, I was just supposed to know how to do those things.

My brother and I received inconsistent direction from our mother. This is not to be confused with any form of favoritism. I postulate this was due to her undiagnosed ASD and OCD. Regardless, it would have been significant to receive it consistently when my brother and I did something meaningful. Praise is a strong motivator. "Parents can start kids on the road to healthy self-esteem by offering praise associated with something concrete."[179] Now that I understand autism, I appreciate Temple Grandin's quote, "The literal concrete mind of the autistic child requires that self-esteem be built through tangible accomplishments coupled with verbal praise."[180] While my mother and I didn't have an ideal relationship growing up, we have been close for about twenty five years. She is a good person, smart and very funny with her blunt sardonic autistic sense of humor!

## Importance of Chores, First Jobs, and Manners

I give my parents credit for making sure my brother and I did our share of chores around the house as we grew up. The regular household duties we completed served a variety of purposes, teaching us life skills, responsibility, self-reliance, and a strong work ethic which I still have today. My brother and I worked as a team to get the jobs done. We made our beds each day, washed clothes, and cleaned the bathroom. Due to our mom's OCD, we also had to clean the baseboards regularly. We hated this job because it seemed we never got it right in mom's eyes. There were times we cleaned them several times in one day. One important thing I learned from doing chores growing up, and which I later practiced in my business with employees, was to always set clear objectives and consistent rewards.

As I got older, I learned additional life skills by working part time jobs in high school. Dr. Temple Grandin noted in her book, *The Way I See It: A Personal Look at Autism*[181] that work experience for those on the spectrum should start before high school graduation. Education of people with ASD goes far beyond book learning. They absolutely require 'life learning skills'. Grandin says, "Working for a year before graduating greatly increases employment from 6.25% to 87.5%."[182] Because my parents and I did not know we were autistic, they did not know how important it was for me to gain skills from a part time job. But I was fortunate that some high school friends had jobs and I needed to earn some money. I also wanted to hang out and have fun.

I remember my first job working in a yacht club restaurant kitchen. This experience was invaluable because I learned to take directions from a boss. But I hated it. This was an early indicator I wanted to become an entrepreneur someday, and it was not from an ego standpoint of being in charge. I simply could not tolerate seeing tasks that could easily become more effective, efficient, and improved upon and not have the authority to fix them.

Learning compliance was not taught much at home because of the way my brother and I were raised. I could not 'mouth off' to my employer just because I did not want to do a particular task. If I had, I would have been fired, and I did not want that to happen. I may not have liked everything in my job description or the way a manager behaved at the restaurant, but I still had to comply. These early lessons support many parts of my life today. I don't like grocery shopping, but I know it is an unavoidable task. I don't like filing my taxes each year, but it is the law. Too many young individuals on the spectrum who have never had early learning experiences like mine could find themselves in distress later in life if they don't learn from the structure of an early job experience. Having said all the above, I strongly believe that many of us on the spectrum are born entrepreneurs. I encourage this when teaching my students and life coaching adults through my foundation.

Manners are something else I appreciated learning when I was young. Mostly I mirrored the behaviors of what I saw others do, specifically my father, who has impeccable manners, even if old-fashioned. When people said, "Thank you", "Please", and "Excuse me", I paid attention. I interacted with many kinds of people before I was fifteen years old, and I found the act of observing became the best teacher for me. Parents of children with autism will often wait to teach their son or daughter manners and respect, because other issues seem to take priority. But I have discovered it is very important to begin teaching these skills as early as possible. 'Autism is not an excuse to be rude.'[183] Individuals on the spectrum need to learn that manners are not just kind *words*, they include the *practiced behaviors* of sharing and taking turns. Children and adults with ASD can struggle with seeing social cues and body language (lack of cognitive empathy), which can make it difficult for them to show consideration for others. It is clear, then, that learning manners and respect will help people with ASD navigate everyday situations more smoothly.

## Non-Nuclear Families

I am not sure how many children growing up in non-nuclear families, as I did, could say that this type of family dynamic *saved* their life, but I can! If just my mother and father had raised me, I believe I would have harmed myself or someone else. I realize these words sound harsh, but it is true. Because I can describe my parents as 'distant' and 'uninvolved', it is easy to see that stepparents helped balance my childhood. My stepmother and stepfather were perfect partners for their spouses because they had positive parenting styles that my biological parents did not. To this day, my stepdad (Dad Southworth)) has always been my greatest advocate. Also, having stepsiblings (as well as a brother) made me feel heard and regarded as a valued part of the family.

Lastly, I cannot understate the contributions of Pierce's parents (Marvin and Judy) to my upbringing. As I mentioned earlier, we basically grew up as brothers and I spent almost as much time with them as I did my parents and stepparents. Unfortunately, they have both passed away. Their funerals were exceptionally difficult for me and in most regards like losing yet another set of parents. Their influence and understanding throughout my life have been profound. All these combined dynamics- from parents to stepparents to Marvin and Judy- have been a lifesaver for me.

As I learned more about autism, I understood that my parents were extremely *unfamiliar* with its signs. It is important to note that symptoms are always present in early development years, even if not noticed until later in life.[184] As described to me by my psychologist Dr. Robinson, my parents most likely had an extreme stereotypical view of autism and felt that I in no way fit their understanding of it. In addition, he pointed out most importantly that many parents of autistic people who are now adults are very defensive when questioned about their son's or daughter's early years. This was true when we interviewed my parents for this book. Parents take the suggestion that their child is autistic very personally, considering it an accusation that they were neglectful, uncaring, or emotionally unavailable. Even though my parents are well-educated and very familiar with medicine, they remained unaware of my ASD. Dr. Robinson added, "I've observed that parents who are well-educated, especially in medicine, don't know what they don't know." That my parents relied on their professional training and careers unfortunately made them even more confident that there was nothing different about me. On their behalf I will say that when I was a child, Asperger's was completely unknown to physicians. Autism was viewed only through the lens of classical, profoundly, 'low functioning' individuals, and I did not look like that.

## Early Childhood Screening for ASD

I am happy to say that today the American Academy of Pediatrics suggests all children should receive a formalized ASD screening at their 18-and 24-month well-child doctor visits.[185] Health providers look for signs of developmental and communication challenges during these exams. Behavioral observations (baby giggles, points, waves, responses to their name, crying), family history, health examinations and parents' perspectives help pediatricians identify children at risk of ASD. I find these recommendations and screenings a huge step forward, but I think that even today I would 'slip through the cracks'-especially when it comes to developmental milestones.

Tools used to screen for ASD include:[186]

○ *Ages and Stages Questionnaires SE-2 (ASQ-SE2).* Parent-completed questionnaire; series of 19 age-specific questionnaires screening communication, gross motor, fine motor, problem-solving, and personal adaptive skills; results in a pass/fail score for domains.

○ *Pervasive Developmental Disorders Screening Test II (PDDST-II).* This is a 22-item questionnaire that is designed to be completed by the child's parent/caregiver. It takes parents between 10 to 20 minutes to complete and is easily scored and interpreted by providers.

○ *Communication & Symbolic Behavior Scales (CSBS).* Standardized tool for screening of communication and symbolic abilities up to the 24-month level; the Infant Toddler Checklist is a 1-page, parent-completed screening tool.

○ *Modified Checklist for Autism in Toddlers-Revised with Follow Up (M-CHAT-R/F).* Parent-completed questionnaire designed to identify children at risk for autism in the general population.

It is interesting to note that a recent Duke University study indicated signs of autism can be picked up as early as the first month of life.[187] Children's health records were used to create an algorithm to predict the babies who were later diagnosed as autistic, distinguishing them from those who later developed ADHD or other neurodevelopmental diagnoses. The study reveals how important it is to see that autism is not just a *behavioral* health condition, but also a condition that involves *physical* health (digestion, sleep, neurological, vision and other issues).[188] The director of the Duke Center for Autism and Brain Development, Geraldine Dawson, says, "Infants who will go on to get a diagnosis of autism show very different early patterns of health care utilization."[189]

If I had been screened for autism before 2 years old, I know I would not have been diagnosed. I met too many 'normal' childhood markers early, and never exhibited any of the more common early symptoms of autism, like lack of eye contact, repetitive behaviors, or challenged socialization. Because every child is unique, it is important to remember that screening is not diagnosing. The American Academy of Pediatrics reports:[190] 1) If a child has a positive screen for ASD, it doesn't mean he or she will be diagnosed on the spectrum. 2) If a child screens 'normal' but as their parent you continue to worry about ASD, seek further evaluations. Screenings do not identify all children with ASD.

# Benefits of Travel

All children benefit from traveling; but for autistic individuals *and* their families, the rewards of travel are immense. The destination does not matter. It could be a trip to the zoo, a beach, a museum, or a national park. The travel opportunities I had before high school shaped who I am today: they taught me lessons and skills I would never have learned without them. Some of the benefits of family travel include:[191]

○ *Reduced isolation.* When parenting a child with special needs, isolation is a very real concern. It is all too easy to become isolated at home because of your child's needs, which is not healthy for you or for your child. Traveling allows your entire family to move out of your unchallenged comfort zone and avoid the trap of isolation.

○ *Enjoyment of family time.* Travel brings the opportunity to bond as a family. Your child with special needs *and* your other children need time together to build strong relationships. You can use travel experiences to visit relatives that you may not see regularly. The family bonds and memories you create are worth the challenges and logistics you must tackle.

○ *Development of Life skills.* Your goal when raising a child with autism is to encourage as much independence as possible, and that requires developing life skills. Being able to travel is a life skill that will benefit your child long after the trip. You can use travel to teach skills like social interaction, map reading, budgeting, and more, depending on your child's abilities and age. Learning flexibility is important too, especially as a contrast to the strict routines often required to manage neurological differences.

○ *Educational benefits.* Seeing different cultures, exploring historic sites, and interacting with nature are all important for your children's education—things that they cannot learn in the classroom. It will increase your child's cultural

appreciation, and empathy for others who think or act differently than your child.

○ *Sensory desensitization.* Most children with autism have sensory
needs, and many respond negatively to sensory stimulation.
One of the best ways to help them overcome this hurdle is
to desensitize them to the sensory stimulation that they find
challenging. Travel exposes your child to new things that can
help with this process, and because you don't have access to the
comforts of home, it makes desensitization more automatic.

○ *Spreading autism awareness.* For many parents of children with
autism, spreading awareness about neurodiversity becomes a
passion. When you travel, you can expand that message even
further. Exposing other people to the neurodiverse world
(i.e., people on the spectrum) will make the future world
more accepting of diversity and of people with autism, which
benefits not only your family, but also the rest of the world.

My parents divorced when I was an infant. Before I was
three years old, my father's clinical foundation was already
successful. He began to travel out of the country often to
conduct courses and seminars. When I was three, I made
my first trips to Mexico and Europe with my father and
my stepmother. As I got older, I traveled with my parents
all around the United States, and I traveled internationally
once a quarter to countries like England, France, Germany,
and others throughout western Europe. Being on the
spectrum, I 'soaked' up all the information and lessons
as possible.

When I was 6 years old, I remember traveling to London,
where we stayed at the exclusive Stafford Hotel. I learned
about the quintessential tradition of British 'high tea'.
I enjoyed sitting like a little gentleman at a lovely table
with high back chairs eating small sandwiches, quiches,
pastries, and scones. I learned a great deal at a young
age about proper manners. I was taught about the table

settings for a seven-course meal, and how to participate correctly in continental European style service at dinner. Over the years, my father, his various wives, and I stayed at this hotel more than twenty times.

When I was almost 8 years old, my father had a seminar planned in Paris. He asked me what I wanted to do for my birthday while we were there. Like every 8-year-old, I said, "I want to have dinner at the top of the Eiffel Tower". My stepmother said no. But my father, who always got his way, said yes. He even sent out birthday invitations to my friends in Gainesville! Can you imagine getting a children's birthday invitation to dinner in the Eiffel Tower? This is an example of how my father directed the attention to himself. He wanted the families to 'Ooh' and 'Ahh' at this extravagance. My birthday dinner was fine, but I was very lonely. I wish I had had my Texas friends around me while the waiters sang *The Eyes of Texas are Upon You*. I blew out a candle on my baked Alaska dessert in front of a huge crowd, but that made me feel uncomfortable and alone. (My 9th birthday was at McDonald's in Gainesville with my 'crew'. Guess which birthday I preferred?)

By the time I was twelve years old, our travels overseas always looked the same. We stayed at the same hotels, spoke with the same people, and ate at the same restaurants *because my father had to repeat things over and over: his preference for routine was obvious*. I observed at hotels, like The Stafford in London, that he liked the staff to know him personally. At seminars and conferences, he wanted to see the same faces he saw the last time he lectured. At restaurants, my father wanted the same head waiters to dote on us. He had to know them by name, and they had to know exactly what he liked to eat. I didn't know then, but I do now, that this behavior was a symptom of autism; I find that I generally do the same thing now, albeit to a lesser extent.

When my father presented at seminars, I observed closely. I often felt I could teach, like he did, about maxillo-facial orthopedics, orthodontics and TMD. Another big part of my learning on these trips was engaging with the sales teams and other representatives at the conventions. I learned how to sell products and entertain other dentists. These people taught me how to hire and incentivize employees, which became very useful later in my own business career. Interacting with so many types of people was crucial to my success today.

When I turned fifteen, I made my first trip around the world. At this stage in my life, the only continent I have not been to is Antarctica. (It is on my bucket list.) Bouncing around the globe has been organic for me. One month I could be in Texas, and the next month in Switzerland, Germany, South Africa, or Australia. School was never a problem because when travelling during the school year, I brought school assignments with me. All of my parents felt that the unique developmental, cultural, and educational benefits of traveling abroad were impossible to replicate in a class-room environment. I wholeheartedly agree.

The lasting friendships made during our travels have also impacted me in a very meaningful way. One family we met in France became like my own. Their daughters became like sisters to me. I was invited to stay with them during three different summer vacations, and I became immersed in their culture. We visited the fish markets at 5:00 am, brought oysters back to shuck and cook in the backyard, ate freshly prepared meals like escargots, mustard rabbit, and 'fromage' of all kinds. We returned the invitation to this family, and they visited us in Texas. We introduced them to American culture, including a taste of Texas BBQ. This experience felt much like the foreign exchange program some students experience today. Our perspectives were broadened about each other's culture. My French 'sisters' and I expanded our personalities, improved our self-confidence, and gained maturity. We knew our lives were forever changed in a good way because the experiences we had together framed the rest of our lives.

When I returned home after each global excursion, I always had interesting discussions with my family. My little brother wanted to hear all about everything. Once I told him the funny story of a well-educated doctor I had met in France who told me I pronounced 'water' incorrectly. He said I could not travel around the world saying it the way I did. With my Texas accent, I pronounced it 'wadder'. My mother always told me when I returned from a trip abroad that I had a markedly different personality for a few days. She would say, "John, you are just like your father." I took this to mean she was *not* happy. My stepfather would buffer her by saying, "Give it a couple days, and he'll be fine." It drove her crazy until I settled back into my American small-town personality again.

After being gone from home, sometimes for a whole summer, I was happy to see my friends and my maternal grandparents when I returned. My friends made me feel included, but my Mamaw and Papaw made me feel loved. They owned a 120-acre farm not far from Rockwall, Texas. The land there has gentle rolling hills with hundreds of beautiful oak trees. My Papaw raised some cattle and Mamaw grew fruits and vegetables. I spent lots of time there hunting, cutting firewood, shooting guns, and riding four-wheelers. When it came time to eat dinner, Mamaw would cook meals like 'poke salad' (pokeweed is like spinach) with catfish, homemade cornbread, and jam. When I sat to eat Mamaw's delicious food, I would remember that just weeks before I had been in an exclusive restaurant in Paris eating foie gras. My two very different worlds became a fundamental part of who I am today.

Today there are few places, if any, where I can relax, not have anxiety, and sleep well like I did on my grandparents' farm. I would stay up until dark, go to bed early, and wake up with Papaw at 5 am to have coffee. Then we would go out and I helped him work the land. Today, I would rather live on a farm or in a cabin in the country than in a city. I learned from my 'spectrum of extremes' that I am very connected to the land. (It must be the Irish in me.) What did Dorothy say in the movie *The Wizard of Oz*? She said, "There's no place like home." Land, and utilizing it in some manner, are essential to my happiness. Traveling the world helped me clearly see that I am my best self when on the farm.

## Schools

Twice-exceptional students were unidentified when I went to school for the reasons mentioned in Chapter 2. It is sad that this special group of students are still overlooked today. The periods before and during elementary school are very important because, when identifications are made earlier in a child's life, and supports are put into place, the child will have more success at school and at home. I am certain my teachers and parents knew I was gifted. But they were not aware of my Asperger's and dyslexia. I feel certain that if by age 5 the adults in my life had had the tools to support my twice-exceptionality, my life would be very different. Again, in today's world where there is far greater understanding and acceptance of neurodivergent children, I strongly encourage early diagnosis.

### Montessori Education/Learning Styles

Pierce and I began attending a Montessori type school at 4 years old. I remember enjoying it because I could learn at my own pace, which meant very quickly and differently than the other children. The philosophy for this type of education is based on the belief that children are naturally smart and curious and should have the freedom to explore the world around them in an orderly, disciplined environment.[192] The development of the whole child (cognitive, physical, social, and emotional) is emphasized by identifying the child's learning styles. This is important because identifying strengths to compensate for weaknesses, without a label, enables a student to learn without struggling through school: if a student has visual-spatial problems (difficulty picturing things) but is outstanding in English, the student can learn math by putting everything into their own words.

There are many learning styles, and not all people fit neatly into one category. Some individuals may learn with a combination of them. Here is a list of learning styles to help identify and support a student in their classroom:[193]

○ *Visual Learners*: A preference for visual learning emphasizes seeing and observing things, including pictures, diagrams, written directions. This is also referred to as the 'spatial' learning style. Students who learn through sight understand information better when it's presented in a visual way. These are your doodling students, your list makers and your students who take notes, for whom educators should use smartboards or whiteboards: allow students to draw pictures and diagrams, provide handouts to students, use visual presentations, and allow time to process the material.

○ *Auditory Learners*: Auditory learners learn better when the subject matter is reinforced by sound. These students would much rather listen to a lecture than read written notes, and they often use their own voices to reinforce new concepts and ideas. This type of learner prefers reading out loud to themselves. They aren't afraid to speak up in class and are great at verbally explaining things. Additionally, they may be slower at reading and may often repeat things a teacher tells them. Educators need to involve these students in their lectures by asking them to repeat new concepts back to the class, asking lots of questions, and invoking group discussions. Using mnemonics, watching videos, using audiotapes, and incorporating non-obtrusive music will also help auditory learners.

○ *Reading/Writing Learners*: Reading/writing learners prefer to learn through written words. While there is some overlap with visual learning, these learners are drawn to expression through writing, reading, writing in diaries, looking up words in the dictionary and searching the internet for just about everything. Most traditional educators cater to this learning style: students write essays, do research, and read books. With these students it is important that teachers be mindful and allow plenty of time for students to absorb written information and give them opportunities to express themselves on paper as well.

○ *Linguistic Learners* (similar to reading/writing learners): These individuals learn by vocal expression and articulation. They are typically strong orators and writers and need time and space to think out loud and on paper. One way to engage linguistic leaners is to always provide written instructions. Picturesque charts are useful but can be limited by the teacher's expectations. Word problems in math and writing, to explain science concepts, are effective for linguistic learners.

○ *Logical/Mathematical Learners*: These learners excel at math, but they dislike the ambiguity of literary analysis. They learn through logic and love the absolute quality of numbers. Logical/mathematical learners thrive when structure is abundant and may struggle with the in precision of creative projects. For these students teachers should provide rubrics and checklists with clear expectations. Goals should be measurable and provide students with the information and tools necessary to self-monitor progress.[194] 'Sequencing' activities, technology, and building projects are great for this type of learner.

○ *Interpersonal Learners*: Students who consistently ask to work in groups is likely an interpersonal learner. They thrive during collaborative work because *communication is the key to their comprehension.* Group work is obviously their strength. When some assignments must be completed individually, teachers could allow interpersonal learners to work with others during the planning phase of such assignments, like offering activities that include literature circles or 'think-pair-share'. *Think-pair-share* is a collaborative learning strategy where students work together to solve a problem or answer a question about an assigned reading. This strategy requires students to (1) think individually about a topic or answer to a question; and (2) share ideas with classmates. Discussing with a partner maximizes participation, focuses attention, and engages students in comprehending the reading material.

○ *Intrapersonal Learners*: These learners are the exact opposite of *interpersonal* learners: they thrive working alone. They will request to work alone on group projects. Independent study time and a quiet, secluded workspace are extremely helpful. Intrapersonal learners do well with self-directed research, so providing resources for them to study independently is beneficial. When these learners must work collaboratively, provide defined roles and let them identify the role to which they are best suited.[195]

○ *Kinesthetic Learners*: Also known as tactile learners, these students retain information through action. They like to get involved by acting out events or using their hands to touch to understand concepts. Kinesthetic learners might struggle to sit still, and often excel at sports or dance. They may need more frequent breaks when studying. Planning lessons which include physical movement and manual creativity will help kinesthetic children succeed. Activities like 'gallery walks' that allow students to move about the classroom are helpful. Flexible seating options that allow students to work while standing, laying down, etc., are also helpful. Products like *fidget cubes* and *bouncy bands* are great ways for these learners to discreetly maintain movement while working.

[*Fidget cubes* are small, handheld gadgets that provide one with a series of sensory tools across its six sides. They are small enough to hold easily in one hand, making the other hand free to do something else. *Bouncy bands* are simply resistance band 'fidgets' for one's feet, designed to go around the legs of a desk or chair so one can rest their feet on them and move them whenever necessary.]

### Early Public-School Experiences/Teachers

I was enrolled in public schools in Gainesville when I turned six years old. I loved attending school because I am a sponge when it comes to learning something new. Unlike many Aspies, I enjoyed socializing. I was well-liked by my peers and teachers for the most part, and I was never bullied. It seemed that my teachers accepted my *quirky* nature (unconventional qualities and behavior) and 'cut me some breaks' because they recognized I was smart. This was also a time when teachers were allowed to really educate as opposed to having to focus on administration and statewide metrics. Few of my elementary teachers taught directly from a textbook and their freedom to teach in different styles was of great benefit to me.

Teachers can have an enormous impact on their students, positive and negative. The few negative ones I remember impeded my learning. In third grade I had just been to Paris, and I was very excited to tell my classmates and teacher about what I had learned on this trip, but my teacher was not interested in me sharing. She wanted to 'put me in my place' by making me feel unimportant. It was also in third grade that I began to hear from my teacher, 'try harder', and 'don't be lazy'. This happened specifically in math because I was challenged to learn the multiplication times tables. No one considered dyscalculia to be the issue. I began to *hear* the 'tic- tic- tic' of the classroom clock and air conditioner. These things were all very distracting to my learning.

What is *wild* to me about math since I have dyscalculia is that I love statistics, fractions, decimals, and percentages. The sad thing is because I thought I was horrible at *all* math, I skipped statistics and economics in high school and college. Today my math calculation is at a 10th grade level. But pragmatically, I can apply math at **graduate school level**. In business, I created profit and loss statements as well as *pro forma* forecasts (based on projected company income and cash flow), but I cannot balance a check book. The great news is there is this amazing device I can use for free called a 'calculator'.

In fourth grade, my teacher preferred girls to boys. I remember writing my first 'civil disobedience' letter to the principal. It must have made an impact, because my teacher began calling on boys more in our class. The same year, when I did well in math, I heard, "Oh look, John is trying now!" (I was extremely good at fractions and ratios.) When I struggled with math skills that involved lots of calculation, I got the opposite reaction. My teacher said, "Look, John is not trying anymore". She never thought that a learning difference could be the reason for my 'hot and cold' reaction to math.

In kindergarten, I was reading at the 5th grade level. By fifth grade, I was reading high school material. However, my teacher decided that since I was challenged at reading aloud, I must not be a good reader. She had several reading groups, and I was placed at the mid-fifth grade level. It is unfortunate that I was not given credit for comprehending at an advanced level if I was allowed to take my time with unfamiliar material. Reading fluency (the ability to read with speed, accuracy, and expression) is not the only determination of a student's reading ability. If a student's comprehension is high and their reading fluency is low, this discrepancy may indicate a learning difference. In my case, I am dyslexic.

My positive school experiences involved teachers who enjoyed my personality and took time to speak with me. I also appreciated the teachers who allowed me to use my strengths to demonstrate what I learned. For example, when large projects were assigned, many of my teachers allowed students to select their partners. Because our school district was small, my friend Pierce was always in my class. We knew we had complimentary skill sets and we enjoyed working together. We would split up tasks and work on the parts of the project that played to our strengths. I always felt successful in school when this was an option. Additionally, when Pierce would travel with my family and me, we would complete our school assignments together the night before we left. We finished a week's worth of work in one night using the same team dynamic.

### Disorders or Differences Never Recognized

When I reflect on my early times in school, I consider a paraphrased line from Robert Burn's poem *To a Mouse*. "The best-laid plans of mice and men often go awry" translates to no matter how carefully we plan, something still may go wrong. Because I always put my best foot forward in school and my intelligence masked some of my issues, teachers never suspected that I had learning differences and therefore were not able to support me. Here are a few important issues that I was later diagnosed with:

### Processing Speed Disorder:

Slow processing speed means that a child cannot keep up with the pace of learning in the classroom. But because of my giftedness I already knew much of the curriculum being taught, so it appeared that I learned everything faster than my peers. I was also a very verbal child, and always wanted to share what I knew. Many 2e children show substantial differences between their verbal abilities and their working memory capacity, and between their nonverbal abilities and processing speed, so working memory and processing speed scores are often low in 2e children.[196]

Slow processing speed can play a part in learning and attention issues like dyslexia, dyscalculia, dysgraphia, ADD/ADHD, and auditory processing disorder.[197] I was not surprised to learn that studies done at Massachusetts General Hospital in the Learning and Emotional Assessment Program (LEAP) showed that 70% more boys are affected by significant processing deficits than girls.[198]

*Dyslexia:*

I now understand that I was *hyperlexic* in school. Children with hyperlexia are often self-taught readers who can read well above what is expected at their age, but they struggle to understand what they are reading.[199] The perplexing part about this term for me is that in school I always read above grade level, but I *also* always understood and remembered everything I read. I have never been challenged by comprehension as a child or adult. I realized late in life and only after my diagnosis at 45, my comprehension was excellent, but I needed to slow down when reading large amounts of text or long books. This was confirmed when I took the WAIS test as an adult. If I am unaccommodated, I will scan the reading material and retain it only at the 20th percentile. But when given more time to read, my scores jump back to the 99th percentile. (I must read at roughly half the speed of my peers.) My formal diagnosis now is dyslexia and I inherited it from my father. Additionally, we are both poor spellers. I have come to learn through my psychologist that having dyslexia and being a poor speller is common. He said, "It is often very easy to help a dyslexic person to read, but difficult to get them to spell well." Dyslexia can be categorized as:[200]

1. *Phonological*: People with this type of dyslexia have difficulty processing the sounds of the individual letters and syllables and cannot match them with the written forms.

2. *Rapid Naming Deficit*: This individual finds it difficult to name a letter, number, color, or object quickly and automatically. Their processing speed is low, and it takes time for the person to name them. I fit in this category.

3. *Surface Dyslexia*: This type of dyslexia is marked by difficulty recognizing whole words, which probably results from vision issues or visual processing difficulties in the brain. With trouble recognizing what is written, these people may have a hard time learning and memorizing words.

4. *Double Deficit Dyslexia*: This form of dyslexia shows deficits in both the phonological process and naming speed. Most of the weakest readers fall into this category.

*Dyscalculia:*

As young as 8 years old, I knew something was wrong with my ability to do math calculations. In third grade when peers started learning their multiplication tables, I was one of the few students who struggled. I felt perplexed because I knew I could do complex math extremely well. Unfortunately, my parents or teachers never realized anything was different.

Dyscalculia makes learning or comprehending arithmetic challenging: there is difficulty understanding numbers, learning how to manipulate numbers, and learning math facts.[201] Dyscalculia can make it hard to do everyday tasks like cooking, grocery shopping, and getting to places on time, because all of these involve 'number sense', i.e., basic math skills. Today I am challenged with balancing a check book and making change at the store.

I have said throughout my life, 'please don't put any letters with my numbers.' I cannot comprehend or execute the calculations required in algebra, geometry, and advanced math. Yet, I automatically know how to apply the concepts. Funnily enough, I have never seen any letters in the numbers when it comes to a P/L or pro forma (profit and loss statement) other than the assumptions running down the left-hand side of a spreadsheet.

This disorder can show up as early as preschool or it can reveal itself when math becomes more difficult.[202] Young children can find it difficult to understand that a number stands for a quantity; or a child finds it hard to grasp the meaning of terms like 'more' and 'less' and 'biggest to smallest'. Multisensory techniques can help, like clapping five times for the number 5. Other accommodations for school and home should include extended time to finish math work, using manipulatives like blocks, and playing math games.

*Obsessive Compulsive Disorder:*

I believe my OCD was first noticed at home. Per our mother's insistence, my brother and I had to arrange our clothes by the colors of the rainbow, ROYGBIV. We also had to arrange our pants from short to long, and our shirts from short sleeve to long sleeve. When we were young, my brother and I would observe our mother try to vacuum the lines out of the carpet and mow the lawn in different directions. She would do these tasks over and over. When I started school, I enjoyed lining things up on my desk. I insisted everything had a place and a place had a thing. Today, lining things up on my desk at home relaxes me and helps me perform better.

Obsessive compulsive disorder was formerly classified as an anxiety disorder because the characteristic obsessive thoughts can lead to severe anxiety.[203] The compulsions or rituals performed are an attempt to reduce the anxiety. The DSM-5 has moved OCD to its own class, 'Obsessive-Compulsive and Related Disorders'.[204]

There is no exact cause identified for OCD in children. Researchers feel that several factors play a role, including brain structure, early-life trauma, stress, and genetics.[205] The average onset of childhood OCD is at approximately ten years old, although children as young as five can be diagnosed. In rare cases, children show symptoms as early as age three.[206] I feel strongly that my OCD is genetic. There is no 'OCD gene', no evidence for certain genes that may signal greater vulnerability. But OCD *has* been found to run in families. The closer the family member, and the younger the child was when symptoms started, the higher the risk of OCD.[207]

*Motor Issues:*

My handwriting has been terrible since the time I began to learn how to write. I also have miserable eye-hand coordination. In elementary school grade, I could never play catch with balls and frisbees or skip at recess like the rest of the children. But I was very good at kicking, and I enjoyed running and tackling in football, wrestling, soccer, and kickball. As an adult, you will never see me playing a game of golf. Partially because I am simply not good at it, but primarily because I find it a fundamental waste of time with no tangible results. But I occasionally 'play' golf with my friends which essentially entails drinking beer and driving the cart.

According to the latest estimates, 87% of autistic people have some sort of motor difficulty ranging from atypical gait to problems with handwriting.[208] (These problems are not considered a core trait of autism because they also occur in other conditions like ADHD.) There are many motor issues autistic individuals can have. In my case, I have trouble with actions requiring hand-eye coordination, such as catching an object or imitating the movements of others, and with planning a series of movements or gestures, known as praxis. I enjoy participating in sports if I can utilize my strengths, such as running or kicking.

Today teachers are becoming more aware of the many differences that affect a child's learning. Schools have intervention assistance teams who help identify and support children with unique needs. We believe, though, that parents are the first adults to notice when their children are not meeting age-appropriate benchmarks; nonetheless it is extremely important to remember that *smart children often mask learning differences, at school and at home*. We must be very careful not to incorrectly label students with hidden talents as underachievers or lazy.

### *Middle School/ Stressor*

Transitioning from elementary to middle school is an adjustment for any student. Three of the main stressors in making this concern procedure, social life, and academics. Procedural change involves adjusting to more students in a larger school, visiting a different teacher for each subject, and managing the transition time between classes, including using a locker and fitting in bathroom and lunch breaks. Social stressors include students moving from the 'top rung of the ladder' in elementary school to the bottom in middle school. Seventh graders have different schedules that may not include friends from elementary years, and so the challenge of meeting new people is inevitable. And academic stressors affect many middle schoolers. It is typical for academic performance to drop slightly while adjusting to middle school.[209] More difficult classes require more homework and taking charge of larger assignments and projects. There is much less day-to-day guidance and personalized instruction compared to elementary school. Middle school teachers are training students to become stakeholders in their own learning success.

I encountered all three stressors transitioning to middle school, some more than others. *Procedurally*, I found it difficult adjusting to different types of teachers. If I had a teacher I respected because they offered me new knowledge, I would be invested in their class. But if I was in a class where I knew more than the teacher, my attitude soured: I would have preferred to be anywhere than sit in a class that offered me nothing but a schedule place-holder. Next, I am a holistic thinker or what some call a 'leaper'. My brain needs time to connect a new concept or new information to my greater body of knowledge and way of thinking. In middle school, I realized that parents, teachers, and classmates were not going to take my notes or oversee my assignment due dates anymore. I wish someone had suggested to me the following holistic thinker study tips.[210]

○ *Pay attention to outlines.* Outlines provide a framework for 'storing' new information.

○ *Make your own outline.* This visual tool helps the brain organize more quickly.

○ *Don't skip the introduction or summary.* This helps establish a framework for storing and applying concepts found in the subsequent reading.

○ *Look for boundaries.* Holistic learners may have trouble discerning where one concept or event ends and another begins. It is helpful to establish the beginning and ending points.

○ *Ask for examples.* The holistic brain likes to make comparisons, so the more examples the better. Label these examples to avoid disorganized notes.

○ *Use images.* Make pictures and charts after reading a long passage or explanation.

○ *Draw timelines.* This is another way of creating guidelines for organization.

○ *Look at sample assignments.* The holistic brain likes to use examples as a frame of reference. Without them, it is hard to know where to start.

○ *Make drawings of concepts.* The more one can sketch out and characterize concepts the better. Examples include Venn diagrams and other graphic organizers.

I have always been outgoing and able to make friends. But middle school surprised me *socially*. It was during this part of my schooling that I found I connected with all types of students. I had friends in the 'jock' or sports crowd, although I was not an athlete; and friends among the musicians in the 'rock' and 'band geek' groups. I 'hung out' with other smart students, too. They provided the most mental stimulation for me when I needed truly in-depth conversations.

By 8th grade I was challenged to read facial cues and body gestures of other teens. When fourteen-year-old boys and girls started interacting with each other in ways that didn't happen in elementary school, I was not prepared. Although I had friends and girlfriends, I sometimes felt like an 'outsider'. One significant event occurred in the summer between 7th and 8th grade: I had my first negative experience with alcohol. My mother and father had moved to Rockwall, Texas and I made a couple of new friends in their neighborhood. One night we went to a mutual friend's house and drank a lot. To make a long story short, I got drunk and was out of control. I got 'sucker punched' and my jaw was broken. At fourteen years old, I learned a valuable lesson: if you decide to drink with a group to socially fit in, there will be unwanted outcomes. I also learned another important lesson that night: when someone swings at you, you duck!

The third and final stressor in middle school was *academics*. I found it challenging to be in a class where I felt truly stimulated. Since most elementary to middle-school students are of average-ability, the classes tend to be geared toward *their* learning needs. As a gifted individual, I found that the curriculum did not keep up with my interests and abilities.

Some of the lessons were mind-numbingly dull. This is a problem for gifted kids when boredom transforms into underachievement, social isolation, and disinterest in school. In some cases, underachievement among profoundly gifted students does not reveal itself until they are finally in environments in which challenge them appropriately. Challenge leads these students to work hard in school, employing new study skills and independently discovering ways to increase their knowledge. Without such challenge they are at risk of becoming disillusioned with their own intellect, which will cause poor self-esteem, anxiety, and academic underachievement.[211] It was far too often that I sat in middle school classes daydreaming about high school and the possibility of finally being academically challenged.

In addition to the three stressors of middle school, I always dealt with the complication of family dynamics. I was still a pawn in the ugliness that existed between my mother and father, who overtly battled each other at every turn. Because my mother and stepfather moved to Rockwall in the middle of this year, I asked myself, "Where do I belong now? Should I stay in Gainesville, or move to another school in Rockwall with only a semester to finish the year? Which way should I turn for advice?" It was a very difficult time for me.

When my jaw was wired shut for six weeks, I didn't really do a lot of talking, which was probably a good thing. Right after I decided to stay in Gainesville with my father and stepmother to finish the school year, they unexpectedly announced they were getting a divorce! I couldn't scream or make any deafening disapproval comments. This news impacted me like it would most kids confronted with their parents' divorce: I was devastated. Because I was an infant during the first divorce, I was oblivious to the effects that this divorce would have on me. My father moved out of our house immediately, and the only words he said to me were, "Please don't speak with your stepmother anymore". How was I going to do that? I still lived in the house with her and loved her very much. My world was now spinning. I knew I would be attending boarding school with Pierce in the fall, but the changes in my family dynamic gave me a great deal of anxiety and it did not set me up for success.

## Boarding School and Public High School

From about the age of eleven, I knew I would be attending McCallie boarding school in Chattanooga, Tennessee. Pierce's father and uncle had both attended this elite school, and Pierce and I had heard all about it from a very young age. When I further investigated the school on my own, I liked that the academic and extracurricular programs were tailored specifically for boys. The school focused on teaching boys responsibility, leadership, and citizenship, all things I think are extremely important for students to learn. In addition, I felt living away in Tennessee would give me some space from dysfunctional family dynamics. My father paid the tuition, and my stepmother helped me pack.

When it was time to move to Tennessee, I thought I was prepared. I traveled internationally, I did well in school academically, and I enjoyed meeting new people. But there were some obstacles I never considered which would negatively affect my experience at McCallie. First, my parents' divorce had more of an impact on me than I expected. I wanted to stay in touch with my stepmother, but I kept getting inordinate amounts of pressure from my father to stop speaking with her. Then, once school began, I realized I had been placed in a sophomore dorm as a freshman, while Pierce was in a different dorm. At first glance, this should not have been a problem, but over the course of the year I realized it was not socially coherent for me to be with students who had already been at McCallie for a year. I got along with them well and they helped 'show me the ropes', but I really had more liberty than I should have. Finally, without any accommodations for learning differences that I did not know I had, like ASD and dyslexia, I was not prepared for the rigorous reading freshman course load expected at McCallie. The only thing the school knew about me upon enrolling was that I was coming from an ugly family divorce, which was the only reason I saw the school counselor. In addition, I had no support in place for poor executive function skills or social and emotional needs. I was truly trying to figure out everything on my own.

The massive change in routine (including moving from middle school to a boarding school and my parents' divorce) caused an odd 'homesick' feeling to wash over me. Even when I saw my best friend Pierce, I felt a tug inside that suggested maybe I should go back home. I guess this is how many college students feel about their freshman year: everything is challengingly new and different. But I was only fifteen years old. I gave everything my best shot, but in the second semester, I had a massive meltdown in my dorm one night that was triggered by a phone call from my father. I demanded someone get my friend Pierce from his nearby dorm. He was the only one who could calm me down. All he had to do was walk into my room and chat with me and I would feel better. This emotional 'spinning out of control' was the first real 'red flag' that indicated it might be difficult for me to continue at McCallie.

I like to use my 'funnel analogy' when describing meltdowns as a person with ASD. I have slow executive function, but everything around me, including noise, lights, and information, is sucked into me at very high speed. I take in twice as much sensory stimulation and information as a neurotypical individual, but it takes longer to process it. Too much is going into the 'funnel', like fuel into a car's gas tank, and it spills over. A meltdown is often inevitable.

I started my sophomore year at McCallie with a fresh outlook. Pierce and I were roommates, and I tried my very best in school. But I had cultivated the persona of a discontented, misplaced guy who hated being at school. The irony in this was that I liked attending McCallie because the curriculum was finally challenging, and the other guys I met were outstanding. But the 'die was cast' from my freshman year: the challenges overwhelmed the benefits. By the middle of the year, I decided to go back to Texas to finish high school.

My decision to leave McCallie disoriented me. I felt like the character Holden in J.D. Salinger's *Catcher in the Rye*. I was at a prep school unable to relate to some people; I had trauma (parents' divorce); I was confused, angry, and often anxious. My perfectionism made me uneasy with my own differences (remember, I had no idea I was autistic). My mother, stepfather, and brother came to pick me up at the end of my first sophomore semester. I felt general disappointment from my father that I was leaving McCallie, but my brother, mother and stepdad were glad I decided to come home. As we were driving back to Texas, I had the overwhelming sensation that I wanted to go back to McCallie, but I knew I couldn't.

I put my experiences at McCallie behind me and looked forward to a more 'normal' high school life at Rockwall High School. I looked at it as a clean start because it was refreshingly different from Gainesville, where I had grown up. Everyone I met was new and they did not know my family history. I wanted to have my 'John Hughes *16 Candles, Breakfast Club*' kind of moments in school. I had a car, I dated, and I got along well with everyone. I was even in a rock band. The town of Rockwall also appealed to me. It is situated on Lake Ray Hubbard, 22 miles east of Dallas and there were always interesting things to do.

Although my public high school experience in Rockwall was enjoyable, the learning differences that always challenged me did not disappear. My social interactions with others were hindered by the challenge to read the facial cues and body gestures of older teens, especially girls. Academically, I just listened and learned, and I never did homework. I enjoyed taking exams, but I never studied for them. If I scored 90% on a test instead of 100%, it was because I sometimes transposed answers. I either loved what I learned or found the subject matter mundane. If an assignment did not interest me, I would 'argue' my case with the teacher to change the assignment. For example, if there was an assignment to do a report on Emily Brontë in literature class, I would ask to do one on Oscar Wilde instead. By the time I pleaded my case with a teacher, he or she would say to me, "Ok, Ok, Ok, you can do it!" I got the nickname 'Spin' because everyone thought I would become an attorney due to my ability to influence others' opinions and state solid facts and logic.

In my junior year, I decided to explore the sensations of getting high using drugs and alcohol with my friends. Beyond the physical sensations caused by these substances, they helped me be more comfortable socially. I could make friends in school, but I sometimes had trouble keeping them. Drinking made me feel comfortable in a group, but I also had to endure the obvious negative side effects of consuming alcohol. I did not know it at the time, but for people with autism, alcohol tends to cause increased agitation, irritability, and anger, thus affecting social interactions.[212] The person may act aggressively towards themselves, or even towards others. When I drank, I often got angry and got into arguments with peers. As I approached graduation, I had to decide if I would continue using such substances in college.

(More about autism and addiction will be discussed in Chapter 5.)

### College

As the transition to college approached, I felt as burdened as I had been four years ago at the beginning of high school. Many seniors select a school based on their interests and possible future career (business, political science, pre-med, etc.), or students have a family legacy and attend the college other family members attended. For me, I had no plan; I had not chosen a major, and I did not want to attend the same schools as my parents. So, with little support from family, I decided to attend The University of North Texas in Denton. This was a significant disappointment for my family because I had considered other purportedly 'better' schools like William and Mary and Washington and Lee University when I was attending McCallie.

I selected UNT because a few of my friends were attending. Upon enrolling, I thought I could bide my time until I decided on a major by taking freshman level courses in philosophy and literature. I knew I did not want to follow in my grandfather's and father's footsteps of becoming dentists. I thought I might perhaps be good at business. In the meantime, I started meeting new people and I joined a fraternity. After only three weeks in a dorm, I got permission to move off campus into a house with ten friends.

My first year of college was enjoyable. I liked the freedom I had when I wasn't attending classes. It was less boring than high school, but academically still not as challenging as I had hoped. But I was learning more about myself. As the year passed, I was beginning to feel like I did in high school: I was overstimulated, I had no goals or degree plans, and I began having more difficulty with dating, especially reading facial expressions and body language. I was drinking and partying too much with fraternity brothers. I still had no accommodations to support my academic needs, and I was repeating a pattern from grade school. I was excited about the newness of college, but my interest was beginning to wane.

After a year and a half at UNT, I was not doing well. Academically I was bored, and emotionally I kept trying to figure out what I was doing here if I did not have a plan. I never received any comfort from family about my problems, how I felt, or ways I could get the support I desperately needed to succeed. All I heard, loud and clear, was "Get your act together!" During semester break, I withdrew from college, and returned home extremely disappointed with myself. This decline led to me being hospitalized for a breakdown, with the *misdiagnosis* of bipolar disorder. I was only nineteen years old.

Later in life, my psychologist Dr. Robinson concluded in his clinical report that my high school and college years were marked with high performance anxiety, as well as social and generalized anxiety. My perfectionism always led to fatigue, frustration, and damaged self-esteem. This anxiety and perfectionism caused challenges in personal relationships with friends, family, and while dating. If I had only been provided with the following academic accommodations, my doctor feels I would have had less anxiety and better performance in school.

### *Academic Testing Accommodations*

○ Be allowed to take tests and quizzes in privacy and quiet. This includes an area with minimal distractions, or a seat away from the door, and should include frequent breaks, and the ability to wear noise-canceling earplugs. (Headphones can cause some to experience discomfort with something over the ear.)

○ Be offered extended time on standardized and classroom tests and quizzes.

○ Be allowed to use 'non-scan' answer sheets, primarily because some learning disorders make transposition mistakes inevitable, and the time required to fill in boxes reduces the time for answering questions. With 'scanned' answer sheets, the additional effort devoted to hyper-focusing on preventing careless mistakes when filling in answer boxes is fatiguing.

○ A student should not be penalized on tests and assignments for spelling errors, letter reversals, or for poor handwriting. A student should be graded on the *content* of his test answers and assignments, as opposed to just procedural or graphic accuracy.

○ A student should be permitted to use The Kurzweil 3000 or similar instrumentation, along with software that converts written text to voice output. If this is not available, the student should have someone who can read aloud each question on the test, one at a time. When possible, the reader should clarify any misperceptions about the specific meaning of the question and clarify any confusion about how a question is worded.

○ Multiple choice questions on tests must be clear and distinct from one another. A reading disability can limit the student's ability to distinguish between words that look alike. Some college professors create 'distractor' alternative answers that look like the real answer but have only minor differences in spelling and phrases. These items are also 'nonsense' items with no meaning or basis in fact. This type of test severely limits a student's ability to access and share his knowledge of a subject and could clearly make the difference between his receiving a grade of 'F' versus 'A' or 'B'.

○ Students should be allowed to use technological learning, reading, conversation, and language and math aids, like those afforded by a computer, sound recorder, calculator, or assisted listening device whenever possible. This applies to completing a writing sample on a standardized test. Typing answers instead of handwriting them will enhance the length and quality of answers. The student should also be afforded the opportunity to correct spelling with 'spell-check', and to use a dictionary to edit his wording.

## Classroom Accommodations

○ Students should be provided with their preferred seating during class and standardized conferences, especially if the administration includes any audio-visuals. They should be granted permission to make video and audio recordings of class lectures; to use a recording pen as an aid in note taking; and be provided with a set of notes from the teacher during class. They should also be allowed to use text-to-voice and voice-to-text software.

○ Having empathy and support from test administrators and professors is critical to a student's success. Professors are strongly encouraged to provide detailed outlines of each lecture at least a week in advance. The student should be offered class notes and reading assignments in advance of each lecture so they can have the required accommodating time to be fully prepared.

○ The student should be permitted extra breaks during class when feeling anxious or overwhelmed.

○ Under no circumstances should instructors be permitted to use the 'cold-calling' questioning technique during class. If participation is required, a significant 'wait time' is necessary so the student can prepare their answer.

## Assignment Accommodations

○ Professors should provide directions for homework and long-term assignments orally as well as in writing.

○ Students will benefit from meeting with instructors on a regular basis to review progress. This will help avoid information-processing mistakes that lead to distracting tangents when studying for exams or when completing class projects. This assistance will help re-clarify the objectives of assignments.

○ An established class syllabus should be provided for all classes, whenever possible. Professors can help by providing advanced notice of all tests and assignments, and their relative percentage of the overall grade. Students with anxiety can better focus on completing their work if they know what to expect.

○ Professors and teaching assistants need to reinforce awareness of the goal of an assignment by clarifying its purpose and part of the curriculum. Students will also benefit from a clear understanding of what has already been learned to assist in 'connecting the dots', creating a holistic understanding. To this end, assignments and testing should follow and reflect the sequence and coherence of the curriculum.

○ Students should be provided with examples of good work and shown the features of the work that contribute to its quality. Professors should ensure that students understand what characteristics distinguish good work from poor work.

○ When appropriate, a student should be allowed to demonstrate his knowledge of a subject orally rather than in writing, and be offered alternatives to written assignments, like oral or taped or video presentations, projects, collages, posters, etc. When possible, the student should be given the option to present assignments to the instructor only, or allowed an alternative assignment, because his social anxiety and other deficits cause him to get overwhelmed when speaking in front of an audience.

### Other Academic Accommodations

○ The student will benefit from working with a reading coach.

○ The student will benefit from working with a counselor to help him reduce his stress and overdependence on perfectionism and help control his anxiety and tendencies to be angry or get frustrated with himself and others. Counseling will also help the student self-monitor the unintentional negative effects of his neurocognitive deficits and help keep them from disrupting his self-esteem and his working and social relationships.

○ The student will benefit from personal counseling to help navigate the transitions and unexpected changes in life.

# CHAPTER 5:
# Jobs

*"Now you're climbin' to the top of the company ladder,
hope it doesn't take too long. Can't cha see there'll come a
day when it won't matter, come a day when you'll be gone."*
~Boston

Have you ever asked yourself, "What if?" I think it is only human nature to wonder about the opportunities missed in life simply because of being afraid to execute or take the risk. I, however, have always believed that when I take a course of action and it doesn't work out, I can correct my course. I am never afraid to make mistakes. In fact, the excitement of risk taking inspires me to get things done. It's like rocket fuel for me!

My life offers a unique vantage point on neurodiversity when it comes to jobs. I have worked in many different fields and found all of them fulfilling in some way. Many believe that those with Asperger's fall into subtypes, and each of these contains its own skill set. Some consider themselves artists, or visual thinkers; some feel they are verbal or nonverbal; some love patterns and gravitate towards areas such as math, engineering, or music: there are countless potential good fits between individuals and modes of expression.[213] I would ask all neurodiverse individuals to think about their interests and skills, and how they can realistically translate these into a plan of action that is achievable within the foreseeable future.[214]

When I withdrew from college after a year and a half, I had already started thinking about my next journey. I took a huge leap of faith and enlisted in the Army. I knew the Army offered a variety of training programs, leadership courses, and ways to continue one's education. I took the Armed Services Vocational Aptitude Battery test (ASVAB, like the SAT), and an IQ test for military personnel. At the time I enlisted, the job that required the highest score was combat medic. A GT score (overall aptitude) of 110 qualified an individual for the

'Green to Gold' program, which helps soldiers earn a degree to qualify for an officer's commission. My GT score was well over 125, so I joined the Army on March 17, 1993, with the desire to be a combat medic, and most importantly, to jump out of helicopters!

## Army

*This section of the book is about my Army experience. I was an Air Assault qualified Light Infantry Combat Medic in 4/87th Battalion 25th Infantry Division (Light). Nothing more and nothing less. I was assigned to headquarters company and permanently attached to Bravo company 2nd Platoon. I did not deploy to a combat theater. I was our platoon medic, and as all combat medics, I had the dual role of training with my infantry counterparts as well as overseeing their medical safety while training. The references and stories here do not in any way imply that I was in combat. We 'live fire' trained, threw live grenades in combat scenarios, conducted joint service exercises, and we did a lot of road marching and air assaults. My comments here are based on my experiences from 1993-1995 and are in no way intended to glorify war. These are stories of brotherhood, the positives, and negatives of service as I saw them, and express the overwhelming appreciation of the logistics, operations, brotherhood, and leadership that I experienced and witnessed.*

As my flight to Fort Leonard Wood in Missouri took off from Dallas, it came to mind that just a few days earlier I was in college partying freely with fraternity brothers. Life would be very different now, but I had a plan. I arrived for military entrance processing (MEPS) at 5:00 am. The next step is called *Basic Training Reception*: your head is shaved, and everyone is pumped with gamma-globulin to fight off dangerous infections.

In *reception*, 'black hats' or tech sergeants (not drill sergeants) show everyone the basics of the army, things like introduction to formation, how to salute, and the standards for uniform and dress. This training took about ten days. One day during Reception, the tech sergeants came into our barracks early with a very different demeanor from the previous days of training. They were yelling, "GET UP! GRAB YOUR GEAR, YOUR BUS IS HERE!" I am not sure why but two of the sergeants whispered to me, "Get ready, keep your head down, chin up, and do EXACTLY what they tell you to do!" As the bus rolled up, out stepped Sergeant First Class Lambert. At first glance he looked like he could have probably killed all of us, bury our bodies, and NO ONE would have asked him any questions.

We were packed onto the bus like sardines; everyone called it the 'cattle car'. The bus's windows were all boarded up. Sergeant Lambert did not want us to know where on the base we had been taken. We were driven around for a couple of hours as the beginning of the 'break down' phase of basic training. Then the bus came to a stop and mayhem began. As we departed the bus, we were given a 'D bag', a roughly 35-pound duffle bag with all our necessary gear. We entered the 'Gauntlet', a 100-yard walk from the bus to our barracks, with drill sergeants along the way screaming at us and popping us on the nose with the brim of their hats. We were instructed not to ever let our bag touch the ground. If it did, the entire platoon would be 'smoked' or punished for one person's mistake. During this long walk to our barracks, the commands to line up, parade, rest, and stand at attention were shouted continually. Mind you, we did not yet know how to do anything correctly. Nonetheless, if we made mistakes, everyone was punished. This chaos went on outside for many hours.

Once we got inside the barracks, we were instructed to take inventory of everything in our D bag. We did this with one hand holding the bag (never allowed to touch the floor) and the other hand pulling each item out when named by the sergeant. For example, he would yell, "Glove, black, left hand". Then, in unison, every platoon member had to find that item, repeat its name, and put it in our wall locker. Imagine the hundreds of push-ups we did for all our mistakes, and the number of hours it took to complete this procedure correctly. There are countless stories I could tell these grueling tasks, from one about the saw dust pit to one about the 'gas chamber'. Suffice it to say everyone was very happy to have basic training completed, and to be ready for Advanced Individual Training (AIT).

I left Fort Wood in Missouri and traveled to Fort Houston in San Antonio for combat medic training. I was very excited to finally start learning my real job. The classroom and practical training experience earned soldiers in our program the title of Emergency Medical Technician (EMT). This training was then combined with infantry experience, and how to perform the medic's job while under fire.

Soon after becoming an army medic, I realized that I had tacitly gained authority through my vocational position, and not my rank. Although sergeants (also known as noncommissioned officers, NCO's) could invoke their rank, they generally did not. It afforded me the ability to get out of certain work details that others were forced to do. It also permitted me to get some great temporary duty assignments, like teaching combat lifesaver courses. Then, there is an old army adage that one shouldn't mess with *doc* because he could throw your shot records away. Although this is a little extreme, and rarely if ever actually happens, it is a joke more than a reality. I also knew this was unnecessary because I had the respect of my men.

I enjoyed the time I was stationed in San Antonio for a couple of reasons. First, my training was rigorous, and it motivated me to be the best army medic I could be. I felt that when it was time to ship out to *permanent party* (25th Infantry Light), I was very prepared. Second, I liked being in San Antonio because my best friend from childhood, Pierce, was a student at Trinity University. We spent time together during the weekend leave. Also, I discovered one of my fraternity brothers, Bill from UNT, had moved to San Antonio to finish college at the University of Texas San Antonio (UTSA). This surprise re-connection provided opportunities to blow off a little steam with another good friend.

I always wanted to be an infantry medic who rode in helicopters after watching on television the 1975 evacuation of Saigon during the Vietnam War. My wish came true when I was assigned to an air assault light infantry unit in Hawaii. I was assigned to the 25th Infantry (Light) at Schofield Barracks. I remember riding a bus from Honolulu Airport up the mountain through sugar cane and pineapple fields. As I entered the base, I saw a platoon returning from a training exercise that replicated real combat. They were covered in mud, blood, and camouflage gear. I was hoping that would soon be me!

One significant training exercise I remember involved a thirty-hour march carrying 50 pounds of gear plus water and weapons. As an army medic, I was trained in close-contact jungle and urban warfare. I had to participate in both and watch for real-world casualties and injuries. I would train like everyone else, but if someone got hurt, I would perform triage and begin treatment. Regardless of how long a field exercise lasted, each became a *gut check* for me. We never had tents or sleeping bags, just an improvised 'hooch' made from a poncho. I truly felt part of the military at this point, and I loved my time in the field as opposed to the barracks.

The next step was to be assigned to a company (120-140 soldiers) and battalion (550-600 soldiers). I also met my squad leader, our platoon leader, and Physician's Assistant (PA). This was considered our first real day in the United States Army. Less than a week after arriving in Hawaii, I received orders for Air Assault School. This training is called 'The toughest ten days in the Army'. Although it is very good training, it is by no means the toughest ten days in the Army. My friends who completed Ranger School experienced far more rigorous training in their first ten days of a 62-day program.

The physically and mentally demanding program I experienced included being taught to rappel from helicopters. (Be careful what you wish for!) Once during training, we were forced into the 'L' shaped position (basically turning around and sitting backwards with your feet on a 50- foot tower) and taught to rappel. The first time was very difficult as it is an unnatural and frankly a scary thing to do. When it was my turn, I couldn't let myself get fully in position and was hanging halfway off the tower with my boots on the edge. One of the sergeants (who were all yelling) came over to me and quietly said, "Doc, those guys down there are your infantry counterparts. You have been on island a week and are already at air assault school. You can't back down and let them see you wash out of this course." I was still 'frozen' in my position and couldn't move. He put his hand out like he was going to help me back up on the top of the tower, then he faked me out and kicked my boots. I immediately bounced into a perfect L-shape position, and he yelled, 'Lane one on rappel.' I did a perfect bounding rappel, and I never had any other issues with the school. I looked back up towards the top of the tower, and he gave me a quick head nod, meaning 'well done". He then moved on to the next soldier. This was an indication of great leadership and one of many examples of which I experienced while in the army. Our sergeants and officers were very committed to providing the best training possible.

When this training was completed, I was no longer referred to as private first-class Truitt: I was now officially 'Doc' the platoon medic and received my air assault 'wings' patch. I flew in Blackhawk helicopters during training missions that simulated trench fighting with air and artillery support.

My first field exercise with my new platoon was a simulation assault of Makua Valley. Watching a 105mm artillery round hit the side of the valley and an Apache gunship dump 30mm rounds at night was unbelievable. The feelings I had of brotherhood and the overwhelming appreciation for logistics, operations, and leadership were exactly what I was looking for in the army. But after returning to the barracks, I reflected on several moments that made me question, "What have I done?" The first was when I learned how to throw live grenades in basic training. While it is a rush, one cannot describe the concussion and noise the first time you 'cook off' a live grenade. They can do a lot of damage not only to me, but more importantly to people who were now my friends. The second was seeing the bloody platoon return from field exercises and realizing this is real. I could very likely be in a scenario (training or combat) where I would have to use my skills as a medic to potentially save my friends. There was never a question as to whether I could do the heavy lifting under real battle combat circumstances. I was prepared well. But after a year or so, something began weighing heavily on my mind, and I didn't know if I should remain in the army.

My lieutenant called me into his office one day and said he had heard I was unhappy. He asked me to speak freely about my concerns. I told him I was considering leaving the army for two reasons. First, it was very difficult for me to transition back and forth from the dynamic of essentially a nobody in the barracks to a very important person in the field. (I imagine this would have been difficult for anyone on the spectrum.) Secondly, and most importantly, as I spent more time with the men in my company, they became like friends and brothers, as opposed to faceless infantrymen. This is not good in real war, critical care/emergency scenarios. (I knew from my father and grandfather that doctors rarely work on family or friends.) I was very good at emergency and trauma medicine, but very uncomfortable when the patients were people I knew. These dynamics made day-to-day army life difficult and unenjoyable.

As my lieutenant and I discussed my situation, he offered me the opportunity to enter the 'Green to Gold' program. This allows a qualified enlisted person to train to be an officer. I knew it was an honor to be considered because good leadership skills and high aptitude are required to become an officer. However, we both agreed that the politics in the military just increases after becoming an officer. I have always found it difficult to be put 'in a box', and I knew if I stayed in the army, the political environment would be impossible for me. We decided I would leave with the 'Clinton deferment', which reduced my commitment time in the army. I was honorably discharged from the military with full GI bill benefits after two years.

I will always appreciate my experience in the military. It taught me many valuable lessons, and I made friendships which have lasted to this day. However, after over two years in the army, including basic training, Advanced Individual Training, Air Assault School, and permanent party training, my entire 'out-processing' to leave took only 24 hours, which seemed to crush the meaning of my memories and experience and leave me unprepared for the 'real world'. Americans wonder why there is such a mental health problem with veterans. I sincerely believe the instant separation after intense experience is one of the reasons. Even today, combat veterans who have deployed for years receive only minimal time to transition back to being civilians, and they are given little support when reintegrating into society. As I closed this chapter of my life, I thought about the famous quote by Mike Tyson: "Everyone has a plan until they get punched in the mouth." I now needed another plan.

## School or Business

Forty-eight hours after leaving the army, I was back in Texas, where I got the news that my father had divorced his third wife who was from Australia, and married his next wife who was from England (my father was not a faithful man, and this caused trouble in his marriages). Although our relationship was still not good, I began working for his company. The plan was that I would set up a telemarketing element for the company. I also took a few night classes at The University of North Texas, which turned out to be unbearably boring after what I had just experienced in the army. My good time and effort at my father's company led me to realize he needed someone who was good at running the business, which he was not. I started working on global marketing and operations for NAOL and did not continue at UNT. I traveled around the United States,

England, continental Europe, Asia, and Australia spending time restructuring the company.

Along the way, I began dating a former high school class-mate who still lived in the Dallas area. She had a four-year old son from a previous relationship. We married and I became a stepfather. I enjoyed being a parent very much. I hoped to do things very differently from the way I was raised. After two years of marriage, my wife and I had our own son, Nash. Things were tolerable until my father decided to sell his business. I was supposed to get 30% of the profits, but that never happened as he was getting *another* divorce. What did I say about "Get punched, need another plan?" Well, I had another plan. I was heading to a place I had been before and dearly loved.

My father was only married to his fourth wife for two years. I believe his fondness for all things British influenced this marriage. During the short union, they had a daughter, but sadly my half-sister and I never had a chance at a good relationship. She was taught negative and untrue things about me by my father and my aunt (my dad's sister is also autistic, but she does not recognize it). As my half-sister grew up, she received encouragement and accommo-dations for a dyslexia diagnosis, which disturbed me, since my neurodiversity was treated with disdain by my parents. This dichotomy of how we siblings were treated differently is a source of bitterness for me to this day. However, I hope in the future my sister and I can have a more amicable relationship.

## Utilizing My Business Talents in Australia

I didn't speak with my father for seventeen years after leaving Texas. Moving to Australia felt like a fresh start for my family and me. I started an orthodontic supply and laboratory business with my father's third wife. (Weird I know!) This job was a good fit for me because I could use my gifts and talents, which included getting investors, business development, marketing, problem solving, and guiding the strategic part of the business. As good as my job was, it was the opposite for my marriage, which failed, and my wife and son moved back to Texas.

I was devastated that I would not see my son every day. My hope was that he and I would reunite sometime after my ex-wife settled back in America. Regardless of this emotional upheaval, I had to keep moving forward with work. In Australia, I ran into a woman I had known for fifteen years from previous trips with my father. Now that we were older—and a bit wiser—Ashley and I connected romantically. We dated for two years and then got married. Six years later, we got the amazing news that we would get full custody of my son Nash because my ex-wife could no longer be a responsible parent. We were thrilled we would now raise him.

After two and a half years with our orthodontic supply business, my wife and I were invited by a venture capital group and inventor to create a medical device company. It manufactured and marketed an oral device, uniquely designed for mandibular advancement splint for snoring and obstructive sleep apnea (OSA). It was a competitive product to CPAP, which also treats sleep apnea. We had the right industry and business experience to make this company successful. Our high growth potential brought venture capital help, and we ended up listing the company on the Australian Stock Exchange. We designed a custom-built facility in Crows Nest, Australia, developed the initial strategy for the Asia Pacific region, and oversaw all aspects of global sales and marketing for the company. We also created an international network of dentists and sleep physicians loyal to our company and willing to choose us above other devices. (I guess I didn't need that diploma from The University of North Texas after all!)

## Golden Handcuffs in Business

In December of 2005, my wife and I evaluated the global markets and determined America held the most to offer for our company. We devised an entry strategy and relocated to Dallas-Fort Worth, Texas. Once again, we created a business plan, designed, and constructed a facility, hired, and trained employees, implemented, and managed all operations, and reported the results of the company to the chairman and board of directors. We created the fastest growing region in the world and were the first to achieve profit for the company. We consistently exceeded sales targets and revenue while keeping costs below budget. The company went on to become a global leader in America, facilitating expansion into other world markets. Because of our success, we kept getting amazing bonuses and stock options thrown at us. So, we put on the 'Golden Handcuffs' and stayed in America as opposed to returning to Australia. Our plan had been to return home after one year, but the money and autonomy of running the American operation was too tempting to resist.

Why does it seem there is always a downside to success? As the global Chief Marketing Officer then Executive Vice President of the company and my wife running the international markets and continuing education side of the business, we realized we were working a full schedule in the United States. In addition, we worked another 5 to 6 hours after that to accommodate the time change to Australia. The song lyric "Working Man" by the Canadian rock band Rush says it all about our life at that time- "I get up at seven, and I go to work at nine. I got no time for living; I'm working all the time." We were running out of steam with those 14+ hour days. Then a new investor came on board, and he became the chairman and largest shareholder, as well as my boss. My position had been restructured, and I became the Executive Vice President in America. Although we continued to get paid well and receive stock options, we were unhappy. We made the decision to work for two more years with the company, and then made our next plan.

## Change of Scenery

When we left our previous company in 2010, I was looking for a new business concept. I approached an old friend about becoming my partner and starting a sleep diagnostics and therapy company. I had the experience and background to get a startup off the ground. My partner had experience in the operational side of running a business. We moved forward to secure the investors, write the business plan, and implement all the marketing and advertising.

While getting our new business off the ground, I became overwhelmed with the constant noise, lights, and other uncomfortable aspects of living in Dallas. I began drinking too much to cope with the stress. It seemed this was the only way to blow off steam. The strain of overworking and drinking caused serious problems in our marriage and with my business partner. Ashley and I discussed that it might be best if we moved to another location, one that was more tranquil. We thought we could manage our company from anywhere, and my business partner could remain in charge in Dallas.

We relocated to Durango, Colorado in 2016 because of its serene environment, four distinct seasons, and a good variety of outdoor activities. Although Durango was a very good choice for our new home, our marriage was still in trouble. Fortunately, marriage counseling led to a formal diagnosis in 2018 of autism, and it was an epiphany moment for both my wife and me. We learned how to better communicate with each other and appreciate each other's differences. By the third year in Colorado our marriage was improving, but our company would ultimately not survive. My partner did not handle my diagnosis well. He used it against me to make excuses for his failures to keep the Texas end of our company going. Our company ended in 2019. What do people say about going into business with friends? Oh yes, they say, *"Don't do it!"*

Medical diagnoses are often excuses for others to point fingers when jobs are not done correctly. For example, "Susan missed her deadlines because she has ADHD". Or "Bill has ASD, he cannot possibly be smart enough to figure out this business plan and execute it well". My partner, who I had thought was a friend, lied to our business investors, claiming that the business problems in Texas were my fault; more importantly, he hid information from me, which spoke volumes about his character. His behavior told me that he feared anything different (like the uniqueness of my intelligence), and that he did not understand the distinction between 'different good' and 'different bad'. I realized he was not a true friend at all, and that I must be careful not to be taken advantage of again or otherwise be *gaslighted* in future working and personal relationships.

Ultimately the fault lies with me that our business never got the exit we were trying to achieve, although it made great money along the way. I take responsibility for selecting the wrong person as a partner. I had been advised by several trusted friends that this man was a poor choice because they thought he would not live up to his end of our deal due to our work experiences and skill sets. This certainly turned out to be the case. It should have been an early indicator for me when the investors took out a one-million-dollar *key man life insurance* policy on me and nothing on him. I hold no animosity towards him from a business perspective. We both experienced successes and setbacks in the business. However, the way he handled my diagnosis was, for lack of a better word, pathetic.

## *Autism Exploitation in the Workspace*

Since my diagnosis, I now understand it is common for individuals with ASD to prefer to work with others they know. We struggle with change, and this includes the people we work with. Even after trusted friends suggested that I should not go into business with this other 'friend', I ignored them all and then paid the price. Some people with autism can be manipulated and taken advantage of, and it can take the form of emotional exploitation. We often struggle to notice and understand motive (Theory of Mind challenges). We often doubt that someone could act maliciously, although experience tells us they can.[215] We tend to take people at their word; neurodiverse individuals are more vulnerable to manipulation than someone who is neurotypical.[216] And so I learned the hard way to be on guard for such unscrupulous individuals.

In a 2015 survey, 80% of people with autism reported they had been taken advantage of by someone considered to be a friend.[217] This is a huge leap from a previous report of 48%. A person with autism can feel isolated and welcome the opportunity for friendship, unaware of the ulterior motive or ignorant selfishness of their acquaintance.

There are ways to overcome exploitation by a friend, work colleague, or romantic partner:[218]

- ○ *What's Yours is Yours*: Whether it be time, property or your body, a true friend will never demand anything that you don't want to part with. That's why teaching autistic people that it can be okay not to share is crucial for our protection.

- ○ *Avoid the Pressure*: Manipulators like to work by putting someone under pressure and pushing them for an immediate response. This is usually because the manipulator themselves has run out of time which—too bad for them--isn't your problem.

○ *Identify When It's Happening*: This happened to me: 'Gaslighting' is a term used to describe when someone manipulates their victim into doubting their version of stories over time, and it is incredibly common. Although difficult to detect, gaslighting becomes more problematic in the autism community, where many of its signs, such as increased anxiety and depression, are already frequent.

○ *Take Action*: One of the bizarre things about any kind of 'wrong-doer' is that they can be oblivious to the fact that what they are doing is wrong. If you are a potential victim, or if you can act in the interest of a potential victim, simply sitting down with the manipulator and explaining the negative impact of their actions can make a difference and help to put a relationship back on the right track. Of course, in some cases the situation must be handled by experts, like the human resource officer in a company.

### Alcohol/Drug Use

I am a firm believer in taking responsibility for one's actions. This was instilled in me by my parents and during my time in the army. During my last business enterprise, I knew I had some culpability in how things turned out. The stress that kept mounting in our company led me to drink at night to cope and sleep. I have since seen current studies which suggest that autistic people more frequently turn to alcohol and drugs as a method of self-medication.[219]

Alcohol impacts everyone differently, especially when they are wired differently. Without any preparation or knowledge of how alcohol impacts a person's neurodivergent brain, trying alcohol for the first time in a public place or on a date may be dangerous.[220] I never drank during the day when I was working. But if I had a business call at night and had been drinking, I could experience a complete loss of self-control; my thoughts slowed down, and my memories were hazy. These conditions only exacerbated my relationship with my partner and our business decisions.

There are some neurological factors that predispose people with autism to addiction. This may be related to the tendency to prefer sameness, to form repetitive behaviors or habits.[221] Others find their way to addiction through prescribed medications. Even in early childhood years, autistic kids can be prescribed powerful medications, like stimulants for co-occurring ADHD, anti-depressants, anti-psychotics, mood stabilizers, and sleep aids.[222] Without being given access to sensory or academic accommodations first, individuals can form patterns of addiction and then seek increasingly stronger dosages to cope.

When I was a senior in high school, I tried cocaine. It gave me an endorphin rush, but I did not like it. I tried it again when I was in my thirties because I saw a lot of it being used in the corporate world and I was under a tremendous amount of stress. It seemed my friends who had tried it liked the fact that they could work longer because it made them feel more alert and energetic. It was odd for me because it did the opposite. I used cocaine a lot for about three months because it made me relax at first. Then I started getting more anxious, so I quit. It was a textbook case of self-medicating. Today I still drink socially, but I have not used recreational drugs for a long time. With alcohol I must be careful because I can overdo it. If there was a pill that did the same as alcohol for me in social situations, I would take it.

It has always fascinated me that neurotypical people are too often prescribed antidepressants and stimulants to deal with depression and anxiety. They believe if a doctor prescribes a substance, it is a medicine and not a drug. Two good examples are Oxycontin and Adderall. According to the Health Policy Institute, 66% of adults today in the United States take prescription drugs.[223] An even more alarming statistic is that every year in America more than 4 billion prescriptions are dispensed, and that is expected to increase by 2024. [224] The United States consumes more prescribed and recreational illicit drugs than any other country in the world.[225]

Self-medicating for autistics is a big problem. In a recent study at the University of Cambridge's Autism Research Center, Dr. Elizabeth Weir spoke with many autistic individuals coping with mental health as well as autism. She discovered that they want to manage symptoms but experience little support from physicians.[226] One reason is that autism is frequently undiagnosed, or misdiagnosed, as other conditions, which then makes it difficult for things like sensory issue to be properly identified and addressed. This same Cambridge University study reported that autistic adults were almost nine times more likely than non-autistic peers to report recreational drug use to manage symptoms of mental illness.[227]

Without access to mental health care, autistics are at a greater risk of a downward spiral of mental health and a higher rate of suicide.[228] According to Dr. Marcia Eckerd, psychologist and autism expert, research emphasizes the failure of the current social and medical system to meet the urgent needs of autistic individuals, who then resort to substances to self-medicate for pain.[229] Because approximately 1 in 36 children in America have been identified with autism spectrum disorder (ASD)[230], we need to acknowledge the hypocrisy of our medical system, which allows law makers to let the drug problem in our country grow because humans with life altering differences have to fend for themselves.

## Neurodiversity in the Workplace

From the military to the cooperate board room, I have worked in diverse environments. Now that I understand myself better, in considering my life experiences, I believe the journeys I have taken would have been smoother had I known to ask for specific accommodations to support my specific needs. Even so, after reading current statistics about the challenge for neurodiverse individuals to find and keep jobs, I realize I am fortunate because I have been employed most of my life. Some reports state 85% of people with autism are unemployed.[231] Although most companies today focus on diversity, equity, and inclusion (DE&I), the neurodivergent group is often overlooked. We must broaden the lens on DE&I to include the wide range of mental orientations, including but not limited to autism, dyslexia, attention deficit hyperactivity disorder (ADHD), dysgraphia, and dyspraxia.[232]

The leading nonprofit organization called Disability: IN (https://disabilityin.org/who-we-are/about/) is doing just that. They are the leading resource for business disability inclusion worldwide. Their network of over 500 corporations expands opportunities for people with disabilities/differences across enterprises. Cooperate leaders are exceedingly aware of how diversity impacts culture, management, and financial performance and are increasing their commitments to ensure people with disabilities are represented at all levels of a company.[233] Disability: IN offers the CEO of a company the opportunity to sign a letter of disability inclusion that confirms their company takes action to build inclusive, accessible, and equitable workplaces through their company's participation in the Disability Equality Index.

The Disability Equality Index (DEI), a joint initiative with the American Association of People with Disabilities, is the only global tool for analyzing and measuring disability progress across the enterprise and gives companies a comprehensive assessment of their own disability inclusion and equality practices.[234] Each company that requests to be reviewed receives a score, on a scale of zero to 100. Those companies earning 80 or above are recognized as "Best Places to Work for Disability and Inclusion."[235] Some top scoring companies in 2023 were: Amazon, American Airlines, Best Buy, Charles Schwab, Dell Technologies, Freddie Mac, Ford, Kellogg's, and Lowe's. For a full list of these top scoring companies see: https://disabilityin.org/what-we-do/disability-equality-index/2023companies/.

In addition to these companies proactively supporting neurodiverse individuals, my psychologist told me his practice helped a patient secure a lucrative job with the financial services company Goldman Sachs. He also told me that in 2012 the Israel Defense Force harnessed the unique skills sets of autistics by creating Unit 9900, comprised of autistic soldiers.[236] Recruits are screened and trained (including learning coping skills for the stresses and rigor of the job) to use maps, analyze data, and decipher the aerial reconnaissance photos that provide information to soldiers ahead of combat missions. After military service is completed, an individual can often find a path to jobs in Israel's booming technology sector, especially the intelligence field.[237] The following are just some of the assets an individual with autism can bring to their job.

○ Attention to detail and sustained concentration which results in accurate, high-quality work.

○ Excellent long-term memory with a recall of details that can be astonishing.

○ Tolerance of repetition and routine, which is valuable in all kinds of jobs.

○ Strong logic and analytic skills.

○ Vast knowledge of specialized fields.

○ Ability to think outside the box and discover creative solutions to complex problems.

○ Absence of social filtering.

○ Perseverance.

○ Honesty, loyalty, and a great desire to do well on the job.

Note: If I look back on my Army experience, I think it would have been ideal for me to be part of Unit 9900. This unique military unit would have allowed me to use my talents, as well as make me feel part of a group because all the soldiers would have been on the spectrum. Being part of Unit 9900 would have negated many of the unaccommodated and therefore challenging experiences I had in the

Army. Having said that, in the same breath I wouldn't take my time as a combat medic for anything!

### The Hiring Process Needs to Change

It is unfortunate that during a hiring process, neurodiverse individuals fall prey to the following myths:[238]

- ○ Disabled people are difficult employees.
- ○ Disabled people are too expensive to employ.
- ○ Disabled people aren't reliable.
- ○ Disabled people can't carry a full workload.
- ○ Disabled people can't be leaders.

If the screening and interviewing process were modified to accommodate the differences of neurodivergent applicants, more individuals would get past the first step of getting a job. To do this we must first minimize both recruiter and hiring algorithm biases.[239] Artificial Intelligence (AI) hiring systems are coded using data from neurotypical candidates that is likely biased against applicants with autism because they have atypical facial or speech expressions. Recruiters may have unconscious biases, so it's important to make recruiters and hiring managers aware of and sensitive to different personality types and warn them against drawing conclusions based on eye contact, handshakes, and gestures which they erroneously perceive as deviations from a norm that they expect. Finally, companies need to use talent matching software in their screening process to better understand an applicant's unique abilities, which might include risk taking and emotional intelligence, along with traditional traits such as logical reasoning and quantitative and verbal abilities.

Traditional job interviews could be tweaked to consider a wider range of applicants for a given job. To better support neurodivergent job candidates, questions need to be less abstract and more specific. *All* interviewees should be given a list of speaking points that will be discussed in the interview; a description of how the interview process will be handled; and who will do the interviewing from the company. Interviewees also would like to know if they will be offered breaks in the interview process and provided a second opportunity to interview if the first one does not go well. Candidates will feel more comfortable if they are allowed to use their own laptops for tests instead of company-provided devices. Finally, interviewers should allow the job candidate to have a say in their future relationship with the employer and provide opportunities for the applicant to demonstrate their skills during a trial period.

### Educate Employees about Neurodiversity

If companies would do a better job educating all employees about neurodiversity in the workplace, they could easily eliminate the stigma, lack of awareness, and lack of appropriate infrastructure that cause exclusion of people with neurodevelopmental differences.[240] Employers can make simple improvements to create a workplace that is more neurodiverse friendly. Some examples are:[241]

- Offer adjustments to an employee's workspace to accommodate sensory needs, such as sound sensitivity. Offer a quiet break space, warn of expected loud noises like fire drills, offer noise cancelling headphones.

- Allow modifications to the work uniform for those with tactile sensitivities.

- Allow extra movement breaks, the use of fidget toys, and offer flexible seating options.

- Use clear communication: avoid sarcasm, euphemisms, and implied messages.

- Provide concise verbal and written instructions for tasks and break them down into small steps.

- Inform employees about workplace and social etiquette, and don't assume someone is deliberately breaking the rules or being rude.

- Try to give advance notice and a clear explanation if plans are changing.

Neurodiverse people may need coaching before entering a specific work environment: readiness for life in a corporate job may be very different than a job in law, medicine, or the military. Individuals need to consider which part of a certain field is best for them: someone interested in law may do better with forensic law than litigation; someone going into medicine may be better suited to surgery and radiology than pediatrics. Regardless of the job, if employers refuse to deal with an individual's differences, like executive dysfunction, they will not have access to that person's hyper-focused abstract thinking, and inductive reasoning.[242]

## Interests and Strengths

For as long as I can remember I have had an interest in helping others. My training as a medic allowed me to care for those in need of medical attention during maneuvers and field missions. And I knew my strengths and interests were being utilized to their fullest when I worked in businesses that offered people solutions to snoring and sleep apnea. People who are neurodiverse must follow their strengths and interests so that they find jobs which utilize them.

Finding the right fit may require taking a valid research-based career test. John Holland's *Self-Directed Search*[243] is an online assessment of easy to answer questions about interests and skills. For a small fee it generates a report with information about potentially appropriate careers. If the report says you would make a good zookeeper, look for any jobs that might be connected to zookeeping. It is also important to make as many connections as possible because these can lead to a long-term project or career. Deborah and I met on LinkedIn, and that connection is how we started writing this book.

There are many vocations in which autistic people excel. It probably wouldn't surprise anyone that engineering, computer technology, research and science are good fits. These jobs are performance based and productivity is easily measured. Jobs like these usually have quite a bit of flexibility in their work schedule and often the individual can work alone if that is their preference. However, a large range of options for careers should be considered, such as psychologist, artist, lawyer, and even medicine. I have always succeeded when I matched my passion and strengths to the job.

## Organizations and Companies Offering Support

There are organizations available that offer job search and on-the-job training for people with autism. One is LIME, www.limeconnect. com, a non-profit organization that is 'rebranding disability through achievement'. LIME helps connect university students and alumni to internships and careers with high profile and prestigious corporate partners, and also offers webinars that provide job training and job search skills.[244] Stereotypes are being broken; leading companies of every size, industry, and location are coming to understand the importance and value of the talent and strengths that 'disabled' employees bring to the workplace.[245] California-based company Zavikon is also having great success with supporting neurodiversity in the workplace. Founder and CEO Rebecca Beam helps challenged candidates find the right career path, helps employers find the right talent, and supports success for all. Beam states on the company website (www.zavikon. net): "Zavikon serves any individual seeking career employment who has a visible or invisible disability." They have programs set up for the blind and visually impaired, the deaf and hard of hearing, and neurodivergent people, to name a few. Zavikon focuses on an individual's talents and skills, placing employees in all types of careers, including finance, technology, clerical work, and creative jobs.[246] Once an individual is placed, professional career coaches work with the employee, their new co-workers, and hiring manager to ensure everyone is set up for long-term success.

## *Self-Advocacy and Disclosure*

Self-advocacy is the ability to communicate one's needs. Both neuro-typicals and neurodiverse individuals need these skills. They can be learned at any age, and they create a sense of independence. People who self-advocate are more likely to thrive in school, work, and life.[247] Self-advocacy has three elements:[248]

○ Understanding one's needs.
○ Knowing what kind of support might help.
○ Communicating these needs to others.

Neurodiverse individuals often have the most difficulty advocating for themselves because they are not taught these special skills when they are younger. For example, in school, taking notes may be difficult, so if the student does not know how to ask the teacher for pre-printed class notes, the outcome could be a poor test grade. In the process of a job interview, if an individual does not tell the interviewer they need extra time to process the answers to questions, the applicant will not be fairly assessed. To begin learning about self-advocacy, individuals must start by understanding their challenges and determine if and how they will disclose them.

Do you tell an employer about neurodiversity before you are hired? This is a very personal decision. The advantages to disclosure are evident: if you ask for accommodations at work or school, you are more likely to do your best work. It is an empowering act to say, "I know I work best when...", and it is helpful that many universities and companies today support individuals with dyslexia, ADHD, autism, and other learning differences. Once an individual discloses their neurodiversity, other students and coworkers will have a better context for understanding the specific behaviors they observe.[249] For example, if a neurodivergent coworker comes across as rude due to lack of eye contact, or provides blunt answers to questions, when others in the office understand the behavior in the context of autism, they will look deeper into *what* is said, rather than just *how* it is said.

The choice of not disclosing one's differences can have negative repercussions. If managers and supervisors are not aware that a prospective employee (who constantly fidgets and looks at the floor when speaking) has a learning difference, it is likely that a job will not be offered. In addition, an individual trait that is positive in one context can create challenges in another. Saying what you think can be viewed as honesty, which is a desirable trait; but if one is viewed as uncomfortably direct when they speak in the office, it won't be long before the employee is terminated from their job. There is no way to know if this is discrimination under Diversity, Equity, and Inclusion (DEI), because companies do not report such data due to fear of discrimination lawsuits.

I feel it is important to share a personal example of a time I chose to disclose my autism to an employer. After the end of my last business, I had the opportunity to join a local combat medical manufacturing and supply company in Durango, CO as Director of Sales and Marketing. I considered this job a trade-off from my last jobs as I would no longer be the key decision maker, but I would have great input on the important aspects of the business.

In my interview, I chose to disclose I was on the spectrum, and that it had benefits and drawbacks. The owner of the company viewed this information positively and I was hired. However, soon after beginning the job, I learned the company had significant employee turnover due to lack of respect the owner had for his employees. (My position alone had been replaced three times.) The owner began to observe my team was confident that I had added great value to the company, and they also enjoyed my management style. But he became insecure and viewed my successes and abilities as a threat to his 'leadership'. I learned that he really did not support any employee, let alone one with differences. After five months we separated. But I felt proud of how my team was supported and personally cared for in the company.

Ultimately there are pros and cons to both sides of the disclosure debate. I fall on the side of disclosing one's differences. Besides being tired of masking, I know too many neurodiverse individuals who work for as little as a week before either leaving a job on their own due to stress and lack of accommodations or getting fired. Self-advocacy requires knowing when and how to approach others to negotiate desired accommodations. In the process, some degree of disclosure about oneself is necessary, particularly if the accommodation(s) requested require further explanation.[250] If you cannot own your own company, try to find one that embraces different types of employees, and takes the time to understand how different people work and operate in their environments. Such companies, and there are more and more of them out there, provide the necessary accommodations so everyone can be successful and happy.

## Celebrated Neurodiverse People

It is important to be reminded of all the celebrated individuals who are neurodiverse and nonetheless succeed with great accomplishment because of their gifts, talents, and special traits. Being neurodiverse may be a hurdle, but it does not need to be a barrier to success.[251] Well-known individuals like Henry Ford, Nikola Tesla, Thomas Jefferson, and Marie Curie were likely 2e (on the spectrum). But twice-exceptionality is not exclusive to the spectrum. Consider the information in the charts below. Then for additional famous people see: https://www.onthespectrumfoundation.org/famous-people-with-asperger-s.

*Table 5.1. Celebrated twice-exceptional individuals*

| Examples of Differences | Successful 2e Individuals |
| --- | --- |
| **Area of Difference: Physical** | |
| • Tourette syndrome<br>• Paralysis<br>• ALS<br>• Muscular dystrophy<br>• Cerebral palsy<br>• Chronic or acute health problem such as a heart condition | • Steven Hawkins, Jacob Javits (ALS)<br>• Franklin D. Roosevelt (Paralysis)<br>• Paula Abdul, Toni Braxton, Nick Cannon, Selena Gomez (Lupus)<br>• Shawn White (Tetralogy of Fallot)<br>• Larry Byrd, Barry Manilow (Atrial fibrillation) |
| **Area of Difference: Sensory** | |
| • Deaf/hearing impaired<br>• Blindness | • Ludwig von Beethoven, Jim Kyte, Marlee Matlin (Deaf)<br>• Steven Colbert, Thomas Edison (Hearing impairment)<br>• Andrea Bocelli, Ray Charles, Jose Feliciano, Governor David Paterson, Marla Runyan, Erik Weihenmayer, Stevie Wonder (Blind)<br>• Helen Keller (Deaf & blind) |
| **Area of Difference: Deficit in Social Functioning** | |
| • Autism spectrum disorder | • Temple Grandin, Dan Aykroyd, Daryl Hannah, Michael Burry, Tim Burton, Hannah Gadsby, Barbara McClintock, Greta Thunberg, Dan Harmon, Stephen Fry (Autistic & bipolar disorder) |

| Examples of Differences | Successful 2e Individuals |
|---|---|
| **Area of Difference: Emotional and/or Behavioral** | |
| • Schizophrenia<br>• Depression<br>• Anxiety<br>• Bipolar disorder<br>• Obsessive compulsive disorder | • Winston Churchill, Sheryl Crow, Abraham Lincoln, J, K. Rowling (Depression)<br>• Patty Duke, Demi Lovato, Jane Pauley, Jean-Claude Fan Damme, Catherine Zeta Jones (Bipolar disorder)<br>• John Nash, Jr. (Schizophrenia)<br>• Justin Timberlake (OCD/ADHD)<br>• Howie Mandel (ADHD/depression/OCD<br>• David Beckham, Cameron Diaz, Howard Hughes, Steve Jobs (OCD) |
| **Area of Difference: Brain-Based Impairments** | |
| • ADHD<br>• Executive function | • Terry Bradshaw, Jim Carrey, James Carville, Scott Kelly, Adam Levine, Lisa Ling, David Neeleman, Ty Pennington, Michael Phelps, Will Smith (ADHD)<br>• Richard Branson, Channing Tatum, Vince Vaughn (ADD & dyslexia) |
| **Area of Difference: Specific Learning Differences** | |
| • Dyslexia<br>• Dysgraphia<br>• Dyscalculia<br>• Sensory deficit disorder | • Anderson Cooper, Tom Cruise, Richard Engel, Whoopi Goldberg, Tommy Hilfiger, Jay Leno, Charles Schwab, Steven Spielberg (Dyslexia)<br>• Henry Winkler, Cher (Dyslexia & dyscalculia)<br>• Agatha Christie, Daniel Radcliff (Dysgraphia) |

| Examples of Differences | Successful 2e Individuals |
|---|---|
| Area of Difference: Speech -Language | |
| • Stuttering<br>• Impaired articulation<br>• Voice impairment | • Joe Biden, Emily Blunt, Samuel L. Jackson, James Earl Jones, Byron Pitts, Carly Simon, Bruce Willis, Lewis Carroll (Stuttering)<br>• B.B King (Stuttering/diabetes |
| Area of Difference: Other health impairments | |
| • Diabetes<br>• Epilepsy | • Nick Jonas, Patti LaBelle, George Lucas, Bret Michaels, Mary Tyler Moore, Jean Smart, Sonia Sotomayor (Type 1 diabetes) |

# Job Accommodations

Unlike neurotypicals, who have no deficits or learning differences and can remain calm and in control throughout their day, I can be in a chronic state of moderate to high stress and vigilance on a daily, and sometimes hourly basis. In addition to the previous academic accommodations mentioned in Chapter 4, my psychologist offered these accommodations to support me in the workplace.

○ Close the office door.

○ Acquire a time management buddy.

○ Ask for voicemail directives from supervisor.

○ Obtain permission to record meetings for later review.

○ Use a recording pen (like a Livescribe) with voice to text and text to voice software.

○ Be assigned projects that match one's intense interests in specific areas.

○ Be allowed front row seating in presentations and have clear access to audio-visuals.

○ Ask presenters to provide copies of their presentations in advance, so the focus is on the presentation and not one's difficulty processing input. It is best when presentations include graphs, pictures, and diagrams.

○ Break tasks into smaller segments.

○ Ask for extended time to complete written projects.

○ Have job concepts and rules presented in context and not just as isolated facts. Ask for an overview of job requirements, and to be offered a clear understanding of the steps needed to achieve projects and objectives.

○ Ask for a full explanation of jargon and the unique terms of a topic before tackling it.

○ Ask supervisors to meet on a regular basis, not only to check progress, but to make sure work is meeting objectives, and to avoid going off on tangents.

○ Suggest to supervisors that job opportunities could include working with other employees that have common interests or on joint projects.

○ Remind others that one might benefit from computer-assisted instruction, and from hands-on, learning-by-doing options.

○ Ask for freedom to control one's work environment, including lighting alternatives, control over sound levels, and controls for heating and air conditioning.

○ Seek opportunities to explore creative options and alternatives to approaching difficult, challenging, and complex problems.

○ Keep working with a counselor to help reduce stress and control anxiety. Continue to see one's psychiatrist to manage medications and adjust them when necessary.

# CHAPTER 6:
# Relationships

*"I don't have to sell my soul,*
*I wanna be adored, you adore me"*
~The Stone Roses

E. B. White's classic children's novel *Charlotte's Web* (1952) takes place on a farm and involves a pig named Wilbur and his devoted friend Charlotte the spider who manages to save his life by writing about him in her web. Charlotte and Wilbur's friendship, despite their differences in nature, teaches us many things, especially tolerance. Successful relationships and friendships begin when both partners are open-minded, patient, and accept each other's differences.

A healthy relationship is one between two separate people who bring different strengths and weaknesses together to compliment, enhance and support each other.[252] Achieving this in neurodivergent and neurodiverse relationships is often challenged by conflicts. Difficulties arise when one person doesn't understand how the other processes information.[253] Jumping to conclusions and misunderstandings happen in any relationship when conflict is based on an individual's one-sided interpretation. When such conflict occurs in a neurodiverse partnership, it can be magnified because of the unusual differences each has in processing information. Neurodiverse people are more likely to misunderstand or misinterpret what happened.[254]

Neurotypicals have the advantage of processing a complex set of signals from other people, including facial expression, speech and sound, and gestures. They deduce what they imagine to be someone's thoughts and intentions from these physical clues.[255] An ASD brain, on the other hand, will have difficulty recognizing and interpreting these clues of body language and vocal inflections; they may not realize at all what another person is thinking or feeling. Autistic people often do *not* have the ability to 'read' another person's whole outer expression.[256] It does not mean they cannot understand people, but they need accommodation to be led to understanding. It is important to realize that there are autism-related 'traits' that are unlikely to change; nonetheless, individuals with this difference are capable of growth, and can have fulfilling and meaningful relationships.[257]

## My Friendships

I usually come into a setting as the awesome new guy who is smart and knows a lot about a myriad of topics and cool stuff to do. Then three to nine months later, someone in the group will say to others, "I thought John was a great guy, but he is a jerk!" The closer people get to one another, the more non-verbal facial gestures and body language they use. Because I miss a lot—sometimes all—of this type of communication, I have sometimes fallen out of core groups of friends quickly. But as I have gotten older, I have learned how to make important relationships last.

One of the most important friendships in my life is with Pierce, who I have known since childhood. We grew up next door to each other and our parents raised us like brothers. His father Marvin often provided guidance when my own father could not. As we grew up, we remained close. We visit each other and take vacations together with our spouses. Our friendship is strong today for several reasons.

Although I've asked Pierce to go into business with me on more than one occasion, he knew it would not be wise. We both feared our friendship would potentially be impacted. Also, if either of us become overwhelmed in the friendship, we take a break and revisit after a short time has passed. And because I can be quite intense in relationships with others, Pierce is patient, objective, non-emotional, and thoughtful. He does not jump to conclusions about things I say or do, and he never becomes defensive when either of us feels misunderstood. This is generally a common source of conflict in a neurodiverse relationship. As a final point, I often say Pierce speaks what I call 'Johneese'. It is based on my unique way of communicating. Simply put, he knows what I am thinking and trying to say due to the closeness and length of our friendship,

There are other individuals I have met during my life who have remained close. All of them have seen me at my best and worst times. They don't see me as different; they just accept me for exactly who I am. I met many individuals who became lifelong friends while I was in the army. Because the men in our cohort were together for three years, a cohesive bond much like a brotherhood was established. Even today we share news about our lives in a text group. When one of us 'goes down' (has significant life challenges), the others rally around to offer support. This happened to me twice with army friends Nick, Rosy, and Matt.

Once I was severely depressed and drinking too much. I called Nick, who realized I was in trouble, and he notified the other men. Matt said, "We will drop everything. It is all hands-on deck. What can we do to help John?" Nick contacted my wife, who then arranged for me to fly to Pennsylvania to stay with him for a couple weeks. Everyone in the group was checking on me to see if I was alright. Although my wife helps me through tough times like this, my army friends were just the right medicine during this episode to get me back on solid ground.

Another time I experienced the meaning of friendship was when army buddies Rosy, Lobo, and Matt came to Texas to be with me after a very close Marine Corps friend committed suicide. This death was very difficult for me to understand. I still have not completely grieved the loss of this important friend. During their stay with me in Texas my army buddies supported my art show. They consoled me when I heard that another important person in my life had passed away, Pierce's father Marvin. My emotions were very high. Without friends who cared about me uncondi- tionally, I don't think I could have made it. Friendship is not about always having to know all the details in a situation. Friends just show up and express how much they care.

Although the U.S. Department of Defense publishes an *Annual Report on Suicide in the Military* and makes efforts to address and prevent suicide across the Department of Defense, the grim statistics never make the national news. Prevention efforts in our military are now more focused on fostering quality of life, reducing stigma, and creating a culture of lethal means safety.[258] (Lethal means are objects like fire- arms, medications, and sharp objects that can be used to engage in suicidal behavior. Safety measures that secure lethal means include safe storage options such as cable locks, locked safes and medication lock boxes.[259]) According to the Secretary of the Department of Defense, General Lloyd James Austin III, "…mental health is health, and so we must continue to work to break down barriers to help-seeking, address stigma, and build healthy climates and a culture of connection where all our Service members can thrive."[260]

There are two other dear friends in my life that I know I could always pick up the phone and talk to about anything and never be judged. One of them is Brian. He and I first met in our college fraternity. We reunited after many years at a fraternity reunion back in Texas. We discovered we both had children the same age and shared many of the same interests, including business. Brian ended up becoming an investor in our company. Along with my other close friend Gus, who was hired to be the head of operations at our sleep apnea business, the three of us were like 'The Three Musketeers'.

When I first met Gus, we just 'clicked'. We trusted each other and worked well together. The relationship never felt like a boss and an employee. We were equals setting and achieving goals that we had established as a team. We enjoyed socializing together with our wives, who also became very close friends.

When I was diagnosed with ASD, Brian and Gus went with me a number of times to see my psychologist Dr. Robinson and discussed how they could understand my differences better. This meant a lot to me because as I told other people in my life about my diagnosis, I discovered some shrugged it off thinking 'that is just how John is'. As Gus and I talked more about ASD, he said his brother Don had a 2e son named Austin. Don often struggled to understand how his son experienced life. So, when Don contacted me about speaking with Austin, I jumped at the chance to not only help a friend, but to help a young boy who was experiencing life like me. Don later told me that Austin said speaking with me was like having a conversation with himself. Austin had never connected like that with anyone in his family. I am now a 'life coach' for this special young man, and along with strong support from his parents, he is excelling in life.

### Adult Friendships

There are many compelling reasons to get out in the world and socialize, rather than spending too much time in solitude.[261] Meeting a person who is like-minded can help with loneliness. People who are lonely crave human contact, but their state of mind makes it more difficult to form connections with other people.[262] Loneliness has a wide range of negative physical and mental side effects, such as alcohol and drug misuse, poor decision making, increased stress levels, and depression.

Talking with someone who shares the same interests can lead to a lifelong friendship. There are many researched benefits for this type of connection. Most importantly, one may live longer and likely enjoy better physical and mental health.[263] A recommendation for finding people with similar interests might be to sign up for classes at a local recreation center, library, community college or university.

Equally important is socializing with others who can help with networking. People can help you find a new interest group, a club, or even a job opportunity. Social network websites allow users to connect with other people around the world. Most networks let users send messages, request and share information, and share connections and friend requests. Some popular online networking platforms are Twitter, Facebook, Instagram, and LinkedIn. I am happy to say I have met friends through social networking, including my newest friend and co-author, Deborah.

In addition to making social connections, interacting with others helps the rules of a neurotypical world become clearer. If you are neurotypical person, you don't have to guess if someone's words are to be taken literally, worry about information gained from asking a question, or figure out what is expected from non-verbal cues. For neurodivergent people, the consequences of getting these rules wrong and misinterpreting people can be severe. There is the danger of losing employment or friendships, awkward public interaction, even being arrested or assaulted because neurotypicals will negatively judge and perhaps act against words and actions they don't understand.[264]

Friends can help you meet a special person who might become a romantic partner: neurodiverse individuals have a deep desire for intimacy and connection in a committed relationship.[265] Unfortunately, romantic relationships are rarely, if ever, addressed in autism related services, especially during the critical adolescent years when relationship skills are usually developed.[266] The key to dating is to begin with simple meetups that allow each person to share a little about themself, remembering that the person one meets doesn't need to be 'the perfect date' or 'love of one's life'.[267] Such an unburdened experience is just a small risk, not putting too much on the line. Such simple dating offers a chance to practice making conversation and connections with other people.

Just like determining if one should disclose to an employer they are on the spectrum, the decision to share this on a date is equally as stressful. Because the way autism affects each person is unique, there isn't any 'key' or 'golden answer' that will serve all people in all circumstances.[268] If you don't expect to date the same person again, perhaps disclosing is not necessary. But if you make a connection and decide to date more than a few times, it may be a good idea to find a comfortable way to share your diagnosis. If they are truly interested in you, they may already be aware of some kind of difference. In his book *Been There, Done That, Try This* (2014), clinical psychologist Dr. Tony Attwood says, "Sometimes the characteristics of ASD are conspicuous, such that a neurotypical may be confused and seek an explanation of certain unusual behaviors or reactions." Below are some helpful ways to be a better friend to one on the spectrum.[269]

○ Don't assume a neurodiverse person is not interested because they don't react or express excitement the way a neurotypical person expects.

○ If plans get canceled, it could be the neurodiverse person is overwhelmed at the time. Don't stop asking them to do things.

○ If a neurodiverse individual is angering you, tell them. If you don't agree with them, say so. Talk it out. Neurodiverse people don't do well with passive- aggressive behavior or silent treatment.

○ Humor the neurodiverse friend by engaging the subjects they like.

○ Remember that neurodiverse individuals can be intense. When they do something, they are fully committed. Their intensity is a positive thing: don't be put off by it. Their hyperfocus is what drives them to accomplish incredible feats; pressure to temper it will keep them from being successful and finding purpose.

○ Remember that neurodiverse people may 'stim' when they are around others. Stimming (self-stimulating) is a neurologically driven behavior that helps a neurodiverse person self-regulate intense emotional and sensory input. This could be rocking back and forth, tapping their hands or feet, standing or pacing while the other person sits, twirling their hair, or fidgeting with their clothes.

○ Neurodiverse people often live in fear that they will say something that offends another person. Look past their word choices and seek the meaning of what the individual is trying to tell you.

○ It is important to know that neurodiverse people have great difficulty lying, so don't ask for their opinion if you don't want the truth.

### Twice-Exceptional Children and Friendships

Making friends can be hard for any child. For socially awkward gifted or twice-exceptional children the challenge is significantly multi-plied.[270] They struggle to find peer groups or successfully interact with others. On one occasion they can have an intelligent conversation with an adult expert in one of their fields of interest. But put them in the same room with children their own age and all bets are off.[271] The gifted/2e child may find it difficult to have conversations at their advanced level. This mismatch between mental and chronical age (asynchrony) provokes a qualitatively different social experience making it difficult to find a place to fit in.[272]

Similarly, depending on the child's particular diagnosis, the learning difference may or may not hinder them in acquiring age-appropriate skills.[273] A child with dyslexia may not have trouble making friends, as his difficulty reading does not necessarily impact his ability to navigate social situations. But it is different for children with challenges like autism, ADHD, or social anxiety, because these differences make them struggle to understand others.

Twice-exceptional children may need help navigating peer interactions. One way to address such social challenges is with social skills groups (although these can be difficult to find for gifted children). When searching for such a group, consider these questions:[274] 1) What are the child's interests? Camps allow a child to study in a field he loves and practice social skills. 2) Where does the child feel safe and accepted? This might be a club, a sport, an art or music studio. Once the child finds such a supportive environment, parents can create opportunities that help the child to get more involved and establish connection.[275]

Finally, most twice-exceptional children will need individualized support to help address lagging social skills. Examples include psychotherapy, occupational therapy, speech/language therapy, and executive functions coaching. To locate these and other services, find your state gifted association, https://www.sengifted.org/, and https://nagc.org/.

## Dating

One of the most *Googled* questions neurotypicals ask about dating someone on the spectrum is, "Can autistic people fall in love?"[276] The answer is a most profound yes! But in couples where one or both partners have a diagnosis or suspected diagnosis of autism spectrum disorder (ASD), there are traits that can make a relationship challenging.[277] The good news is that when the autistic partner focuses on improving the challenging trait, and the couple works together to understand their differences, the relationship can be fulfilling and thrive.

Dating is one of those rights of passage that most teenage boys or girls enjoy in high school. I was very excited for the opportunity when it presented itself in my junior year. I felt that I always picked the prettiest and smartest girls to date. If I really liked a girl I asked out, I thought our initial friendship could possibly turn into something more than just one date and perhaps we could become a couple. Why wouldn't this be possible? If I was happy on a date, shouldn't my partner be happy too? I came to realize that my perception and my date's perception of how things were going was often totally different. I could not read her body language or facial cues, which of course led to misunderstandings. I became exhausted and perplexed by the unclear signs that my date was giving me. "It can feel like reading a book, but you only get to see every fifth word."[278] My goal in dating became to understand the whole book, but it was difficult because misunderstood cues meant that I was missing most of the 'story'. Dating in high school was my first glimpse into the world of neurodiverse relationships. I could see that they tend to grow apart due to the resentment of not being able to understand each other.[279]

Although I didn't know I was autistic when I started dating in high school, I realized as I got a little older there was no reason to turn myself inside out trying to please others. I just looked at dating as making a friend. If I enjoyed someone I met and we shared things in common, I would ask the young lady out for an official date. I did not worry about whether it was going to become romantic, but I did learn to pay more attention to some common signals and body language and react more appropriately. Some of these were: 1) My date would touch my arm or shoulder indicating she was interested in me. 2) If my date sat close to me, I knew she was showing interest or flirting. 3) If my date moved away from me, she may just need space or she may be uninterested in what we were talking about.

Those with Asperger's can find enjoyment dating many types of people. Dating another neurodiverse individual brings understanding along with similar needs and interests. Autistic individuals may also enjoy group dates with several types of people. In this scenario, there is no pressure to be romantic. In my case, I enjoyed dating women with a neurotypical profile who provided another point of view and offered interests and talents that were different than my own. This is how I met my wife, Ashley. We got to know each other first through a working relationship and then we began dating.

As my relationship with Ashley became romantic, I was concerned that it might not last. I have experienced feeling close to someone many times in my life, but after a few months those relationships succumbed to the big differences between me and the other individual. This was the case in my first marriage. But I was determined to make this important relationship with Ashley work. I had never met anyone who had traveled around the world from a young age because of their father's job, as I had done growing up. Most importantly, we enjoyed each other's company very much.

Although I didn't know I was neurodiverse when I began dating Ashley, I understood there were no guarantees that any relationship I had with a woman would work, especially if problematic issues came along.[280] I felt confident, though, if I met someone who was loyal, honest, and appreciated my strengths and accepted my short comings, that there was a good chance that things could work. As I dated Ashley, I felt we had a relationship that was mutually beneficial and caring, with few disagreements or arguments. If we did argue, neither of us wanted it turning into a destructive loop, so we always forgave each other. As a couple, it was refreshing to feel the freedom to be ourselves.

Whether individuals are dating or considering marriage, the partnership should always involve compromise. Neither person should feel entitled.[281] This can become problematic in neurodiverse couples because while one person's brain may view something as acceptable in the relationship, the other may not. Recognizing the needs of each partner and finding a balance becomes paramount.[282]

It has taken me years to realize there are multiple perspectives in a relationship. Both neurodiverse and neurotypical partners need to release judgements they have held about what one person knows or doesn't know and recognize the validity of the other partner's viewpoint.[283] As I have often heard, there is not one owner of reality. Each partner must understand the concept of 'different yet equally valid perspectives.[284] Looking at this picture, one may see a rabbit, or one may see a duck. Neither is wrong, it is their point of view.[285]

*Figure 6.1 Rabbit or duck?*

When two people come together in a relationship, remember that each person has a brain with unique experience 'filters', like one's psychology, neurology, gender, ethnicity, family history, and life experiences.[286] Establishing a good connection and communicating well with your partner, especially about their needs and how best to support them, will lead to a fulfilling and enriched relationship in the long term.[287] If you are fortunate enough to capture the heart of a person, as I did, tread gently and see where it leads. It certainly will not be boring.[288]

## Cohabitation/Marriage

Neurodiverse relationships see a turning point when the couple moves from dating to living together. This is significant for any couple, but for neurodiverse partners there will be unique challenges when personal contact goes from dating to being together all the time. The demand on the autistic or neurotypical partner may not be anticipated.[289] Some of the more common difficulties that arise are managing impulsivity, reading non-verbal cues, sensitivity dysphoria, sensory and emotional overload, executive function challenges, hyper-fixation on special interests, and low frustration tolerance.[290] Also, the neurodivergent partner may feel like they have to explain themselves constantly, which leads to hypervigilance, guilt and shame.[291] This recurring impasse in communication leads to a dynamic where both partners feel they are 'walking on egg shells' when conflicts arise.

After dating for a short period, I decided Ashley was the partner for me. I planned to propose marriage to her at The Jonah's Boutique Hotel on Whale Beach in Sydney, Australia. This was her favorite place to visit with her parents when she was growing up. After an amazing dinner in the hotel, I had two dozen roses waiting for her in our room and the ring in my pocket. I was so happy when she said yes! After a short engagement, we had our wedding on the beach with many family members and friends in attendance, including Pierce, his brother

Marc and their parents Marvin and Judy. My own parents did not attend. The reception was a big party everyone said they would always remember. After our honeymoon on Hayman Island, off the coast of central Queensland, Ashley and I looked forward to a life of adventure and success in Australia.

The first five years of marriage were the most relaxed. We traveled and worked together at our dental laboratory, diagnostics, and supply company, and later a company we would help list on the stock exchange. From our Sydney apartment, we enjoyed walking to nearby restaurants, bars, and the zoo. Because I had been living in Australia for only a couple of years, Ashley showed me the wonderful cities of Brisbane, Melbourne, Perth, and Adelaide, as well as the Blue Mountains, where her father lived. We would also take fun weekend trips to the coast. I felt magic just being around my wife.

Things began to change in our relationship about the same time we decided to move to the United States to run the company. We immersed ourselves in getting the new business up and running. We traveled to Singapore, Bangkok, the United Kingdom, Hong Kong, Canada, and Germany, as we prepared the company for entering new markets. Things got very stressful, and we began to argue a lot when we moved back to America. Our relationship was either euphoric or dreadful. There was no middle ground. Ashley felt I didn't care enough about the relationship to try very hard. I felt she did not have enough patience and that she was difficult to please. At this point in the marriage, we realized we had two different perceptions and the ability to work together constructively was going to be hard to figure out.[292]

While it is true most couples struggle with some aspects of relationship dynamics, neurodivergent brains tend to have more difficulty monitoring and managing emotions and behaviors.[293] If I had known earlier in my life that I was neurodivergent, I would have been more prepared to deal with my emotions as our one-year plan to stay in America turned into a four-year plan. Although we were doing very well professionally, the long office hours and our unhappiness took a toll on both Ashley and me. Our relationship had grown apart due to the deep resentment of not being able to understand each other.[294]

Ashley and I decided we had two choices. We either had to seek marriage counseling, or divorce. Fortunately, we decided to save our marriage. During one appointment with our counselor, she suggested I might be on the spectrum. Although we were both taken by surprise, we agreed it was essential for me to be tested. If the marriage counselor's observation was correct, it would explain a lot of things about me and how I have been challenged in relationships throughout my life. After a thorough battery of tests, my neuropsychologist diagnosed me as 'gifted with autism', or, 'twice exceptional'. Ashley and I were thrilled to have something definitive to 'grab onto' which helped explain why we seemed to be on different planets in our marriage. Our next steps were to learn how neurodiverse couples can thrive with a partner who is not only gifted, but autistic, and with other learning differences.

Being diagnosed as neurodivergent well into adulthood can make you reassess your life, the people in it, the type of partner you seek, and the right fit with employment.[295] I began to think about all these things. I enjoyed the friendships I had maintained over the years, including my childhood friend Pierce, a few former army buddies I have stayed in contact with, and some close business associates. I knew I could count on these people to always be there for me at any time. Even though my job was stressful, I enjoyed the feeling I got when I succeeded in business. I thought long and hard about my marriage. I wanted to make it work with Ashley. Other than Pierce, she was the one person in my life I could count on day in and day out and she appreciates my weaknesses along with my strengths. Although neither one of us knew I was autistic when we met, I would advise others who choose to be in a neurodivergent relationship that they must be open to making a commitment, like my wife did with me. Someone who is flighty, fickle, or irresponsible would not be the best fit and the relationship would most likely fail.[296]

After twenty years of marriage, I am often asked, "What makes a neurodiverse relationship work?" The most successful are the ones where needs and expectations are well matched.[297] A willingness to accommodate each other is essential. Ashley and I coordinate our needs to socialize. She enjoys speaking with many people in large gatherings, which is one reason she is outstanding at her job. I prefer more solitude, which is not to say I don't enjoy visiting the neighborhood bar occasionally to socialize, but I can get overwhelmed quickly in such environments. After time adjusting in our marriage, Ashely and I now better understand our individual social needs, and we don't get upset anymore. We support each other even though we are very different.

In addition to accommodating each other's special needs, successful relationships have good communication. Each partner must understand what their partner needs to offer to approach balance. Unfortunately, not everyone has the same type of communication style. One person might give lengthy explanations about something, but the other person cannot process it all at once,[298] and needs the conversation broken down into smaller pieces. One partner may speak too briefly in only a few sentences, which can be interpreted as rude, abrupt, or as if they don't care. This type of communication doesn't provide any feeling of connection between partners.[299]

A large percentage of good communication is simply listening. Neurotypical partners generally seek an empathetic response, not necessarily wanting a problem solved. On the other hand, neurodiverse people like me listen to our partner describe a problem, and we immediately want to solve it. I think: "Why would one communicate about something that is bothering them and not want to find a solution?" It is illogical to me. Neurotypicals want an emotional connection and if they don't hear something back that makes them feel closer to their partner, they can feel alone. My wife is a feeling and emotional decision maker. I am the exact opposite. I am very logical and harder up front to interact with. We had to learn how to work as a team to make sure we were both being heard.

My best advice for a neurodiverse couple is to make sure each person really appreciates each other's strengths *and* weaknesses. The differences and 'quirks' of the neurodiverse person must be seen as positives, *not* negatives. When Ashley and I were in business together early in our marriage, I saw the dynamics of her personality working with my ability to problem solve as a win-win combination. It is still like that today. She and I complement each other. We are more at peace than we have ever been. Communication is organic for us now that we have developed a true understanding of each other. Each day we keep moving forward with appreciation that we are different, but in sync.

## Useful tools to improve marriage

All marriages are unique and can have their own obstacles. There are tools that a neurodiverse individual (and sometimes neurotypical partner) in a committed relationship can use to create happier, healthier ones for themself. Recently, I read an outstanding article in *Psychology Today* by psychotherapist and couples' counselor Eva Mendes. She found that there are certain ASD traits that make a relationship challenging. But when the Asperger's partner focuses on attenuating these traits, the marriage can often come back from a crisis or even divorce.[300] Here are 8 tools Mendes's clients found useful:[301]

○ *Don't be defensive*. Admit when you are wrong. Asperger's is characterized by a high IQ and strong logical thinking. This can lead individuals on the spectrum to think that they're right and justified in their actions but doesn't work well in marriages which require compromise. The ASD partner must be vigilant and take responsibility to accommodate.

○ *Give up control*: Would you rather be married, or right? Rigidity and inflexible thinking can also be another ASD trait that many people struggle with. They have a hard time changing their perspective even when there's evidence to the contrary, or even if they see that holding on to their close-minded view is creating a schism between their partner and them. They need to work hard to trust, practice being flexible and see their partner's point of view.

○ *Avoid resentment*: Many ASD individuals are known to have an elephant's memory and may remember every little disagreement or conflict. They have trouble letting go of the daily aggravations and instead archive and catalog them, leading to a mind full of resentment, anger, and bitterness. Mendes says she often offers her clients the analogy of 'taking out the garbage'. Just as we empty the trash from our kitchen, we need to take the negative thoughts, upsets, disagreements, fights, and irritations out of our minds daily, and let them go away permanently.

○ *Listen more, talk less*: Sometimes an ASD individual can be an over-talker, especially when anxious. They are often smart, so they have a lot to share. This can get in the way of a two-way communication flow. Control talking over people and listen more.

○ *Control emotions*: Many individuals on the spectrum have trouble regulating their emotions, which range from anger to anxiety. They must practice being aware of and understanding their emotions.

○ *Practice self-awareness*: Invest in building self-awareness through therapy, reading books on autism and Asperger's, relationships, depression, anxiety, OCD, addiction, etc. To understand what drives one's thoughts, feelings, and behaviors, one must understand their triggers and plan ahead to circumvent them. This will help avoid meltdowns and aggressive behaviors.

○ *Trust my partner*: Mental rigidity and slow processing can lead an ASD partner to relate in a way that is negative. They contradict what their partner is saying or criticize them without fully thinking the matter through. They fixate on their own perspective without considering what their partner's thoughts and feelings are.

○ *Work can be an excuse*: Being a workaholic is often an ASD hallmark. Work can be rewarding, especially in their area of interest; but it can become a fixation, such that the ASD partner will get hyper-focused on work to the exclusion of their marriage or relationship. When their partner complains, they infer that their partner doesn't understand the pressures, or that they are getting in the way.

# Additional Slices of Life

*"Gonna have a good time tonight, rock and roll music gonna play all night. Come on baby it won't take long, only take a minute just to sing my song."*
~The Easy Beats/Jimmy Barnes & Michel Hutchence

Although this book contains quite a bit about my life, I find it important to share a few 'slices of life' in more detail, as I experienced them. I understand now I see things through a very different lens than a neurotypical adult. The 'slices' I share here include additional viewpoints on things I have experienced, a few poems I wrote, and important photos to accompany part two of the book.

# Viewpoints

## Childhood

As previously mentioned, I grew up in Gainesville, Texas, which was very 'Rockwellian' in the late 70's and the mid 80's. Remembering my early travels, I knew it was too small for me. But that didn't distract in any way from the many positives of growing up in a small Texas town.

I recall countless nights discussing the intricacies of Star Wars with my friend Pierce in his room while having a sleep over. I remember chasing lightning bugs and running through Pierce's father's giant backyard garden while our parents shucked fresh corn and had a few evening cocktails.

Throughout the summers and most weekends, Pierce, his brother Marc, my brother Bryan, and I would play neighborhood games. Creative play amongst children, unlike today, was how we all learned from one another. Instead of playing Dungeons and Dragons (a popular fantasy tabletop role playing game) with character sheets and dice, we forged our own weapons and armor and 'went to war' outside. At the time, there were still aluminum trashcans with detachable lids with a handle. The lids became shields. Lumber was cut to become swords and barbarian's clubs. Full broomsticks became lances for jousting, and we wore our football helmets. We would mount our faithful Chromoly BMX 'steeds' and face off at opposing ends of Rusk Street. We had a broomstick lance in one hand and trashcan shield in the other. The goal was to dismount your opponent while riding full speed at one another. Each scenario of our outdoor *Dungeons and Dragons* was more memorable than any tabletop version could ever be.

My childhood, although tumultuous at times, has many fun memories from when I traveled outside of Texas with my father and stepmother. One of those memories is from Steamboat, Colorado, where my parents had purchased two condominiums. I fell in love with Colorado the first time we went in 1977.

During a Christmas trip to Steamboat, when I was about 8 years old, my friend Pierce and I took my Yankee Clipper sled to the top of Headwall, the main mountain run, after closing and took a ride. It did not turn out well, it was a debacle from the outset. I fell off the back of the sled, got the rope tangled around my feet, and we hit the bottom of the mountain so fast that we jumped the snowbank and skidded along the pavement. The next day, we decided to take flat lunch trays from the 'mountain house' and use them as sleds. We got the same results as with our 'traditional' sleds in terms of velocity and impact. But this time we noticed a substantial group of observers. When we got to the bottom of the mountain, we realized dozens of kids and adults had hopped on the bandwagon. We were obviously pioneers in 'tray sledding', which we contend to this day is obviously the precursor to snowboarding.

## Teenage Angst

Teenage angst is part of growing up. During my sophomore year at McCallie School, I had just finished wrestling practice. I was leaving my room with a buddy named Brian who lived down the hall and tossed a coat hanger towards the hallway trashcan near my room. It bounced off the can and gently tapped me on the leg. Our eyes immediately locked, and it was 'game on'!

I bent the hook of the hanger down for safety reasons and hurled it back at him but missed. The coat hanger went bouncing down the hall. We both ducked back inside our respective rooms to grab more ammunition and started throwing hangers at each other, popping out of doors, and jumping back in our room for protection. This went on for a few minutes, and when another dormmate walked by, he got hit by a flying hanger and immediately joined in. Soon, everyone in the dorm at the time was upstairs, divided into two teams and battling for roughly 30 minutes. Our dorm head, Mr. Patterson, heard what was going on and called us out for our mischief. We apologized, but Mr. Patterson told us to look up at the ceiling. We had destroyed about fifty ceiling tiles, our parents got the bill, and we had a lot of explaining to do.

In the summer between junior and senior year at Rockwall High School, I was dating a beautiful and intelligent young lady. She asked me what class I was taking for my senior English credit. I had not given the topic any thought until she told me she had been accepted into the AP English program. Besides the possibility of being in her English class for senior year, it intrigued me that this class would meet only on Mondays, Wednesdays, and Fridays, like in college, and also that my girlfriend would receive college credit for passing the AP exam. The only issue for me was that I had not applied for the AP English program. So my girlfriend and I decided I should do the only logical thing. The first day of AP English I sat down to see if anyone would notice I was in the wrong place. Within five minutes, the teacher pegged it. She knew I was trying to sneak into the class because my girlfriend was there. I will never forget the way she handled the situation. Instead of kicking me out, she said, "I think there may have been some scheduling confusion, but we will address it next time we meet for class". She then proceeded to distribute a 20-question general knowledge test, which is not something one studies for, or has assigned as homework. It was just a test to see what we know, and I took the test.

At the next class the teacher started handing out the graded tests. Everyone got their tests back but me; my girlfriend had a high score. Then the teacher moved slowly to my desk and handed me my test, waited for me to see my grade, and said, "I think I may have misspoken last class. Everyone is exactly where they should be". I was the only student in the class to score 100%. This class was one of the few which I really enjoyed, and fully participated in during high school. To this day, whenever I doubt myself about college or other traditional academic education, I reflect on that moment and never forget its positive encouragement.

## Travel

My experiences traveling abroad have benefited me in ways that could not be replicated in a classroom. Flying on a plane in the 70's is something children today will never understand: people dressed in their finest clothing to fly, regardless of the seating class, and the meals served were a true dining experience.

The way I saw Europe then is impossible to experience today. London was a city of mostly brick and there were fewer buildings above 6 stories high. I remember being in London when authorities found an unexploded German bomb from WWII. Back then, Paris was not 'plastic' as it seems today. Fewer people spoke English, menus were in French, and there were no fast-food restaurants. On a visit to Normandy, I witnessed veterans paying homage to their fallen comrades. Every country in Europe was unique.

One of my most memorable European trips was at 8 years old. My father had become a well- known clinician and lecturer by the late 70's and he had a business in France. The taxes at that time were crazy, so my father and my stepmother set up Swiss and Caymanian bank accounts. The decision was made to move cash physically out of France and into Switzerland to avoid large taxes. I recall a close family friend bringing the money to the border. One would have thought this transaction was some 'French Connection' type of drug run or something. Our family friend wore a hat and sunglasses, trying to hide, but he stood out like a sore thumb. A highlight of this trip is when I sat on a duffle bag full of money in the back of a rental car traveling from France into Switzerland. I had one of those switch blade combs that was popular at the time, and it was positioned on top of the bag to look cute and provide levity. It all worked out and no one got arrested.

Living overseas, particularly in Australia, seems to be easier for me. My quirks are mostly taken as being 'American', or more specifically 'Texan'. In Australia, Aussies are very sardonic, and their sarcasm is not mean. It is the kind I understand and find very funny. I remember doing something in business other than the normal way, and my CEO at the time said to others, "Haven't you guys worked with an American, much less a Texan? That is just how they do things". The CEO also nicknamed me 'the little digger'. Digger is an Australian term for a tough infantryman. I took this as a nice compliment.

I did not fare as well when I traveled to other countries. Northern and southern England are very different. Southern England (London, Surrey, etc.) includes stereotypical, aristocratic people or white-collar office professionals. Northern England is more 'blue collar' or working class. These people in the north are much more direct when speaking, as compared to the southern English who use a lot of facial expressions and body language. I fare much better visiting Northern England because of their direct-ness. But in both cultures, I have learned what is not said is much more important than what is said.

Some of my fondest memories of travel, as an adult or a child, are from trips to the Cayman Islands. My father purchased a condo there when I was young. I remember there were no cruise ships coming into port and tourism had not spoiled the greatness of the Caribbean. The locals were kind and hospitable.

Before my 12th birthday and before I was certified to scuba dive, I had somewhere around 100 hours logged under-water. When I became a certified diver, I experienced deep water, wrecks, caves, and night dives. I enjoyed the relaxed feeling of being underwater. I remember each time I went diving as a youth. The dive master would take pictures with his underwater camera and show them at dinner with a Polaroid 610 slide projector that went 'click clunk' with those little white slides.

I had two close friends on the island who were around my age. Their father had a construction business on the island. We built sand forts on the beach and went swimming out to the reef with spear guns. We caught fish, lobsters, and conch to take home for dinner. It was a blast speeding around in their little skiff with its 5hp engine and listening to the latest 'alternative' music, songs I would have never heard in Gainesville.

I also visited the Cayman Islands several times in later life. One fond memory is of my dear friend Pierce's bachelor party. Along with his brother Marc and some McCallie school friends, we had a blast of a time that lasted 12 days. Ashley and I visited a few times, and it was wonderful. But on these later trips the Caymans were nothing like the times I remembered as a kid. In 2014, Ashley and I had an amazing trip with my friend Gus and his family. We were packed into a little condo with his two kids and our son Nash, and it was a great trip. We had beach fires, went fishing, and just enjoyed everyone's company.

## Early Business Mind

After the second semester of my sophomore year of college, I decided to visit my friend Bill in Breckenridge, Colorado, as I did not ship out for the Army until mid-March. Bill had just moved to Breckenridge a couple weeks earlier. He and I stayed with another fraternity brother in his tiny 400-square foot two-bedroom apartment. I slept on the recliner in the living room. Jobs are hard to find in ski towns under the best circumstances, so I really had to improvise.

Bill worked for a high school friend about our age from San Antonio who owned a taco stand called Nacho Taco. The business wasn't big enough to employ me also, but the owner said that I could work there and be paid in tacos and burritos. Luckily, bartering was still alive and well in Colorado ski towns in 1993, so I got a system going. I could trade 10 tacos for a pizza, 20 tacos for rented skis, and about the same for a day-long lift ticket. Had I really explored it, it's my sincere belief that I could have traded around 1000 tacos and burritos for an annual ski pass. But I was only in town for three months before I was to return to Texas and join the Army.

## Business

In 2003 Ashley and I were invited by a venture capital group to list a medical device company on the Australian Stock Exchange. The product was not yet commercialized, so this was a completely *de nova* endeavor, and it took from January until August of 2004 to complete the listing. Joining us was a gentleman who specialized in getting companies on the exchange and had successfully been involved in approximately 20 Initial Public Offerings (IPO).

There were many great twists and turns, and I learned a tremendous amount during the process. One of the wildest experiences was called 'Road Show'. This occurs near the end of the process once an underwriter is secured. We did around 12 pitches over a three- day period, in Sydney, Brisbane, and Melbourne. The three of us were in meetings with a representative of the underwriter. We got in front of some legitimate potential investors, including Queensland Investment Corporation (QIC) and Wachovia.

The Road Show process was amazing: it felt a lot like being a rock star. We hit the meetings all fired up, secured the investment, and hopped back into our limousine. The underwriter would hand us a glass of champaign and then turn into a character like Burgess Meredith as the trainer in the movie Rocky. He rubbed our shoulders, gave us positive feedback, and prepped us for the next pitch. It was like, 'wash, rinse, repeat' for three days and I loved it.

On listing day the venture capital group, the future board, and the three of us went to the exchange floor to 'ring the opening bell'. I had visions of the New York Stock Exchange mayhem, with yelling and screaming, when the 'ding, ding, ding' rings out. It was an awesome experience, albeit not what I expected. We went into a small, well-appointed room where there was a digital ticker running along one side of the wall. Then there was a 'buzz' and the day opened. Immediately our ticker symbol popped up and the shares opened at around a 40% premium. The price bounced around quite a bit that day and closed at over 50% up.

We celebrated with an incredible lunch that lasted four hours. Soon, our hard work paid off. On paper, we were instant millionaires; it was an unbelievable experience. The following day the real work began. Fortunately, Ashley and I came in at the top of the company instead of working our ways through being manager and then supervisor to get to the top. In retrospect, this was essential for me. Due to my neurological differences and lack of ability to play the corporate game, I would have never survived the traditional path up the corporate ladder.

The educational value of this experience could not be replicated today. We worked with the best of the best: everyone was an expert in their respective fields. I was afforded the opportunity to let my talents and abilities shine. I had an inherent ability to make financial forecasts, do marketing, and help with patents. (Our medical device was similar to the orthopedic appliances I had learned about at my father's lectures.) When we worked with a well-respected intellectual property law firm in Sydney, Spruson, & Ferguson, I quickly learned that learning 'over-the-shoulder' as I did there, combined with my autodidactic ability, would become a positive pattern that would repeat itself throughout my career.

Finally, I must mention what people really talk about after board meetings. The simple fact is they don't talk about business. After a day spent voicing opinions, debating with others, having disagreements and sometimes arguments, the work is left at the meeting table.

I can remember one interesting dinner with our chairman, a McKinsey-trained, Swiss-educated, very experienced, and successful man. A new senior executive wanted to look smart and impress the chairman, so he interrupted a conversation I was having about WWII. The chairman ignored him, turned back to me, and continued, "So when they talk about the Rangers taking Pointe Du Hoc, those weren't airborne troops were they?" "No, they weren't", I said. "We had two airborne divisions jump during the invasion, the 101st and the 82nd. But at the time, Rangers didn't have airborne status. They were light infantryman. I can remember going to Normandy for the first time when I was seven and seeing oceans of crosses, and stars of

David as far as one could see. There is even a section for fathers and sons who died the same day during the invasion." Then I thought to myself, I connected with the chairman on a personal level and not by having a Harvard degree. By the way, the other guy lasted about 3 months with the company.

## Miscellaneous

I do not understand envy and I never will. I have known people who got jealous when a friend was successful or did well in their career, and I honestly cannot fathom why someone would think like that. I think the exact opposite way. When my friends do well, I am nothing but happy for them, and swell with pride that they are my friends. I feel that my successful friend is a positive reflection of me. I also have no concept of merely 'playing the game' in business or society. I do not make friends with people because they are wealthy, or because I can gain something from them, such as more popularity or more success. And I never liked using money to 'keep score' of success. Many executives I worked with found it enjoyable to see who could make the most money. For me, money exists only to help execute my plans and dreams. It is a necessary evil that I must contend with, not a tool for measuring friendship.

Additionally, I have never enjoyed *good old boy* 'chit chat'. I prefer direct conversation, which is one of the reasons I always enjoyed doing business in New York, where conversations with people tend to be very direct. Also, when someone makes a comment that others would view as an insult, I flip it to my advantage. Once, early in my career, I was at a medical trade show at the Javits Convention Center in Manhattan. I was working at our company's booth explaining and selling different oral-facial orthopedic devices. Two doctors walked by the booth, and one said to the other in a purposefully loud voice so

I could hear him, "Those things don't work". I immediately retorted, "Oh they work, you just don't know how to use them." He stopped, pivoted, and said, "Ok then, show me". He was not rude or angry. After the demonstration and discussion of the device, he became a client and good friend.

In Texas the chit chat seems to go on for days. For example, the local insurance guy came by my house to discuss a policy, but before we ever got down to business, he asked, "John, how are the kids? What do you think of the weather? What are your plans for the weekend?" I hate it because it seems to be a duplicitous distraction from our common purpose. I just want to see the policy, discuss the insurance rates, and ask what my options might be to shop with other insurance carriers. The more chit chat that occurs, the more it drives me crazy.

# Poems

I started writing poems around fifth grade and continued until about 18 or 19 years old. Writing poetry for me today is a stream of thought in 'one hit'. It is cathartic. I don't choose when I write, it just happens. I wrote *The Pendulum and the Pit* after falling into the dark hole called depression. Things can seem to be going well and then life drops me into a pit that is very hard to escape. I wrote it in hopes that others who encounter similar issues know that they are not alone and there is hope at the end of the tunnel. I wrote *Twenty-Two Per Day* after a close friend who was a Marine Corp veteran took his life in February of 2022. It is a tribute to all veterans who have taken their own lives. I sincerely hope that civilians and government do something soon to help address the mental health issues of discharged service men and women.

## The Pendulum and the Pit

It's a usual day. Woke up, made my bed. Looked in the living room.

The normal.

Couch destroyed. Pillows in disarray.

Pants, shoes, water glass, remote control and light decorative blankets strewn across the room.

Kitchen full of dirty dinner plates I should have washed the night before.

It's a usual day.

There are great times.

This isn't one of them.

I should have run the dog by now.

Showered.

Just gotten my shit together like a normal adult.

Problem is I'm not 'a normal adult'.

Who the hell wants to be normal?

White picket fence?

Corporate job with a cubicle?

And if you kiss and kick ass long enough you win the grand prize.

A pyric victory and office with a view.

2.2 kids. Both in select sports and the country club is impressed.

F*** that.

Those are the thoughts that push me.

Fast, furious, and down.

Into the pit.

Again.

I'm contentedly walking along, enjoying a beautiful day.

I plummet into a crevasse.

Then the fun starts.

It's like tumbling into a dark hole.

When you hit the bottom, it's vicious, viscous concrete.

As dense as a sidewalk, but wet.

I start to sink.

Emotional quicksand.

I look up, but all I see are muddy walls and a tiny light.

100's of feet above me.


I know the job.

I must crawl the hell out of here.

Or die.

Sink and drown in gritty Jell-o.

Or move.


I hear a distant memory from long ago.

"Get up, ruck up and move the f*** out!"


As I gaze upward, I see nothing above me but dirty, slippery walls.

Nothing to grab.

No roots underground.

I climb, I slip, I fall.


Keep going.

I kick into the sides of the muddy pit.

Step by step.

Inch by inch.

I see the light, the rope, my family, and friends.

They are still out of grasp.


Frozen.

Stuck.

Panting.


It's everything Poe described minus the pendulum.

I correct myself, there is a pendulum.

It just doesn't live in the pit.

It's out there and in my head.


I finally grab the frayed and well-worn rope.

Friends, family, and army brothers gaze down into the pit.

They implore "Hold onto the damn rope".

It takes everything I am and can muster to not let go…


Much less climb.

I finally make the last few feet and salvation hits me on the shoulders.

Hands of friends grab me by the collar.

I ascend.

But only never to know when it will happen again.

To my chagrin. It will happen again.


And now I'll wash the dishes.

# Twenty-Two Per Day

Needed a new phone.

Spent all day at AT&T 'uploading' data into the 'cloud'.

It's magic to me.

I wrap it up and get home as the sun is setting.

Today the sun has already set.

Going to be a dark night.

Nadir.


Saw her name on my caller I.D.

Nacho's wife—this is not good.

It's Stormy calling and crying as I watch the alpenglow.

My Id* goes into overdrive.

Phone down all day—no service—then the news.


In many ways Colorado died for me at 7:08am February 21st, 2022.

President's Day.

Nothing up here will ever seem the same.

Purgatory.


We owned the mountain.

Stormy ran the food and fun on the hill.

Over 100 employees. Kindergarteners.

She was a great preschool teacher.

Nacho and I roamed with impunity.

Bear Bar, School House and everything High Country were our domain.

No more.

Thought he was denied his bloody death in the sand.

He was wrong.

He got hit.

It just took him seven years to bleed out.

Early Monday morning, he shot himself in the chest.

Not his head.

In 1999, he promised his mother no hand tattoos and an open casket service.

He died up to his word.

Morphine in his 'gig bag'.

For negating the pain of war.

Stormy left for work.

He crushed the ampuls into a glass of Bourbon.

She forgot something at the house.

Details aren't important, but he ended up doing it the hard way.

Intentionally and accidentally in front of his wife and 14- year- old son.

I'll never forget September 11, 2021.

We stood in my father's living room.

Solemn remembrances on television.


He spoke.

"F*** Dick Cheney and f*** George Bush."

"I killed the wrong brown people."

"They told me it was the right thing to do."


Twenty-two veterans die by their own hand per day.

No idea who the other twenty-one were on February 21st, 2022.

I damn sure knew one.


There are infinite words I could pour out onto these leaves of paper.

But like weeds, words die.

He lost. We lost.

* *The id is driven by the pleasure principle, which strives for immediate gratification of all desires, wants, and needs. If these needs are not satisfied immediately, the result is a state of anxiety or tension.*

# Photos

We thought it might be enjoyable to provide a few photos of people and places John mentioned in the book. These are some of his favorites.

## Childhood photos

*First birthday in bunny ears & Pierce in blue onesie upper left*

*Peewee football age 10*

*Middle school dance with the "Miami Vice" look*

*Neighborhood wars with Bryan, Pierce, and Marc*

*Father and stepmom Joyce*

*Steamboat, CO 1980 with Pierce*

*My French "sister" Carrine*

*Our French family visiting us in Texas and Colorado*

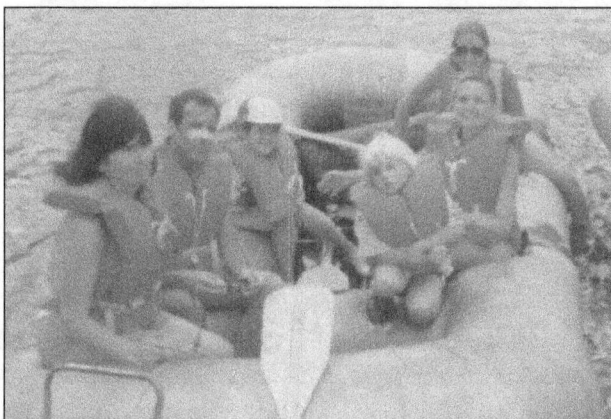

*Our French family visiting us in Texas and Colorado*

# Travel photos

*Mexico*

*Bahamas*

*Venice, Italy*

*Piazza San Marco, Florence, Italy*

*8th Birthday, Eiffel Tower, Paris*

*Natural History Museum London*

# Army

*In the field with friends Nick  (arms crossed) and Capeci (kneeling)*

*Nick to my left and Dan to my right, Kahuku, Hawaii*

*Having a smoke after a long road march*

*My dear friend Nacho. He took his life after suffering from PTSD*

*Nacho and me in better times. May your soul rest in peace!*

# My Wife Ashley

*Our wedding day in Australia*

*Listing our company on the Australian Stock Exchange*

*Enjoying dinner on the Cayman Islands*

## Special People

*Enjoying brunch with mom, stepdad, and Ashley*

*My son Nash*

*My Mamaw and brother Bryan*

*Marc, Pierce, and Bryan, Galveston TX, 2020*

*Army buddies Rosy, Lobo, and Mhoon supporting me
at Galveston Art Walk*

*Fraternity brother Brian and Ashley*

*Gus, his family, Ashley and I vacation in the Cayman Islands*

# My Very Special Companion

*Cassidy hangs out with me
while I paint.*

*Everyone should have a
"Cassidy"*

*Cassidy travels with me everywhere*

# PART III:
# What We Know for Sure

*"All of a sudden, I need to know, I need to know"*
~Tom Petty

# What We Know for Sure

People around the world have often quoted Oprah Winfrey's famous phrase, "*What I know for sure.*"[302] The overarching message of these five words is that no matter how badly one feels in their life, they can turn it around. It is each person's responsibility to do it though, nobody else's. Complaining will not help. It is important to consider our experiences, pleasant and painful, and use them to express our own unique voice.

Chapter 7 emphasizes how John's ability to keep moving forward, regardless of diagnoses of autism and other learning differences, has made a huge improvement in his life. As a matter of fact, his diagnosis as a twice-exceptional adult propelled him on a path to help others like himself. The creation of the *On the Spectrum Foundation* has provided opportunities for him and others to help adults and children who think they might be, or have recently been diagnosed as, twice-exceptional. Regardless of where one might be in their journey, there can always be unanswered questions that may cause a feeling of being unsettled. This chapter shares many helpful tips and strategies that 2e individuals can use to move from surviving to thriving!

Chapter 8 details the bumpy and often unhappy journeys that 2e students and their families experience in schools. It is a myth that all schools (public or private) can adequately support gifted and 2e students. Whether it is lack of funding, lack of teacher training, or simply reliance on harmful myths, 2e students struggle in traditional school settings because of their unique gifts and neurodiversity. This chapter will guide parents on how to become the best advocate for their child and talk about some excellent schools designed specifically for twice exceptional students and why they work.

# Chapter 7:
# Moving from Surviving to Thriving

*"Instead of continuing to try to make life work,*
*I finally let life happen."*
John Truitt

Twice-exceptional adults often carry *baggage-like* messages about their quirkiness, weird habits, and annoying behaviors from childhood. They tend to relive these messages at work and at home with family.[303]. Many of them have learned to cope in a variety of ways. Fortunately, some have learned positive strategies like deep breathing, meditation, exercise, journaling, and talking to a friend. But some strategies are not always healthy, including excessive drinking, using drugs, anger outbursts, ignoring the problem, and even harming oneself.

When 2e adults get stuck or overwhelmed during difficult times, they can shut down very easily. This 'emotional flooding' occurs when working memory impairments allow a momentary emotion to become too strong, flooding the brain with this one intense emotion.[304] When an individual is at this point, and copes in a negative manner, it will take time to unlearn these negative coping mechanisms. They will need to be intentional about incorporating positive strategies into their daily life,[305] but day by day these responses will become more automatic. A fundamental coping strategy for 2e individuals is to recognize and celebrate their own unique strengths, and then formulate additional strategies to manage their challenges.[306]

Today, there is a much greater appreciation for what society gains from including individuals with differently wired brains, and for how these people contribute to our world. There is also a greater awareness of the harmful effects of trying to change neurodiverse individuals and make them behave in ways that are unnatural for them.[307] According to Geraldine Dawson, Director of the Duke Center for Autism and Brain Development in Durham, North Carolina, "We moved away from thinking of autism as a condition that needs to be eliminated or fixed to thinking about autism as a part of the neurodiversity that exists across humankind."[308] Neurodiverse people do not want to be fixed. Rather, they seek ideas, insights, and practical advice that will make their path easier.

## Tips for 2e Individuals

### *Proper identification and labels*

If a person feels it is important to be identified as twice-exceptional or neurodiverse, it should be done by specialists who have experience in this field. The experience of getting 'the label' is not always easy because some feel it can be a detriment to one's progress. A label can be limiting, adversely affect self-image, or help negative stereotypes persist for those who are already marginalized. However, Karen Simmons, Founder and CEO of *Autism Today*, says that being called 2e or neurodiverse can offer a way for people to understand themselves better, and ultimately get support for their differences, instead of being discriminated against because of them.[309]

When an individual knows exactly who they are, they become empowered to stand tall and never hide. Treating learning differences like ADD (attention deficit disorder), dyslexia, giftedness, or autism as unhealthy causes people to suppress their authentic selves,[310] which is wrong and dehumanizing. Whether a child is identified as 2e in school, or an adult decides to seek a diagnosis later in life, acknowledgement of 2e differences can help individuals find support and services to make their lives better.[311]

Even after an individual is diagnosed as neurodiverse, it is important to remember that every person is different: what works for one person may not work for another. Take time to adjust to and integrate new information. Thoroughly educate yourself and others about your condition, which includes learning about your symptoms and how they affect your life. A therapist or counselor can be a great asset in helping you manage symptoms, in addition to providing much needed support and guidance.[312]

### Giftedness is not necessarily a gift

Twice-exceptional adults should realize that their giftedness is not necessarily a 'gift'. This sounds a bit strange, but it is true. People with high intelligence think automatically that everything should come easily for them, which is a hidden burden of expecting too much from themselves; or they feel they should be able to succeed at anything just because they are smart or unusually talented.[313] But when one has learning differences (challenges amongst others) in addition to being smart, the stumbling blocks in daily living can be taxing. Individuals with ADD may not be able to complete tasks in a timely manner. Or individuals with dyslexia can be challenged when trying to read documents necessary for their jobs. Those who are autistic often toil to communicate so others understand them. The good news is that 2e adults can use their strengths and talents to accommodate their learning differences. There are many such adults who think and process information differently yet still succeed in a variety of ways. They nurture what they are good at and refuse to focus on what they do not do well.

### Practice self-compassion

Once 2e adults recognize they can succeed despite learning differences, they must practice self-compassion. Constantly asking "Why can't I do this?" or "Why did I screw this up again?" will not accomplish anything except adding more disappointment to one's life. Self-criticism can cause adverse effects on physical and mental health. When a person does not meet their own high standards and constantly condemns themself, it can lead to anxiety, depression, eating disorders, substance abuse disorders, and even suicide. Eric Tivers, a licensed clinical social worker, asks his 2e clients to practice self-compassion by using the same words but changing the emphasis and tone from negative judgment to curiosity and self-knowledge.[314] Emphasize the excitement of intellectual challenge and the play of curiosity against the unknown, rather than the brief failure at first try. For example, say, "WHY can't I do this?" "WHY did I screw this up again?" "WHY is this hard?" "WHY do I keep making THAT same mistake?" Twice exceptional adults can take a problem-solving approach by challenging themselves to identify what is not working and find solutions.[315] Just as children in school gain more confidence when they experience success with a difficult skill, so do 2e adults.

### Find a community of peers

It is important for neurodivergent individuals to learn more about themselves through a community of peers.[316] Most twice-exceptional adults today probably never heard or understood the term 2e when they were in school. But just as parents of 2e children benefit from sharing stories with other parents like themselves, the same is true for gifted adults. It is always good to read about giftedness and twice-exceptionality or listen to a podcast on the subject. But going beyond that and finding a community to share stories and hear other people share issues they thought were unique to themselves can be truly eye-opening. When we find a group with whom we can share common experiences—whether it is about parenting, medical issues, or a particular job—we discover in ourselves more resilience, self-determination, and self-awareness than we ever thought we had.

One organization that has helped gifted and 2e individuals since 1981 is SENG (Supporting Emotional Needs of the Gifted). Following the suicide of a gifted student in Michigan, the late Dr. James T. Webb founded SENG to offer the gifted community support and guidance through education, research, and connection. With the right intellectual and emotional support, gifted, talented, and twice-exceptional people can accept themselves and fulfill the potential of their incredible capabilities. Perhaps more importantly, they can learn to work with their high sensitivities to feel balanced, happy and at peace.[317] SENG offers a variety of programs, all aimed to be inclusive and accessible. There are online support groups, online SENGinars with leading experts, in person mini-conferences, and their annual conference. There are also occasional events and programs in Canada and an affiliate organization in Europe.

### Take care of physical and mental health

Heathier lifestyles positively affect physical and mental health. People are living longer due to better public health and medical advances. It is imperative to take care of our health, and this begins with making sure you and a trusted individual have a comprehensive copy of your medical records, tests, or at least an overall summary of your health.[318] These are very helpful when visiting a new specialist or hospital. Things like insomnia, anxiety, exercise, and diet should all be managed daily. I have found that hiking with my dog Cassidy, mountain climbing, and scuba diving have helped me stay more centered in my everyday living. I also enjoy socializing with friends, and finding a special interest that I can sink my teeth into. When I started painting, I felt less anxious, more relaxed, and thought more clearly as I worked on and finished a piece of art.

When a person is anxious or feeling on edge, he will blurt out, "That person gets on my nerves," or "That thing really bothers me". Whether a person is frustrating you at work, or something like a neighbor dog's constant barking is bothersome, it is quite normal to become edgy, high strung, or impatient. But neurodivergent individuals are wired differently, and anxiety can more quickly become a serious problem. A health practice called *mindfulness*, a type of meditation that reshapes one's thinking, is a way to prevent anxiety from getting out of control.

Mindfulness helps us become intensely aware of what we are sensing and feeling in the moment *without interpretation or judgement*, and stress is reduced. Spending too much time planning, problem solving, being unfocussed in thought, or thinking negative thoughts can be draining, and lead to stress, anxiety, and symptoms of depression.[319] Breathing practices and guided imagery meditations relax the body and mind.[320] Mindfulness meditation has been studied in many medical trials, and is effective in managing conditions like stress, anxiety, pain, depression, and insomnia. Practicing mindfulness on a regular basis brings greater balance to thoughts and emotions, yielding improved attention, improved sleep, and decreased job burnout.[321]

### Learn more about nonverbal communication

We can all work to become better communicators in today's culture. With technology driving how we share information, including social media, texting, and emails, we miss many important aspects of 'live' communication with other people. Most importantly we lose the *completeness* of the message others are trying to express. A significant portion of face-to-face communication is nonverbal—some researchers suggest up to 80%—so understanding body language is crucial. Because exchanges between neurodiverse individuals, and their experience communicating in the world, can be quite different than 'the norm', missed nonverbal communication can result in feeling misunderstood, unsafe, or not valued as a person.[322]

Body language can communicate interest, lack of interest, acceptance, rejection, tension, and hostility. Nonverbal cues come through facial expressions, hand gestures, posture, eye contact, and micro-expressions (extremely brief facial expressions that happen in less than a second; they occur when one is holding back emotions.[323]) People express interest, engagement, openness, and calmness with relaxed body posture and eye contact. Alternatively, they might express judgement and discomfort, appearing closed off with crossed arms and legs, or by looking away. Practice pausing and being mindful of what the other person is expressing through body language. Body language can be unintentional and not carry 'normal' meaning, especially for people on the spectrum, so don't draw conclusions from body language alone, especially if you are not familiar with an individual.[324] Body language is very different for everyone, especially if you live in another country. It is important to understand the complex dynamics of body language when communicating with others.[325]

## Eyes

○ *Eye gaze*: When one looks directly into another's eyes while having a conversation, it indicates they are paying attention. Breaking eye contact and frequently looking away might indicate that one is distracted, uncomfortable, or trying to conceal real feelings.

○ *Blinking:* When one blinks too much, in distress, or discomfort. If one blinks too little, it may indicate they are intentionally trying to control eye movements or stare at another person.

○ *Pupil size:* Sometimes emotions can cause small changes in pupil size. If one's pupils are highly dilated, it can indicate they are interested or aroused.

## Mouth

○ *Pursed lips*: Tightening the lips might be an indicator of distaste, disapproval, or distrust.

○ *Lip biting:* This can suggest the individual is worried, anxious, or stressed.

○ *Covering the mouth:* This is a sign of hiding an emotional reaction, or a way to avoid displaying unusual smiles or smirks.

○ *Turned up or down mouth*: Slight changes in the mouth can be subtle indicators of feelings. A slightly turned up mouth might mean the person is feeling happy or optimistic, whereas a slightly turned down mouth can suggest sadness or disapproval.

## Arms and Legs

○ *Crossed arms*: This is a sign of a person feeling defensive, self-protective, or closed off.

○ *Hands on hips:* This suggests the individual feels in control, or perhaps aggressive.

○ *Hands clasped behind the back:* This might indicate boredom, anxiety, or anger.

○ *Rapidly tapping fingers or fidgeting*: This indicates one is bored, impatient, or frustrated.

○ *Crossed legs:* This suggests a feeling of being closed off, or in need of privacy.

### Posture

○ *Sitting up straight:* This indicates a person is focused and paying attention.

○ *Body hunched forward:* This can imply the person is bored or indifferent.

○ *Open posture* (the trunk of the body is open and exposed): This indicates a person is friendly, open, and willing.

○ *Closed posture* (hiding the trunk of the body by hunching forward and keeping arms and legs crossed): This can suggest one is hostile, unfriendly, or anxious.

### Personal Space

The term "proxemics" coined by anthropologist Edward T. Hall refers to the distance between people as they interact.

○ *Intimate distance*: Considered to be 6 to 18 inches apart, and usually occurs during intimate contact such as hugging, whispering, and touching.

○ *Personal distance*: Considered to be 1.5 feet to 4 feet apart. It occurs between people who are family members or close friends. The closer people can comfortably stand while interacting can be an indicator of the level of intimacy in their relationship.

○ *Social distance:* Considered to be from 4 feet to 12 feet apart and is normal with individuals who are acquaintances.

○ *Public distance*: Considered to be 12 feet to 25 feet. It is often used in public speaking situations. Different cultures can dictate personal distance. In Latin countries, people tend to feel more comfortable standing closer to one another, whereas people in North America prefer more distance, more personal separation.

Overall, the complex functions of nonverbal communication allow people to earn trust, emphasize a point when speaking with someone, and develop honesty.[326] Engaging in eye contact, nodding your head while listening, and even mirroring another person can show you trust communicating with that person. Then, when *emphasizing a point,* emphasis in conversation includes tone of voice, the way we engage listeners, the way we use hand and arm gestures, and how we take up space, and all have an effect on how message comes across to others. It is important to note when someone's body language does *not* match what they are saying: it might indicate that they are withholding information or perhaps not being honest about how they feel. Body language should never be underestimated in trying to understand interpersonal communications, and it is important to remember how it can be unusual and unexpected in people on the spectrum.

## Strategies To Support Neurodiverse People

### Acceptance

Relationships, institutions, and cultural norms have changed in response to social movements that have focused on human rights, including civil rights, women's rights, and LGBTQIA2S+ rights. The neurodiversity movement is equally focused on increasing acceptance of differences, and recognition that differences *do not* need to be changed or 'corrected'. Accepting neurodiversity means validating the experiences of the neurodiverse, and not dismissing their experiences as deficits.[327]

One important way to show acceptance for those who are different is to learn about them. If you go to school or work with a twice-exceptional individual, politely ask them to share how their differences affect them. They may reveal they are often stressed and anxious throughout their day, which gives them the opportunity to discuss what causes that, and how others can help diffuse it. Not only does this show interest, but it allows the neurodiverse individual to educate others about providing support in everyday settings. Spending time with people who are different promotes personal growth and teaches about what it means to live with those differences. Positively engaging people who are different will make an impact on their life, and lead to new insights and friendships.

By getting to know someone who is different, you learn about their unusual strengths, but also about how they work their challenges to their advantage. An individual with dyslexia can have the ability to flip and rotate shapes in their mind. This skill is necessary in architecture, engineering, design, art, photography, and music. In her book *Differently Wired*, Deborah Reber uses the term 'differently wired' to define neurodivergent people more accurately. She says it frees individuals of the harmful stigmas of words like 'disorder' or 'problem'.[328]

The benefits of getting to know the neurodiverse and their unique abilities should give neurotypical people the goal of *enabling* neurodivergent people, not disabling them. Forcing those who think and work differently to be like neurotypicals is disabling. Years ago left-handed students were forced to write with their right hands, which had negative long-term impacts. Now left-handedness is known to be a difference, not a disorder;[329] children are allowed to write with whichever hand comes naturally to them. When neurodiverse individuals are allowed to be themselves and focus on their gifts, they achieve to their full potential, and their self-esteem is reinforced.[330] By normalizing different ways of learning and working we can create environments that are universally beneficial for all.[331]

## Growth Mindset

As we accept everyone's specific needs, we do away with the negative 'one size fits all' narrative. We remove the neurotypical expectation that everyone—from children at school to adults in the workplace—should adhere to a strict timeline and specific way of doing things. We develop a 'growth mindset'. Stanford University psychologist Dr. Carol Dweck was the first person to describe the growth mindset in her insightful book, *Mindset: The New Psychology of Success*.[332] The growth mindset postulates that a person's capacities and talents can be improved over time,[333] which contrasts with the standard neurotypical fixed mindset, which believes that the capacity to learn and improve cannot be meaningfully developed. People with a fixed mindset are usually averse to change, sensitive to constructive criticism, and fear failure.[334] In contrast, the growth mindset encourages change and growth, even if it takes time. When neurotypical *and* neurodiverse people both adopt a growth mindset, it opens the door for everyone to be more successful.

Following are eleven benefits of growth mindset.[335]

1. *Treat challenges as opportunities for growth.* Avoiding challenges and fearing failure will merely keep one in their comfort zone.

2. *No longer limit your talents and abilities.* You are now willing to *give it a try.* Failure is no longer seen as the limit of your abilities but as an opportunity to grow.

3. *Experience greater career success.* Be adaptable, willing to learn new skills, ready to tackle challenges for career growth. Employers tend to promote prospective employees who have eagerness to learn and be trained in new roles.

4. *Be receptive to feedback.* Almost all facets of life require us to be open to self-improvement. Receiving feedback, fresh perspectives, and new ideas helps us grow personally and professionally.

5. *No longer be threatened by change.* The idea of something new or different is not frightening anymore. Positive change is a part of development.

6. *Be inspired by the success of others.* Learning to draw inspiration from other's success is results from the growth mindset. You should no longer see other people's accomplishments as a threat to your personal or professional life.

7. *Experience less stress.* With a growth mind frame, you are more likely to remain calm, and focus on the *process* rather than performance and outcomes. This prevents obsessive scrutinizing, harsh self-criticism, and rumination over what could have been done better.

8. *Improve romantic relationships.* Relationships evolve and change just as people do. Some behaviors and habits that were once admired or accepted may start becoming a source of conflict. Wanting to do better for the sake of your relationship is important.

9. *Achieve better health.* Continued stress of any kind activates the stress hormone cortisol, which is linked to cardiovascular disease, anxiety, and depression. Seeing the world through the lens of growth tends to put your mind at ease. Instead of stressing over problems, look for solutions.

10. *Greater desire to set "SMART" goals.* S=Specific. M=Measurable. A=Attainable. R=Relevant. T=Time bound. These are designed to be realistic and easier to follow through on.

11. *Change to live the life you dreamed of.* The true definition of success is personal.

As neurotypical individuals consider acceptance of all types of people in our society, we should turn to *The Autism Society of America* for guidance. They have provided support for neurodiverse individuals for over fifty years. One of their core values is: 'Everyone is integrated into society without barriers or exceptions in a collaborative environment.'[336] They shifted terminology from *awareness* to *acceptance* in 2021 because resources and advocacy are needed to support those who are neurodiverse. April is now 'Autism *Acceptance* Month' which aims to not just label people with autism, but to truly understand and appreciate neurodiversity, and positively engage neurodiverse people in daily life.

### Reasonable Accommodations

Twice-exceptional children and adults are finally beginning to see their experiences revealed in a variety of pathways. There are books and podcasts authored by the neurodiverse as well as by people who have immeasurable experience living and working with 2e people. We also see more neurodiverse characters in significant television and movie roles (although most autistic characters in media are portrayed in extreme stereotypical fashion;[337] for example, the character Shaun

Murphy on *The Good Doctor* has stiff body movements and vocal tics that greatly exaggerate the way some people on the spectrum present themselves). Regardless of the extent to which books, podcasts, and other media include 2e people, we must do a better job providing actual and effective accommodations in schools and workplaces so everyone can find success[338]. Only when this happens *effortlessly* will we feel that the steps taken to educate society about 2e people have finally paid off.

It is not easy to change the way we have done things for decades. But when human lives are not in balance, we cannot afford any more waiting for positive transformations to occur. Although the following political efforts *began* a shift in societal thinking regarding people with differences, they were over twenty years apart in their implementation. In 1968, the *Architectural Barriers Act* gained legal backing for curb cuts and ramps. But it wasn't until 1990 when more tangible and effective changes happened, like lifts on busses and the removal of all architectural barriers to access public buildings, which became a reality with the passage of the *Americans with Disabilities Act (ADA)*. The time has come to understand *all* the issues surrounding neurodiversity and promote its full acceptance by providing all the necessary accommodations so everyone is included in our society.

Many accommodations do not have to be difficult or expensive to implement. In May of 2023, the Department of Labor published a favorable report that found nearly half of workplace accommodations that could be made for people with differences could be implemented at no cost to employers.[339] It also stated that of those companies that do incur a cost, the median expenditure has decreased to only $300.00. [340] This is especially noteworthy when we know that neurodiverse people work hard to mask their differences and appear neurotypical, which is contrary to their fundamental character and well-being. It becomes exhausting for them to just get through a day. That fact masking is so detrimental to the health of the neurodiverse is exacerbated by the fact that their gifts and special talents are thereby quashed further isolating them. The small expense of providing easy and inexpensive accommodations is one of the most effective ways to create a truly *inclusive* workplace.[341]

An *inclusive environment* is one where people from different backgrounds, abilities, and beliefs all feel welcomed, respected, supported, and valued. An inclusive environment invites and enables full and meaningful participation for everyone and removes any barriers that prevent some from engaging fully. An inclusive environment fosters open, honest discussion and appreciation of differences.[342]

Dr. Melanie Hayes, author of *Being Twice- Exceptional* and founder of the California-based 2e school Big Minds teaches the idea that we should *provide a longer runway to launch,* i.e., more time and space for 2e students to achieve success in schools.[343] This concept could be applied to adults in the workplace as well. When we force neurodiverse children and adults to work just like their neurotypical classmates and colleagues, we are forcing them to endure unfair challenges with sensory stimulation, language and social communications, and even physical problems that keep the nervous system in a heightened state.[344]

The prospect of providing more time and space for neurodiverse people to be successful seems simple. But invisible differences can be perplexing to others, resulting in unconscious bias or conscious bullying.[345] Workplace and school accommodations are erroneously seen as favoritism and create jealousy amongst colleagues or peers. When employer and employee (or school staff and parents) work together, these behaviors can be eliminated. There are four steps the ADA recommends to successfully accommodate the needs of neurodiverse students and employees:[346]

○ *Establish specific policies and procedures.* With large companies, individuals may make requests through human resources. With smaller companies, individuals may need to work with a staff executive as their 'point person'.

○ *Train managers to be able to identify requests.* Managers, supervisors, and team leaders need to be able to identify when an employee is asking for accommodations, or when an accommodation might be needed. Necessary changes are more straightforward for someone in a wheelchair, but 'invisible disabilities' make them more difficult to identify and be accommodated. An employee with depression might be late to work several times because of their medication, but the untrained manager disciplines them for repeated tardiness: the employee is too embarrassed to disclose their disability. A trained manager would know how to ask the right questions to avoid this unfairness.

○ *Make ADA accommodation requests an interactive process.* Approach requests from a place of positivity by saying, "Let's figure out a way to make this work". An interactive process is one in which employers and employees with differences work together to determine accommodations.

○ *Build ADA accommodations at work that work for everyone.* Look at the essential functions of the job, considering these *with* the employee. What are the options? Some accommodations can be put in place quickly, like a parking space closer to the building. Others take more time. For example, it takes more time to develop a visual checklist of duties for employees with executive function challenges. These could become 'best practices' throughout the organization. Sometimes employer and employee must compromise. For example, an employee may not be allowed to work from home, but they can be accommodated by a private room with noise-canceling headphones.

The following accommodations, in addition to ones mentioned earlier, are becoming increasingly more common for all types of people:[347]

○ *Headphones*: Individuals can wear noise-canceling headphones. These help in open classrooms and office spaces.

○ *Desk placement*: Move those who are challenged by crowds of people away from high traffic areas.

○ *Lighting*: Many schools and businesses still have fluorescent lighting, which can be overstimulating to many people. LED lighting is less expensive than fluorescent lighting, and can improve the aesthetic appearance of a room, our moods, and even our overall health.[348]. Studies have shown that for those on the spectrum, poor lighting causes anxiety, fear, restlessness, loss of focus, and feeling overwhelmed; student behavior and performance improved greatly with a switch to LED (non-fluorescent) lighting.

○ *Mood indicators*: Children and adults can use color indicators (cards, paper, lights) to let people know how they are feeling. Using the colors green, yellow, and red, much like traffic signals, helps those working with neurodiverse individuals to understand their moods. Green indicates approachability, yellow indicates 'stay away', and red indicates the need to step away from one's desk to control anxiety. Unless it is a young child, there is no need for a manager or teacher to question what is going on.

○ *Talk and Listen*: Company managers and teachers should ask 2e individuals how they like to communicate. For adults in an office setting, send complex information in the form of an email or text, so they can prepare for a subsequent face-to-face conversation. For students, provide questions ahead that could be asked in class. If a student is called upon to share, provide enough time for them to process their thoughts before they have to answer or speak. Explore all communication options for everyone's best advantage.

○ *Use Closed Captioning*: Video conferencing software provides an option for closed captioning. Printed text as a guide to or substitute for audio can be a great help to those who need it. It is no longer used for just hearing-impaired individuals.

○ *Record Meetings and Lessons:* Not everyone gets the information they need the first time around. Zoom or Google Meet calls can be recorded and posted for people to review and take notes. In addition, teachers can video record their lessons and upload them to available platforms for students to study.

○ *Intranet Portals:* These are great places to store documents frequently required by employees, such as the paid holiday calendar, time off request forms, and schedules of events. Intranet portals deliver relevant, timely, and consistent information to all audiences.[349] Archived information can be easily accessed when needed.

## Keep Moving Forward

The phrase 'a work in progress' can mean many things. If we are speaking about a human, we are describing someone who is still learning, growing, and improving themselves. There will always be things that we can get better at; there will always be things that challenge us; there will always be mistakes we want to correct.[350] For twice exceptional individuals, every day seems like a work in progress because the struggles are constant and sometimes dramatic. On the best of days, it seems that progress is defined as 'two steps forward and three steps back'. But we learn that our reactions to challenges can determine whether we move forward by learning and adapting, or whether stay still, stagnating and failing to grow.[351] We advocate for always choosing to move forward and grow, thereby building resilience.

## Resilience

Resilience is the ability to adapt to difficult situations. When stress, adversity or trauma strikes, you experience anger, grief, and pain, but are still able to keep functioning, both physically and psychologically.[352] Resilience is an ongoing process that requires effort to build and maintain. Building resilience can help avoid old ways of coping with adversity like numbing our feelings with drugs or alcohol. The more resilient one becomes, the better able they are to tolerate the stress, anxiety, and sadness which result from trauma and adversity and find ways to rebound from setbacks.[353]

While there is no way to avoid things like sorrow, adversity, or distress in life, there are ways to help smooth the rough waters and regain a sense of control.[354] There have been many times in my life when I felt totally out of control and powerless. But I have learned to stay focused, flexible, and productive in good and bad times. If I experience a down time, I work on projects like my art, or go exercise, or talk with friends. I said earlier of myself, "Instead of continuing to try to make life work, I finally let life happen." This has made me fear less about an uncertain future. If I have a problem, I am confident I will eventually find a solution, even when one isn't immediately apparent.

The following tips can help one face hardships with more confidence, cope better with the tumultuous times, and make it through to brighter, more hopeful days ahead:[355]

- ○ *Practice Acceptance:* Many of us try to protect ourselves by refusing to accept the truth of what is happening. But remember, change is an inevitable part of life, and many aspects of the changing world are out of our control. Trying to control this will only drain our energy and leave us feeling anxious and hopeless. Focus on things within one's control. If you are looking for a job, you can control how much time and effort you put into searching for work and how much time you spend brushing up on skills necessary to get the job you seek.

- ○ *Accept Your Feelings:* Trying to prevent our emotions from surfacing will only fuel our stress, delay acceptance of a new situation, and prevent us from moving forward. By allowing ourselves to feel our emotions, we will find a path forward.

- ○ *Grieve Your Loses:* Tough times usually involve some kind of loss. Whether it's the loss of a loved one, a job, or loss of your old life, it's important to take the opportunity to grieve. Only by facing your grief will you heal and move on with your life. I did this when I went from working in the corporate world to teaching at a twice-exceptional high school. Consciously leaving my corporate life behind allowed me to discover that teaching is my 'happy place'.

○ *Reach Out to Others:* Connecting with friends and family when going through tough times can help ease stress, boost your mood, and make sense of all the change and disruption. You can draw strength and build resilience from having others to lean on. The people you reach out to don't need to have answers, they just need to be willing to listen without judging. What you talk about is not the most important thing, it's the human connection that invokes healing. My friends have been invaluable to me in this regard.

○ *Look for Meaning and Purpose:* By pursuing activities that bring purpose and meaning, problems can be kept in perspective, and kept from becoming overwhelming, and you maintain your unique identity. We all have different ways of experiencing purpose and meaning. When I left my previous jobs, I started a foundation to support autistic people, and pursued activities like speaking to groups that help other 2e individuals, it helped me develop and maintain my sense of purpose and has added great satisfaction to my life.

○ *Stay Motivated:* Though tough times are rarely over quickly, they don't last forever. Fostering qualities of persistence and endurance is helpful. Deal with problems one step at a time. Celebrate small wins. Maintain a hopeful outlook. Express gratitude. Being kind to yourself and practicing self-compassion are very important parts of building resilience.

# CHAPTER 8:
# Educating the
# Twice Exceptional Student

*"There needs to be a lot more emphasis on
what a child can do instead of what they cannot do."*
~Temple Grandin

I am not sure how many twice-exceptional students today can say they enjoy school. I guess it is not very many. It is ironic that I liked traditional school because I have many learning differences that should have set me on a path to hate it. I liked elementary and middle school because I have always enjoyed learning anything that is new. Also, I was able to be social at a young age. I never paid attention to the learning differences I had until I was in high school and college. Even then, I wasn't sure why I struggled with some class assignments. It wasn't until I was diagnosed as 2e that I understood if I had been appropriately supported in my early schooling that my later academic years would have been much more successful. We cannot afford to let one twice-exceptional child, or any child for that matter, be so misunderstood, and slip through the cracks of the education system. Everyone deserves an education that fits.[356]

Educating children in America has taken many turns since the earliest schools taught only the virtues of family, religion, and community.

We can read about the one-room multi-age schoolhouses in the 19th century, the Supreme Court overturning school segregation and discrimination in the 20th century, and the United States entering an era of education accountability and reform in the 21st century (*Every Student Succeeds Act*[357]). But regardless of the many positive changes that have taken place in schools in America and around the world, the dichotomy between the 'norm' and twice-exceptional students makes it challenging for most schools to provide effective and appropriate education for this group.

As we have said, 2e students are difficult to identify, which is why we don't have an accurate count of how many 2e children are in schools today. Their characteristics are not readily apparent to educators without looking beyond traditional assessment techniques.[358] Twice-exceptional learners generally have outstanding critical thinking and problem-solving skills, but if they are limited to standard curricula, just a pencil and paper, they will never get a chance to display their skills, the teacher will never see their potential. Twice-exceptional learners have a strong ability to concentrate deeply, especially in areas of interest or curiosity, but this will be missed if they are not allowed to work on project-based assignments of their own choosing. Educating 2e students correctly requires teachers and parents to identify above-average sensitivity to sound, taste, and smell, or poor social skills and low self-esteem due to perfectionism. Debbie Carroll, co-chair of the subcommittee on *Twice Exceptional Advocacy of the Council of Parent Attorneys and Advocates*, says, "Teachers need to be able to recognize when students aren't reaching their potential even though they may be passing their classes. They need to understand that smart kids with behavioral problems may not just be willful or lazy but may in fact need support." [359]

## Barriers for 2e students

One of the biggest barriers to educating 2e students is simply showing that they exist.[360] Under IDEA, all students are entitled to the special services and accommodations necessary to enable them to learn. But to qualify for these services under the law, a student's disability must *adversely* affect academic performance. Many 2e students' challenges don't often show up on their report cards. A gifted student with dyslexia may be able to complete enough work in their language arts class to earn a 'C'. But their learning difference means that this is not a true reflection of their ability. Similarly, a gifted math student with dyscalculia may struggle with algebra but excel at geometry, so their grade will incorrectly assess them as average. Such students are not likely to receive any special services for their learning differences or giftedness. School systems and teachers will merely think that the student is 'doing their best' and miss the hidden gold mine.

When a teacher and parent agree there are concerns about a student and they do not know which path to take to find answers, it is time to engage a team of specialists (i.e., counselor, psychologist, interventionist, administrators) to investigate. These professionals will identify possible ways to help the student achieve greater success. Unfortunately, it is common for such professionals to identify giftedness, or challenges like ASD, *but not both*. If only one area of exception is identified, misunderstandings about the true nature of the child's difficulties will arise, and an *inappropriate* education plan will result.[361] If a child is identified as autistic but not gifted, their giftedness is thus discounted, and their education is compromised.[362] Both kinds of exception must be identified, or the child's schooling will be misdirected by the very professionals who seek to support them.

Twice-exceptional students struggle to succeed due to the lack of effective educational programs; when they are accommodated, it is often in only one area. It is as if we are asking the student to choose: "Are you gifted?" or "Do you have a learning difference?" Uncertainty of how to provide for neurodiverse students is common in most traditional schools. A student's and their family's worst nightmare is the frustration, confusion, sadness, and pervasive sense of being overwhelmed by a system that doesn't know how to meet their unique needs.

Schools cannot just focus (or overfocus) on achievement and ignore all other aspects of a student's education.[363] They must place equal emphasis on the social and emotional aspects of a child's life. In her book *Differently Wired*, Deborah Reber states, "Giftedness isn't a subject thing, it's a true neurological difference that needs to be acknowledged and supported." [364] Because she is the parent of a 2e child, Reber emphasizes that the time has come to "…respect and support how these children move through the world. We must say "no" to frustration and isolation and say "yes" to the gifts of these unique children and everything that goes along with who they are." [365]

## Myths/Misconceptions

Every year educational decisions are made in schools that cause social and emotional harm to students. If educators followed the fundamental guiding principal physicians follow with their patients, i.e., *'first do no harm'*, fewer students would feel frustration and isolation in schools. Important decisions for 2e students, and all students, should depend on everyone who has a stake in them saying that the child's best interest was their primary concern, and that the child is likely to benefit without harm.[366] There are too many instances when myths surrounding the '2e kid' permeate adult decisions, and the child suffers as a result. We must eliminate the myths and clarify and expound the details of what twice-exceptional children need to reach their potential.[367]

Widespread lack of awareness and common misunderstandings have led to damaging myths, misconceptions, and stigmas about twice-exceptional individuals. Teachers and parents must learn the truths and become advocates of facts about what twice-exceptionality is and *is not*. Here are a few important myths, misconceptions, and truths about learning differences outlined by The Janus School in Mount Joy, Pennsylvania.[368]

[The Janus School is the only school dedicated to the education of students with learning differences in south central Pennsylvania. It serves students in grades K-12+ diagnosed with a language- or math-based learning disability, ADHD, autism spectrum disorder (ASD), executive function difficulties (EFD), nonverbal learning disorder, or auditory processing disorder. (https://thejanusschool.org/)]

**Myth/Misconception:** Learning differences are intellectual differences.

**Truth:** Learning differences are the result of the brain being 'wired' differently. Children and adults with learning and attention issues are at least as smart as their 'typical' peers. In the case of twice exceptionality, intelligence is in the gifted range. The symptoms of an undiagnosed learning difference can be complex and misunderstood. A misunderstood and unsupported primary issue can lead to secondary symptoms, such as anxiety and depression. Challenges are misidentified as a behavioral problem or lack of effort, when in fact an underlying learning difference is to blame, and the failed solution compounds the problem.

**Myth/Misconception:** All learning differences are the same.

**Truth:** Learning differences are different than physical, developmental, and intellectual disabilities. While the shared prefix "dys-" (meaning difficult) may link many of the terms we use to describe learning differences, how they impact an individual's ability to learn, and function is dramatically different. In addition, one difference, like autism, can vary significantly from person to person. This is why it's critical for children and adults struggling with learning differences to receive individualized support that helps address their specific learning challenges.

**Myth/Misconception:** A child can 'just work harder' to overcome a learning difference.

**Truth:** When it comes to learning and attention issues, 'trying harder' is a non-functional answer. People with these challenges have brains that process information differently. They need personalized support to be empowered with the tools and strategies they need to manage their learning and processing differences. The attitude, "…well, I made it through, so they will too" is a major barrier to a student s the seeking the help they need to thrive in life. Too many parents and teachers think that any child could do well I school if they 'tried hard enough'. And many impatient educators believe that what people call a learning or attention issue is just laziness. These misconceptions create significant barriers for those struggling with a learning difference.

**Myth/Misconception:** Learning differences fade with time and can be cured.

> **Truth:** The truth is that learning and attention challenges are the result of different brain structure and function, clearly not something you can 'get rid of'. Symptoms can change over time as people grow, and the right support can help people manage their challenges. But the challenges don't 'go away', they are *part* of the individual.

**Myth/Misconception:** A learning difference diagnosis will negatively impact a child's future.

> **Truth:** From the desire to avoid a label, to misconceptions that a diagnosis will negatively impact a child's future job or school opportunities, parents are besieged by misgivings and doubt when they learn their student may be struggling with a learning challenge. But when a child is empowered with tools and strategies to understand and manage their differences, their burden is lifted, and they benefit from the opportunity to excel and unlock their potential. (Review the list of celebrated neurodiverse people in Chapter 5.)

> Just as twice-exceptional students deal with myths and misconceptions about their learning differences (detractions), there are also harmful myths about being gifted. In Deborah Gennarelli's book *Twice Exceptional Boys: A Roadmap to Getting it Right*, she explains several important misconceptions to be aware of when working with this group of students.[369]

**Myth:** Gifted students are capable of teaching themselves and need little academic support.

> **Truth:** There is a kernel of truth in this myth. If a gifted child grabs on to an area of interest, they may become an expert very quickly, sometimes even outstripping the teacher's knowledge. Most gifted students are adept at figuring out many things on their own, but not always. And if they have a learning disability, they may have difficulty applying superior knowledge or conveying it to others, or they may miss some broader

foundational information, which will handicap them later. If they don't understand something, particularly a basic concept, they may be reluctant to tell the teacher or parent for fear of being criticized or 'blowing their cover' as a 'smart kid'. Being thus unsure of fundamentals can trip them up as they move through the curriculum, and it may lead them to doubt their own intelligence.

**Myth:** Gifted students are either happy, popular, well-adjusted, and always excel in school, or they're nerds who will never fit in anywhere.

**Truth:** Many gifted children are indeed friendly, mature, self-aware, and emotionally adjusted. They get their work done, they're happy in school. A good educational fit can make the lives of gifted students tolerable and positive. In her article, *The Impact of Giftedness on Psychological Well-Being,*[370] child psychologist Dr. Maureen Neihart postulates that if intellectually or academically gifted children participate in educational programs geared to their needs and receive support at home, they often will be well-adjusted and happy. But if a smart child feels isolated, helpless, and hopeless, it puts them at risk of developing more serious social and emotional issues.

Being gifted is no guarantee of success in school or life. While high intelligence can help make coursework from kindergarten to college easier to understand, it isn't the only determinant of how well a child will perform in school. One must acknowledge the influence of self-concept, stamina, mindset, organizational and study skills, a supportive family, the handling of stress and social relationships, and they are a big part of a student's overall success.

Unfortunately, these non-intellectual factors cause problems for gifted people. They may become overly anxious, and then stress levels impede their academic performance. For example, they may be a perfectionist: if they can't do it perfectly the first time, they may stop trying to master it altogether.

Though some gifted children struggle, particularly those who are 2e, most gifted students do not. They are often class leaders, athletes, active in music, drama, school clubs, and involved in their communities.

**Myth:** Gifted students are pretty much alike.

**Truth:** No two students are alike, and like other children, each gifted child is unique. In fact, experts have found that gifted children are more diverse than children of average ability.[371] Although there are some characteristics that most gifted children share, like rapid learning, asking probing questions, and mature thinking, not all gifted students exhibit all the characteristics all the time. Teachers and parents should be aware of the broad categories of giftedness. These come from the federal definition of giftedness in the 1972 Marland Report to Congress,[372] and are the basis for most state and local legislation:

- *General intellectual ability*: characterized by an advanced vocabulary and the ability to reason well, even with abstract problems.

- *Specific academic aptitude:* Characterized by very high achievement in a particular academic discipline. Can easily exceed the standard curriculum and may need to be accelerated in that subject area.

- *Creative thinking and production:* Characterized by exceptional ability to come up with original ideas, and by a lively, highly developed imagination.

- *Leadership and Psychosocial ability:* Characterized by the ability to manage and organize other people and projects. They are highly responsible and can be relied upon to get the job done.

- *Psychomotor ability:* Characterized by exceptional performance in such areas as sports, because of their strength, agility, and sense of themselves in space.

- *Ability in the visual and performing arts:* Characterized by exceptional work in art, music, drama, or creative writing. They are original and imaginative in expressing their ideas.

**Myth:** Gifted students come from predominately white, middle- and upper-class families.

> **Truth:** Gifted and talented children are present in all cultural, ethnic, and socioeconomic groups, yet minorities are significantly under-identified and not placed in gifted classes. We are swayed by cultural prejudice against children from minority groups, so that educators overlook giftedness and related issues, and instead conclude simply that a child has a more obvious disability like ADHD or autism spectrum disorder. As Webb, et al (2016) have pointed out, "Many Black American, Hispanic American, or other minority cultural students end up in special education classes or are viewed as having behavior problems by their white teachers. Teachers don't often nominate these students for gifted services. Parents from disenfranchised groups are less likely to know about resources for gifted children and adults, and they are often less able to afford outside testing and assessment, or even that there are options for a second opinion. As a result, gifted programs in many schools are disproportionately white, and minority gifted children are more likely to have their intellectual abilities overlooked and their behaviors classified as disorders."[373]

**Myth:** All children are gifted.

> **Truth:** All children have strengths and positive attributes, but not all children are intellectually gifted. Gifted and talented students have specialized needs when it comes to learning. This is even more the case when the child is 2e. They require specific modifications to the regular curriculum to ensure they are stimulated and challenged by new material; they often must be taught with an approach completely different from the norm.
>
> Many people feel uncomfortable with the term 'gifted', believing it to be elitist. But it is never elitist to give a child the right to

learn something new every day; it *is* elitist to oppress them and make them relearn the same things again and again. People are not all alike, and to say that all children have the same intellectual ability or talents is simply false. We cannot hold children back just because we don't understand the word 'gifted'. If gifted education is elitist, then so are varsity basketball teams, show choirs, and the National Honor Society, all of which require students to be selected from a larger group and given special experiences according to their readiness.

**Myth:** Gifted children's emotions are like other children.

**Truth:** Sometimes this is true, but the more highly gifted the child, the more likely he or she is to demonstrate emotional intensity and particular sensitivity. Just as his thinking is more complex than other students, so are his emotions. Feeling everything more deeply than others can be both painful and frightening. Emotionally intense gifted children cope with inner conflict, self-criticism, anxiety, and feelings of inferiority, often brought on by a sense that they must do more than others, like write the perfect paper or solve one of the world's great problems.

The most important thing we can do to nurture emotionally intense gifted children is accept them and their feelings. Though all children need to feel understood and supported, it is particularly important for gifted children, and they need to know it is normal for them to feel the way they do. We should help them understand that experiencing emotions more intensely than others is part of their *unique* way of being. Parents and teachers can help them use their keen intellect and insight to develop self-awareness and self-acceptance.

## School strategies that work for 2e students

There continues to be the toxic notion that smart people have easier lives by default. Neurotypicals will ask 2e people, "Shouldn't your high intelligence erase your struggles?" Neurotypicals might have good intentions, but such shallow understanding and commentary cause 2e people to feel more ashamed than confident.[374] Teachers and/

or employers might ask, "Why can't you just focus? You are smarter than this". Or they might say, "Stop making excuses, this should be easy for you." Twice-exceptional children often hear at home *and* school, "If you could just pay attention", or "You're not working towards your full potential", when in fact they are focused, but in a way that neurotypicals do not understand. When neurodiverse people are exposed to environments that repeatedly nitpick at their neuro-divergent tendencies, it reinforces the idea that they need fixing.[375] But when positive, research-based strategies are implemented, a 2e student's life can change for the better. The following strategies should be considered:

### Address learning styles

There are many approaches to working with children. One of the most important is to fully understand a child's different thinking patterns or learning styles. (See Chapter 2 for information about learning styles.) Then adults can teach from a new frame of reference, one aligned with the way 2e individual's think.[376] This is best expressed by Dr. Temple Grandin, author of *The Way I See It: A Personal Look at Autism,* and an advocate for neurodiverse people. She says, "Expecting children with ASD to learn via the conventional curriculum and teaching methods that *have always worked* for typical children is to set everyone up for failure right from the start. It would be like placing a young child on a grown-up's chair and expecting his feet to reach the floor."[377] We can no longer ignore that teaching requires multiple ways of helping students learn. It takes patience and commitment, but the benefits are significant.

### Provide a nurturing classroom and teacher(s)

Twice-exceptional students have more success when they experi-ence a nurturing classroom environment with caring and insightful teachers. According to Micaela Bracamonte, founder of The Lang School in New York, "Twice-exceptional students require a nurturing environment that supports the development of their potential by providing appropriately challenging activities. An encouraging approach is recommended over implementing measures from a punitive perspective."[378] For 2e students to reach their potential, teachers should:[379]

- ○ Value individual differences and learning styles.
- ○ Understand the student's readiness, interests, and learning profile.
- ○ Develop activities for a variety of learning styles.
- ○ Provide flexible grouping for instruction.
- ○ Encourage student development so everyone can reach their potential.
- ○ Assess students in accordance with their abilities. *Not every child should be assessed with paper and pencil tests.*
- ○ Define excellence by individual growth.
- ○ Teach with strong intuitive abilities rather than depending on logical deductions. Ex. ASD children are extremely sensitive to the *tone* with which something is said.

In addition, nurturing classrooms are places where differences are accurately identified, accepted, and supported.[380] Teachers should say what they mean and mean what they say, never providing vague instructions to their students. Instructors should use precise numbers, exact times and dates, specific places, and names of people the student will see throughout their instructional day.[381] Affective teachers (those who have a holistic understanding of their student's minds and learning styles) do not leave any room for confusion in their students' minds. If a student has a reservation about anything, they feel comfortable asking for specifics.

## Work with student's strengths/talents

Identifying and supporting twice-exceptional students is often a low priority in schools. But when teachers and parents empower these children by identifying and working with their strengths and talents, they build the student's self-confidence. For 2e students, confidence in their own abilities is *essential* when experiencing problems, whether at school or at home. Changing negative attitudes to positives one will have a profound impact on 2e students' achievement throughout their lives.[382]

Considering the strengths and interests of a student *before* identifying areas for remediation is strongly supported by twice-exceptional research.[383] Many researchers argue that talent development is the most crucial component of the education of 2e students.[384] When educators place *less* emphasis on the *differences* of 2e students, those students demonstrate a greater willingness to attempt difficult tasks, while becoming more creatively productive.[385] To consider student's strengths, review the following:[386]

- ○ Area(s) in which student excels.
- ○ Topic(s) in which student demonstrates advanced knowledge.
- ○ How students use their strengths to mitigate their areas of need.

How to work with students' gifts and talents will vary from child to child. Planning and interventions can be challenging and require focus at school as well as at home. It is also important to remember that as school and home plans are implemented, the adults should observe how these changes are affecting the child. Patience is necessary because changes can take several weeks to produce outcomes. The following is an example of planning for a 2e student named Ricardo from Deborah's book.[387] Mapping out Ricardo's challenges and strengths from the specific categories of giftedness is the best way to customize educational strategies for this student.

## *Figure 8.1 Educational team planning*

## Cognitive Processing

| S=Student Strength C=Student Challenge | Specific Strengths | Specific Challenges/ Concerns |
|---|---|---|
| _S Visual Processing | Remembers what he has read | Mixes up what comes first, next, last |
| __Auditory Processing | Can locate a specific piece of information in a book | Difficulty following through on multistep routines |
| C Sequential Processing | Very good speller | Sustained attention and follow through |
| __Conceptional Processing | | |
| __Processing Speed | | |
| C Attention | | |
| __Memory | | |
| __Executive Function | | |

## Specific Academic

| S=Student Strength C=Student Challenge | Specific Strengths | Specific Challenges/ Concerns |
|---|---|---|
| S Reading | Reads and comprehends at sixth-grade level | Difficulty putting ideas together |
| S Reading Fluency | Reads text quickly and with expression | Poor narrative sequencing |
| C Writing | Advanced vocabulary | Mental fatigue when writing |
| C Writing Fluency | | |
| __Math | | |
| __Math Fluency | | |
| __Science | | |
| __Social Studies | | |
| __Other | | |

## Creativity

| S=Student Strength C=Student Challenge | Specific Strengths | Specific Challenges/ Concerns |
|---|---|---|
| S Creative Thinking | Overflows with ideas | |
| S Creative Productivity | Prefers company of other creative children | |
| __Creative Problem Solving | Enjoys creating new ways to do routine tasks | |
| __Risk Taking | Original thoughts | |
| __Other | | |

## Visual, Spatial, Performing Arts

| S=Student Strength C=Student Challenge | Specific Strengths | Specific Challenges/ Concerns |
|---|---|---|
| __Visual Perception | Shows sensitivity to rhythm, melodies, and sounds | |
| __Spatial Perception | Enjoys music playing in the background when working | |
| S Musical/Rhythmic | Learns easily when information is sung or tapped out in rhythm (math facts) | |
| __Bodily/Kinesthetic | | |
| __Other | | |

## Physical/Psychomotor

| S=Student Strength C=Student Challenge | Specific Strengths | Specific Challenges/ Concerns |
|---|---|---|
| __Sensory Integration | | Restless |
| __Hearing | | Focus is only on self |
| __Vision | | Few tasks or goals are achieved |
| C ADD/ADHD | | |
| __Bodily | | |

## Interpersonal/Leadership

| S=Student Strength C=Student Challenge | Specific Strengths | Specific Challenges/ Concerns |
|---|---|---|
| S Communicating | Advanced vocabulary | Little interaction during unstructured time |
| C Understanding Others | Able to clearly express his own thoughts, ideas, and opinions | Difficulty making friends |
| C Peer Relations | Active listener | |
| __Self-Advocacy | | |
| __Other | | |

## Intrapersonal/Social Emotional

| S=Student Strength C=Student Challenge | Specific Strengths | Specific Challenges/ Concerns |
|---|---|---|
| __Understanding Self | | Negative internal dialogue |
| __Introspective/ Reflection | | Requires use of a "stress ball" most of the day |
| C Resiliency | | Anxieties produce physical ailments |
| C Coping | | Difficulty recovering from stressful school situations |
| __Behavioral Issues | | |
| __Perfectionism | | |

Here are some customized educational strategies suggested for *this* 2e student:

*Figure 8.2: Customized educational strategies*

| Learning Style Observation | | |
| --- | --- | --- |
| **Strengths** | **Interests** | **Challenges** |
| • Advanced reading ability<br>• Creative thinker | • Music<br>• Video games<br>• Non-fiction topics (weather, animals) | • Writing<br>• Incomplete sentences |

| Strength/Interest-Based Accommodations |
| --- |
| • Use flexible, non-permanent instructional grouping practices designed to facilitate accelerated/advanced academic learning. (Cluster grouping, cross-age grouping, interest groups)[388]<br>• Use challenging reading programs/materials. (e.g., Junior Great Books)<br>• Provide high-level materials, activity, and product options that include analytical and critical thinking skills.<br>• Accelerate vocabulary development through a variety of strategies and materials.<br>• Provide opportunities for 'real world' investigation and experiences. Examples: in-depth study on climate change and endangered animals; interviews with meteorologists, zoologists. |

| Accommodations to Access Learning |
| --- |
| • Provide a stimulating educational environment where there are opportunities for critical and creative thinking.<br>• Use advanced organizers for taking notes and outlines to help the students with sequencing information.<br>• Provide adequate workspace with limited distractions.<br>• Use computer/technology to research and complete projects.<br>• Allow student choice to demonstrate learning.<br>• Allow extra time to complete assignments/projects. |

## Explicit Instruction/ Compensatory Strategies

- Instruct the student how to break new learning into manageable segments and use a timeline to plan steps needed to complete project.
- Instruct the student in the use of highlighters and color coding to note key information.
- Teach research strategies and skills essential for in-depth study and advanced learning.
- Teach the student how to avoid fatigue by taking frequent breaks.
- Use software programs (e.g., teach Inspiration software to aid students in organizing information, writing, and projects.)
- Ask the student to write down how long he thinks an assignment will take, and record how long it actually took to complete.

## Specific Instruction: Intervention/Remediation

- Teach typing and word processing.
- Teach how to organize reports and projects.
- Teach strategies for planning, revising, and editing written products.
- Teach how to prioritize assignments.
- Teach the student to use checklists to mark his progress.

### Provide counseling support

Twice-exceptional students face a number of challenges in their psychosocial development. Stress and frustration can negatively influence self-esteem and create challenges with identity development. Self-perception is influenced by challenges during extracurricular activities, difficulties with peer relationships, and struggling to manage the experience of being both gifted and having learning differences. As a result, these students will require specific counseling support.[389]

It is important to remember that gifted students tend to experience greater asynchronicity in their social-emotional development than their neurotypical peers, and the gap is even more pronounced in 2e students. Traditional academic interventions and counseling that are effective in supporting remedial students (those who have fallen below the rest of the class in areas such as language or mathematics) can be counterproductive for twice-exceptional students, who are aware of their strengths and difficulties and often feel inadequate. These students may display elevated levels of anxiety, poor academic self-concept, and executive functioning deficits due to the significant discrepancies between strengths and weaknesses[390].

The drive to achieve perfection is common in gifted children. So when they have difficulty achieving, they are susceptible to significant psychological conflict. Twice-exceptional students can be very self-critical, which can lead to a particularly dysfunctional form of perfectionism.[391] Some children prefer individual counseling because it helps them deal with their unique challenges. But some prefer group counseling, because they are supported by realizing that other people have experiences similar to their own. Parents need to be an integral part of their child's counseling by obtaining information that will help them understand their special needs.

When counseling takes part at the child's school, as compared to a private practice, the in-school professionals can bridge the gaps between personal, social, and academic domains, thus taking the 'whole' student into account.[392] Too often teachers get caught up in academic achievement, or behavior problems, or social problems which challenge a student. This causes neglect in other areas important to a student's success, and this is no different with 2e students. The neglect is perhaps enhanced by overly complex educational plans. School counselors help teachers remember to focus on *all* the students' needs, providing resources and strategies to help with social and emotional struggles. Counselors communicate with school administrators, teachers, and parents, which allows them to advocate for students in all areas of a student's life. Importantly, counselors attend meetings when an Individual Education Plan (IEP) or a *504 Plan* is being formed.[393]

> [*IEP and 504 Plans are both plans that provide accommodation(s), but they serve different purposes. A 504 Plan is used*

*when a student needs accommodation(s) in the classroom. They do not require specialized instruction or a formal written plan. An IEP includes a formal written plan with learning goals and objectives. It focuses on educational benefits, and often includes direct services such as speech or occupational therapy. Both are free. Some students have both, and some just have one or the other. 504 Plans are typically available to students with a broader range of disabilities, including attention deficit disorders.*

*Currently, gifted students are not considered under the same umbrella of federal laws that mandate special education rights and services. Instead, they are supported to various degrees through a patchwork of state and local laws.[394] Therefore, it is essential that 2e stakeholders are familiar with these requirements, and also that they make significant efforts to achieve effective collaborations through the lens of the student's individual education program.[395]]*

## Parent strategies that work for twice-exceptional students

It is natural for parents to speak with each other about how their children are doing in school. Such conversations flow effortlessly, for the most part. For the parents of a gifted or twice-exceptional child, however, the conversations are not quite so easy. If they describe their second-grade child to a neighbor as smart and reading *Harry Potter* books, the reaction from the neighbor can be one of disbelief. Then, if this parent adds to the conversation that their child cannot spell or write at grade level, the reaction quickly changes: "How can that be?" Parents of 2e children will find it uncomfortable, even with relatives, to describe how difficult it is to parent their exceptional child.

It is true that other adults often add to the challenge of raising gifted and 2e kids. Parents of bright children rarely get to revel in their child's accomplishments, because of the learning differences, like dyslexia, ADD, or autism, which must be explained or defended. They feel others are jealous, or that they are perceived as bragging about their child's awards. This certainly adds to the difficulty of raising high ability children. Instead of merely enduring the comments of other parents who don't understand the real difficulties, the parent of a gifted child could respond:[396]

- ○ You are so lucky your child can hit a ball.

- ○ You are so lucky the first parenting manual you tried worked.

- ○ You are so lucky you can spell words out loud to your spouse and expect that your two-year-old child won't understand.

- ○ You are so lucky your child hasn't been thoroughly bored to tears in their classroom.

- ○ You are so lucky your teachers are always happy to see your child in the classroom.

## Collaborate with important stakeholders

As parents continue to travel the frequent bumpy roads in school and at home with their child, it is very important to maintain and increase the list of stakeholders who can collaborate for support of the child. Following is a list of potential stakeholders to consider for effective collaboration in supporting twice-exceptional students.[397]

*Table 8.1: Collaborative stakeholders*

| Stakeholder | Sample Consideration |
|---|---|
| Gifted Teacher | Are the students' strengths being maximized? Is the student bored? How can teaching better incorporate higher-level thinking skills? |
| Special Education Teacher | Are the students' needs sufficiently supported? Are IEP goals appropriate and relevant? Are accommodations appropriate and utilized? |
| General Education Teacher | Is a general education classroom the appropriate learning environment for the student? Is differentiated instruction an appropriate strategy? How does the student socialize with classmates? |

| Stakeholder | Sample Consideration |
|---|---|
| Family/Guardian(s) | How can the family nurture the student's social and emotional development outside of the school day? Are there any current family events that may impact learning? Do you feel that the other stakeholders view you as a valued and respected team member? |

## Promote social/emotional development

All 2e children are different, but parents should empower their child to manage their differences with their own unique self-understanding and motivation. They should never rush to 'rescue' them when they appear to struggle, nor should they make them feel that they are not good enough. By helping a child meet their challenges with their own skills and ambition, parents enable the child to build functional self-esteem. This will be a great victory for a child who often doesn't feel they satisfy adult ideals. Here are some strategies to promote social and emotional development.[398]

*Table 8.2: Strategies to promote social and emotional development*

| Strategy | Description |
|---|---|
| Create a safe home environment. | Reassure the child they are loved and appreciated, allow the child to vent frustrations at home that may have built up at school, make sure the child contributes at home with ideas and plans and the contributions are valued. |
| Nurture strengths and interests. | Encourage the child to explore their strengths and interests so they become motivated to learn; this builds confidence that they can succeed in the face of challenges. |
| Foster 'I can do it' attitude. | Help the child learn that all tasks require effort and persistence to complete; praise the child's effort without judging ability; encourage the child to use positive self-talk. |

| Strategy | Description |
|---|---|
| Support the development of compensatory strategies. | Encourage the use of graphic organizers (homework and projects), technology (increase productivity), spelling and grammar checkups (for editing papers), and calendar tools like Microsoft Outlook (organize time and projects) |
| Promote positive coping strategies. | Discourage avoidance, distancing from a problem, and learned helplessness; promote and encourage accepting responsibility for one's actions, accepting proper help, and becoming a self-advocate. |
| Encourage and assist realistic goal setting. | Begin with short-term goals that result in success. Increased success leads to motivation to strive for long-term goals when they are broken into several achievable short-term goals. Celebrate successes. |

### *Be a strong parent advocate*

Advocacy has been cited numerous times in this book because of its importance in raising awareness. Becoming an advocate is an especially important role for parents of gifted and twice-exceptional children. They have power as an advocate for their child (and other children) because their voices can promote positive change in schools. Modeling advocacy also sets a good example for the child as they grow up because it teaches them to advocate for themselves.

Parents should not assume that school staff will initiate changes in the curriculum for special students. They must be prepared to ask the right questions, and to do so they must learn about gifted educational strategies and options and find out what is offered at school to support the child. They will become prepared to ask questions like:

1. "Would my child benefit from being assigned a teacher who understands twice-exceptionality?"

2. "Could the curriculum be compacted so my child can move more quickly through the material in their area of strength?"

3. "Should my child be accelerated in a particular subject, or should he skip an entire grade?"

Strong advocacy means to champion, encourage, and uphold the child. It does *not* mean to attack, demean, or blame school officials or others. Parents who work *cooperatively* with teachers and schools have much greater success than those who 'go to war' with them.[399] This is particularly important for parents of twice-exceptional children to understand. Because frequent contacts will be necessary between home and school to support the special needs of the child and help them reach their potential, parents should remember:[400]

○ Approach problems as an opportunity to learn.

○ After all the facts are collected about a problem, approach the teacher and school staff with care and sensitivity to schedule a meeting.

○ Start a conference with positive comments and then communicate clearly and without blame. Keep the focus on the child's needs.

○ Always express a willingness to help resolve the problem and work collaboratively toward a positive solution.

○ Keep the lines of communication open for all follow-up meetings that will occur.

### Finding the right school fit

Parents want to find the best educational fit for their smart child so they can stay engaged, motivated, and feel accepted in school, but sometimes they don't know how to go about it.[401] As a gifted specialist, Deborah has experienced too many parents of 2e students feeling like they are 'rocking the boat' if they ask for special accommodations. She has also heard parents say, "I don't want any special treatment for my child. I want them to feel like everyone else in school". As an advocate for not only children but parents too, Deborah gently explains that their child *is* different, and their special needs must be addressed individually to see continued growth *and* avoid possible harm in school and at home.

All adults who live or work with 2e children must keep in mind that *one size does not fit all*. This expression is perfect to keep in mind when thinking about a child's education. Most children start kindergarten in a neighborhood public school or a faith-based school. However, after some time passes, a parent begins to see their child withdraw, beg not to go to school, and/or begin to exhibit problematic behaviors ranging from underachievement to defiant outbursts.[402] After some deep reflection and investigation, including speaking at length with their child, the parents may conclude that their child's learning environment is not meeting their needs. Then it becomes time to explore other educational options which are clearly focused on meeting the needs of gifted and twice-exceptional learners.[403]

As Head of School for Quest Academy in Illinois, Dr. Vicki Phelps reminds us, "…the goal is to recognize when your child needs a change before these negative outcomes become reality." Understandably, kids have unhappy moments in school, but when these become too frequent, it is a sign that the school is not meeting your child's needs. Phelps asks parents to consider these questions:[404]

○ Is my child excited about learning and eager to take on new challenges?

○ Does my child have an opportunity to pursue areas of interest and engage in learning that removes the 'ceiling' on what is expected?

○ Does my child have opportunities to engage and connect with cognitive peers who share similar interests and ways of learning and processing information?

○ Does my child have additional exceptionalities that could be better supported through programming that understands and addresses the needs of 2e learners?

○ Does my child have a passion that is currently overlooked within the current education setting?

○ Does my child have ample opportunities to develop talent across various contexts?

How do parents attempt to find the right school fit for their gifted and 2e child when children and school programs are so different? There are many educational options for providing for the gifted student, like public, private, and independent schools; after-school enrichment classes; summer camps; residential schools; online school options; and homeschooling, to name only some. Nevertheless, when a parent thinks they have found a good fit, they might discover that the school addresses only giftedness, or only learning differences (challenges), but not both.

In the July 2023 issue of *Parenting for High Potential* (National Association for Gifted Children), Vicki Phelps's article *The Right Fit: Finding the Best Educational Program for Your Gifted Child* explains the steps and considerations for parents attempting to navigate the many options to support their child' education.[405]

○ *Reflect on your child's current educational experience, needs, and future goals.* This is a process that the child should be a part of, regardless of age. Not only does this send the message that your child's voice is valued, but it also provides insights that otherwise might not be heard. To begin this conversation, one might create a *'Plus, Minus, Interesting'* reflection known as *PMI.*[406] This *reflection* captures the parents' and student's perspective by creating three columns on paper and labeling them 'Plus, Minus, Interesting'. This is for reflecting upon what is presently going well in the child's current learning environment as well as what is lacking and helps the family begin to explore future educational options.

○ *Research thoroughly to learn as much as possible about each school and program being considered.* Make sure to use the information collected from the PMI Reflection.

○ *Learning Environment.* Consider the times your child is most engaged in learning. What physical learning environment(s) contributes to that level of engagement? Key considerations include classroom and learning lab set up, dedicated resource areas for continued talent development, and accessibility to restrooms, water fountains, and safety areas.

The learning environment is like a 'third teacher'. We should acknowledge the significance which the materials, the space, and the mood of the classroom and other designated spaces have in the child's education.[407]

○ *Programs Purpose.* Parent(s) may need to ask explicitly, "What is the purpose of the school?", because it may not be totally clear through the school's or program's mission statement. It is important to ask school administrators about opportunities for students to pursue areas of interest, the instructional pacing provided for gifted learners, and the connection to real-world applications for specific areas of specialization. This is key to keeping gifted learners engaged and motivated.[408]

○ *Curriculum.* Parents must ask school administrators, "What curriculum model does your educational program follow to meet the needs of gifted/2e learners?" or "What type of evidence-based strategies are implemented to stimulate critical thinking?" If the school or program cannot answer these basic questions, find the next option! Additionally, parents need to know if a school offers whole-grade or subject acceleration, or both. If not, ask explicitly how gifted and 2e students' needs are met when they show mastery prior to a unit of study. At *NO* time should merely increasing workload compensate for prior mastery of content. Differentiated learning means *different and new* learning, not just more of the same.

○ *Additional Attributes.* Parents need to understand, when selecting the best school and program for their child, that there are additional areas of a school to consider. Depending on the needs of your child, the optimal desired *class size* will vary. Consider how often your child will be in attendance: does your child need the consistency of a daily educational program, or would a weekly enrichment class better meet their needs? Inquire about frequency of gifted services, curricular options like sports, fine arts and academic teams, and elective courses such as Advanced Placement, languages, career tracks, and technical educational opportunities.

○ *Supplemental Supports.* Schools have a variety of specialists, but parents cannot assume that every school has the specialists their gifted or 2e learner might need, so be certain to ask. Specialists include: a gifted intervention specialist, a school counselor, a speech/language pathologist, a special education/resource teacher, a school nurse, an ESL (English as a Second Language) teacher, a Librarian, and Technology Specialists.

○ *Cost.* Parents should never hesitate to ask about financial and supplemental resources to help pay for the special programs or services necessary to educate their child. Ask for clarity about the additional costs associated with specific programs like field trips, school uniforms, meals, and participation fees for extracurricular options.

## Successful twice-exceptional schools

There are many schools designed especially for twice-exceptional learners across the United States. Most, if not all, have been founded by parents of 2e children. Their frustration with former schools led them to seek a better way to educate their 2e children. The parent and student knew what worked and what did not work in previous schools. The 2e schools described here are just a snapshot to help people understand the importance of *prioritizing the child* when designing an education program or curriculum. The student must be embraced for who they are, and should never have to change, mask, or try to 'fit into a box' that was never made for them.

We realize not every 2e student can attend one of these amazing schools, but we wanted to shine a bright light on the good work being done around the country to support this special group of children. It is our hope that more public, private, and independent schools integrate the strategies and educational models that have been proven to be successful for 2e students.

### Big Minds (Pinole, CA; Pleasanton, CA)

*Big Minds* school's (https://www.bigmindsunschool.org/) motto is 'A different kind of school for a different kind of student'. Founded by

Dr. Melanie Hayes in 2015, *Big Minds* began as a homeschooling situation to accommodate Dr. Hayes' 2e twins. It grew into a grassroots movement involving other 2e parents. These families recognized the need for an approach to education that is holistic, community-driven, strengths-based, and responsive to students' needs. The learner profile of twice-exceptional students is often overlooked or ignored by traditional educational settings. *Big Minds'* pedagogical methodology is designed explicitly for the 2e learner, catering to their strengths, and accommodating their challenges.

*Big Minds* is an *attachment-based*, community-focused school designed to give 2e students the time and support necessary to grow into thoughtful citizens. The student-to-teacher ratio is 4:1. All learning is done in project-based and strengths-led 1:1 or small group settings. The school uses what the students are passionate about as building blocks to manage the struggles caused by their learning differences. In addition, *Big Minds* also focuses on social and emotional development which supports both cognitive and creative growth. Students and teachers are continually engaged in a passionate and reciprocal learning process.

Children learn according to their own unique patterns. *Big Minds'* school schedule allows for social-emotional learning, group work, one-on-one learning, individual projects, free time, and creativity. Every semester courses change based on student feedback, level of interest, and degree of development. Students also receive an hour of individual coaching in literacy, math, science, programming, coding, art, or music, based on interest and assessment levels.

Since 2e children are not 'morning people', they can arrive between 8:30-10:00am, known as a flexible start day. *Big Minds* strives to provide the least stressful start to the day since 2e students already struggle with sensory and anxiety issues. When children arrive, they are invited to ease into their day by socializing, playing with others, reading, creating art, working on a computer, or working on personal projects.

*Big Minds'* overarching goal is for students to graduate with the skills to navigate the world as it is, and as 'socially literate' humans who feel comfortable advancing themselves. It might seem to many that this 2e school is radically different. But 2e children *need* a school to be *different* so they are set up for success.[409]

### Bridges Academy (Studio City, CA; Seattle, WA)

*Bridges Academy's* (https://bridges.edu/) motto is 'Imagine, Persevere, Achieve, Educating the Exceptional'. Founded by Carolyn McWilliams, *Bridges Academy* began as a private tutorial endeavor in her home in 1994. McWilliams was providing education for gifted youngsters with organizational deficits who were struggling in the regular school setting. She called this home study program 'Bridges to Learning'. In the first year she found herself with thirty students. Four years later, *Bridges Academy* was accredited as a non-profit organization. Today, it is a full-fledged accredited college preparatory school offering classes for grades 4-12. *Bridges Academy* opened its sister school in Seattle, WA for the 2022-2023 academic school year.

*Bridges Academy* prides itself on understanding the whole learner. Students complete detailed learning profiles. Staff work closely with each student during day-to-day project- and problem-based learning, observe students at play, and have conversations with their students at lunch. Learning profiles as well as a deep understanding of each child's readiness helps teachers design curricula and activities that motivate, engage, and increase learning. Differentiation, a teaching approach that enables teachers to accommodate the various learning needs of a group or individual, is ongoing throughout the learning process with respect to content, processes, environments, products, and assessments.[410]

*Bridges Academy* educators take a complexity of variables into consideration. The *Multiple Perspectives Model*[411] addresses seven critical educational variables necessary to consider in understanding the whole child.

*Figure 8.3: Bridges Academy multiple perspectives model*

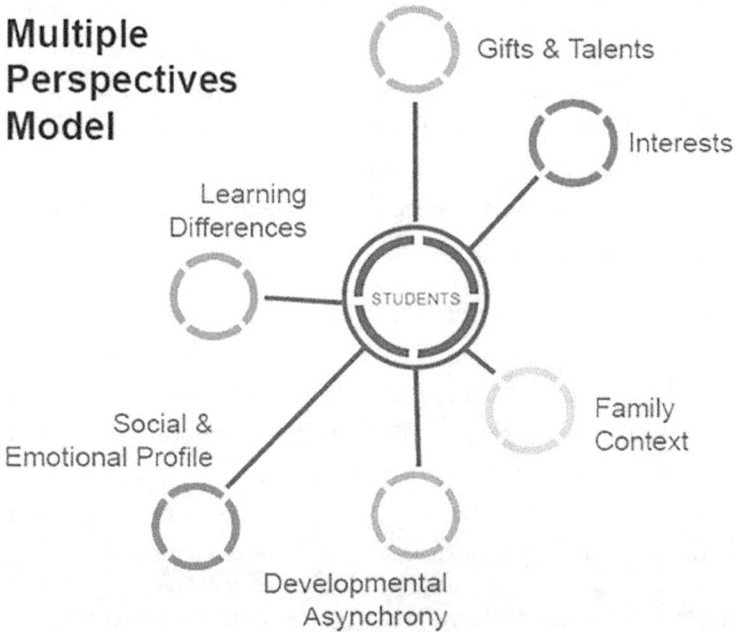

**Multiple Perspectives Model**

Gifts & Talents

Interests

Learning Differences

STUDENTS

Social & Emotional Profile

Family Context

Developmental Asynchrony

In addition to addressing these seven fundamental elements shown in the *Multiples Perspectives Model,* classes are small with no more than eight students. Every Wednesday is enrichment day, when students can choose an activities cluster: they might go on a field trip or invite special guests to school who provide seminars on topics selected by the students. The school prepares their students for the 21st century with many opportunities, including university studies, and artistic and entrepreneurial endeavors.

Twice-exceptional students are capable of developing expertise at a very young age. *Bridges Academy* firmly believes that if the student and the school are the right fit for each other, the student has a greater chance of success in a variety of fields, from robotics to religion, string theory to Sanskrit, and politics to poetry. Utilizing a strength-based program like the one at *Bridges Academy* can unlock the human potential of a 2e learner.

### The Heron School (Moab, Utah)

*The Heron School*'s (https://www.heronschool.com/) motto is: 'Unlocking the gifts of twice-exceptional students. Founder and Head of School Emily Neihaus's inspiration for a 2e school was "…one hundred percent to help my 2e son become a successful adult." [412] After discovering the local school district, although good, was not set up to support 2e learners, she realized she either had to move her family or bring the resources to Moab. Fortunately, she decided to open a special school designed especially for twice-exceptional students.

The Heron School is a secondary school serving neurodivergent learners ages thirteen to eighteen years old. Students thrive through individualized, project-based curriculum that is developed around their strengths and interests. Driven by instructional scaffolding, Heron School encourages students to participate in college-level coursework opportunities and guides students to be ready for independent living after graduation.

Twice-exceptional students struggle socially, emotionally, and academically in a public school system due to their unusual gifts and neurodiversity. So Heron School utilizes a variety of classroom experiences, such as one-on-one instruction, small classes with a 6:1 ratio, project-based courses, online coursework with oversight and facilitation, and an educational setting with minimal external stimulation. Neihaus's overarching goal is to ensure that each student is 'given love and space to be their unique selves, a place to feel loved, safe and serene'.

# Final Thoughts

We encourage you to watch Deborah Reber's (author of *Differently Wired* and creator of Tilt Parenting) TED Talk ( https://www.ted.com/talks/deborah_reber_differently_wired). Her words sum up what we are trying to share with readers in this book. Neurodiversity describes the idea that people experience and interact with the world around them in many ways; there is no one 'right' way of thinking, learning, and behaving, and differences should *not* be viewed as deficits. When approximately 1 in 5 individuals is neurodiverse, we can no longer call them outliers or disrupters. In Reber's words, "We need big changes for differently wired people, especially kids, in the way they are perceived, treated, and supported at school, home, and society".

Our society is finally shifting toward valuing authenticity and being self-aware. Many more people today are willing to understand that diversity is not just a term related to race, religion, or gender. Diversity is now a term which refers to everyone's willingness to acknowledge and accept differences in the way people's brains are wired. As John expresses so eloquently, "When we embrace differences as opportunities for positive change, we allow 2e people to face the world with a positive outlook and strong sense of self-esteem. This newfound confidence and clarity will empower the individual to drop their defensive demeanor, become 'unstuck', and advance with determination".

It is every individual's responsibility to pay attention to how *they* react to a person who is different from themself. It should not be the other way around, whereby we try to change the 2e person's behavior around us.[413] A perfect example is in 2e parent Marianne

Sunderland's article, *What Parents Can Learn from the Story of Gillian Lynn*.[414] Gillian always needed to move around and never sat still. Gillian's mother took her to a doctor when she was 7, because she questioned Gillian's teacher's assumption that something was wrong with Gillian because she moved around so much. Fortunately, the doctor was a keen observer and told her mother, "There is nothing wrong with your daughter, she just needs to be a dancer." Gillian Lynn went on to have a wonderful career with the Royal Ballet in Europe and met Andrew Lloyd Webber. She is responsible for some of the most successful theater productions in history, such as *Cats* and *Phantom of the Opera*.

Finally, in Brené Brown's book, *The Gifts of Imperfection*, she says, "A deep sense of love and belonging is an irreducible need of all women, men, and children. We are biologically, cognitively, physically, and spiritually wired to love, to be loved, and *to belong*. When those needs are not met, we don't function as we were meant to. We break, fall apart, we numb, we ache, we hurt others, and we get sick."[415] If we simply did a better job of understanding individual differences, no one would feel broken or isolated. Neurodiverse people need to let go of what others think about them, and neurotypical people need to be willing to call out others when harmful things are said about someone who is different. Famous American poet Maya Angelou said it best: "When people know better, they do better."

# Epilogue

*"When you finally find your shit,*
*most everyone else will say that you've lost it."*
~John Truitt

While this has been a very abridged version of my 2e life, I hope you have found it both helpful and entertaining. I have attempted to explain the challenges and benefits of being twice exceptional. I also hope you can see that those of us who are neurodiverse can have normal experiences and enjoy life just like anyone else.

I currently live in Durango, Colorado with my wife Ashley and dog Cassidy. I teach at The Heron School for twice-exceptional students in Moab, Utah four days a week, and I love every minute of the time I am there. I have recently thought 'what if': what if I had started doing what I love and pursued a career in teaching earlier in my life? I concluded that it would not have worked. I could never have sat in college classes being taught how to teach. Without accommodations, I could not have kept up with the outside reading and assignments. Most notably, without my successes **and** failures, I realize that I would be of little value to my students. Mark Twain once said, *"Good judgement is the result of experience and experience the result of bad judgement."* By no means have all my decisions been poor ones, but I had to lead the life I have led to finally have what I truly love…teaching.

I came to know the world of twice-exceptionality and neurodiversity when my wife and I met with an astute marriage counselor. At the time we had been married 18 years. Our relationship had become tumultuous and nonfunctioning. I was convinced that my wife was pretty much wrong about everything. The counselor suspected that I might be on the spectrum when during a therapy session she observed me misinterpreting my wife's body language and facial expressions. It was at that moment that the counselor proposed ASD as a potential diagnosis.

I was familiar with the term autism, but I was only aware of the typical stereotype (male, good at math calculation, limited eye contact, reserved socially, and awkward). At first, other than being a male, none of those traits seemed to apply to me. My ASD 'tells' are extremely subtle, like when I uncontrollably and quickly divert my eyes away from someone at the exact wrong moment, or when I can't seem to smile the right way in a photograph.

The symptoms made sense with his diagnosis, even though I didn't exhibit the external traits commonly associated with autism. What I came to know as self-pres-ervation, internal rumination and anxiety were impacting my life in crippling and destructive ways. I accepted a referral to a PhD specializing in adult neurodiversity and learning differences. It was the first step towards a fulfilling life that I never realized could be possible.

I have learned over the years that everyone is a work in progress, including me. I've also learned that twice-excep-tional giftedness is in many ways a difference of extremes, especially in sensitivity. The impact of sensory issues cannot be understated, and I find them more complicated than traditionally explained. While sensitivity to loud repetitive noises and bright lights are common, so are delicate sensitivities to things like vague smells and mild tactile stimulations. For example, the tag on the collar of my shirt can bother me more than breaking a bone.

I no longer 'live' in boardrooms or travel the world. I don't own expensive cars or houses. I rarely go out to dinner and usually cook at home. I now live a life of contentment and normalcy. I encourage anyone reading this book who believes they may be twice-exceptional or neurodiverse to seek a formal diagnosis, especially if you feel your uniqueness is negatively impacting your life. I also hope you will share this information and my experiences with not only anyone you believe to be 2e, but the broader community as well. The more general awareness of our unique talents and limitations the better.

We invite you to join us on our journey to increase twice-exceptional awareness and advocacy. More information can be found at www.onthespectrumfoundation.org and www.deborahgennarelli.com. Our goal is to help the world understand that twice-exceptional people are different, but we are different *good*, not different *bad*!

# References

ABA Centers of America. (2023). *Do I have autism? 10 questions to ask yourslef.* Retrieved from https://www.abacenters.com/do-i-have-autism/

Adams, A. (2017). *How counselors can help twice exceptional students.* Retrieved from https://2eadvocate.wordpress.com/2017/12/07/how-counselors-can-help-twice-exceptional-students/

Amend, E., Schuler, P., Gavin, K., & Beights, R. (2009). A unique challenge: Sorting out the differences between giftedness and Asperger's disorder. *Gifted Child Today, 32*(4).

American Academy of Pediatrics. (2019). *How pediatricians screen for autism.* Retrieved from https://www.healthychildren.org/English/health-issues/conditions/Autism/Pages/How-Doctors-Screen-for-Autism.aspx

American Psychiatrict Association. (2013). *Diagnostic and statistical manual of mental health disorders: DSM-5-TR* (5 ed.). Washington, D.C.: American Pcyshiatirc Association.

American Psychological Association. (2017). *Diagnosing and mangaging autism spectrum disorder (ASD).* Retrieved from https://www.apa.org/topics/autism-spectrum-disorder/diagnosing

Anas, D. (2022). *5 pieces of advice for gifted adults iwth ADHD.* Retrieved from https://www.getinflow.io/post/twice-exceptional-gifted-adults-with-adhd

Anderson, C. H. (2021). *What is an empath and can you become one?* Retrieved from https://www.thehealthy.com/mental-health/what-is-an-empath/

Ansari, D. (2023). *What is dyscalculia?* Retrieved from https://www. understood.org/en/articles/what-is-dyscalculia

Arkansas State University. (2016). *The history of special education in the United States.* Retrieved from https://degree.astate.edu/articles/k-12-education/the-history-of-special-education-in-the-u-s.aspx

Arky, B. (2022). *Twice exceptional kids: Both gifted and challenged.* Retrieved from https://childmind.org/article/twice-exceptional-kids-both-gifted-and-challenged/

Armstrong, T. (2015). *The myth of the normal brain and embracing neurodiversity.* Retrieved from https://journalofethics.ama-assn.org/article/myth-normal-brain-embracing-neurodiversity/2015-04

Attwood, T. (2014). *Been there, done that, try this: An aspie's guide to life on earth.* Philadelphia: Jessica King Publshers.

Attwood, T., & Evans, C. (2018). *Ask Dr. Tony: Answers from the world's leading authority on Asperger's syndrom/high functioning autism.* Arlington, TX: Future Horizons, Inc.

Austism Society. (2022). *The autism experience: Understanding autism.* Retrieved from https://autismsociety.org/the-autism-experience/

Azpeitia, L. (2021). *The unique challenges of gifted and creative adults.* Retrieved from https://gifted-adults.com/challenges/

Bailey, A. (2022). *Coping mechanisms: Everything you need to know.* Retrieved from https://www.verywellhealth.com/coping-mechanisms-5272135

Bargiela, S., Steward, R., & Mandy, W. (2016). The experiences of late diagnosed women with autism spectrum conditions: An investigation of the female autism prototype. *Journal of Autism and Developmental Disorders, 46*(10), 3281-3294.

Baum, S., & Olenchak, R. (2002). The alphabet children; GT, ADHD, and more. *Exceptionality, 10,* 77-91.

Baumer, N., & Frueh, J. (2021). *What is neurodiversity?* Retrieved from https://www.health.harvard.edu/blog/what-is-neurodiversity

Beam, R. (2021). *Zavikon: Bridge to inclusion.* Retrieved from https://www.zavikon.net/

Bel Marra Health. (2015). *Asperger syndrome: An autism spectrum disorder raises suicidal thoughts, depression, and anxiety risk.* Retrieved from https://www.belmarrahealth.com/asperger-syndrome-an-autism-spectrum-disorder-raises-suicidal-thoughts-depression-and-anxiety-risk/

Beljan, P. (2011). Misdiagnosis of culturally diverse students. In J. A. Castellano, & A. Frazier (Eds.), *Special population in gifted education: Understanding our most able* (pp. 317-332). Waco, TX: Prufrock Press.

Better Help. (2023). *22 body language communication.* Retrieved from https://www.betterhelp.com/advice/body-language/22-body-language-examples-and-what-they-show/

Blustain, R. (2019). *Twice exceptional, doubly disadvantaged? How schools struggle to serve gifted students with disabilities.* Retrieved from https://hechingerreport.org/twice-exceptional-doubly-disadvantaged-how-schools-struggle-to-serve-gifted-students-with-disabilities/

Braaten, E. (2023). *Intro to processing speed.* Retrieved from https://www.mghclaycenter.org/parenting-concerns/grade-school/intro-processing-speed/

Bracamonte, M. (2010). *Twice exceptional students: Who they are and what they need.* Retrieved from https://www.davidsongifted.org/gifted-blog/2e-students-who-they-are-and-what-they-need/

Brain Balance Achievement Centers. (2023). *Proprioception explained.* Retrieved from https://www.brainbalancecenters.com/blog/proprioception-explained

Brain Wave Watch. (2022). *Asperger syndrome: How to cope and thrive.* Retrieved from https://brainwave.watch/asperger-syndrome-how-to-cope-and-thrive

Bridges Academy. (2023). *Approach.* Retrieved from http://losangeles.bridges.edu/approach.html

Brody, B. (2021). *What are the different parenting styles?* Retrieved from https://www.webmd.com/parenting/features/parenting-styles

Brown, B. (2022). *The gifts of imperfection* (10th ed.). Center City, MN: Hazeldon Publishing.

Bruelles, D., Brown, K. L., & Winebrenner, S. (2016). *Differentiated lessons for every learner: Standards based activities and extensions for middle school.* New York, NY: Routledge.

Butnik, S. (2020). *Understanding, diagnosing, and coping with slow processing speed.* Retrieved from https://www.davidsongifted.org/gifted-blog/understanding-diagnosing-and-coping-with-slow-processing-speed/

Butter, E. (2017). *Autism spectrum disorders: The difference between boys and girls.* Retrieved from https://www.nationwidechildrens.org/family-resources-education/700childrens/2017/04/autism-spectrum-disorders-the-difference-between-boys-and-girls

Cage, E., & Troxell-Witman, Z. (2019). Understanding the reasons, contexts, and costs of camouflaging for autistic adults. *Journal of Autism and Developmental Disorders, 49*(5), 1899-1011.

Cage, E., DiMonaco, J., & Newell, V. (2018). Experience of autism acceptance and mental health in autistic adults. *Journal of Autism and Developmental Disorders, 48*(2), 473-484.

Center for Disease Control and Prevention. (2022-a). *What is autism spectrum disorder?* . Retrieved from https://www.cdc.gov/ncbddd/autism/facts.html

Center for Disease Control and Prevention. (2022-b). *Screening and diagnosis of autism spectrum disorder.* Retrieved from https://www.cdc.gov/ncbddd/autism/screening.html

Center for Disease Control and Prevention. (2022-c). *Help your child grow and thrive: CDC's free milestone tracker app.* Retrieved from https://www.cdc.gov/ncbddd/actearly/milestones-app.html

Center for Disease Control and Prevention. (2022-d). *CDC's developmental milestones.* Retrieved from https://www.cdc.gov/ncbddd/actearly/milestones/index.html

Center for Disease Control and Prevention. (2022-e). *Data and statistics on autism spectrum disorder.* Retrieved from https://www.cdc.gov/ncbddd/autism/data.html

Center for Disease Control and Prevention. (2022-f). *Autism spectrum disorder in teenagers and adults.* Retrieved from https://www.cdc.gov/ncbddd/autism/autism-spectrum-disorder-in-teenagers-adults.html

Center for Disease Control and Prevention. (2022-g). *Autism spectrum disorder, family health history and genetics.* Retrieved from https://www.cdc.gov/genomics/disease/autism.htm

Center for Disease Control and Prevention. (2022-h). Retrieved from https://www.cdc.gov/ncbddd/autism/addm-community-report/addm-network-methods.html

Center for Disease Control and Prevention. (2022-i). *National center on birth defects and developmental disabilities.* Retrieved from https://www.cdc.gov/ncbddd/autism/addm-community-report/index.html

Center for Disease Control and Prevention. (2022-j). *Key findings from the ADDM network.* Retrieved from https://www.cdc.gov/ncbddd/autism/addm-community-report/key-findings.html

Center for Disease Control and Prevention. (2022-k). *Learn the signes, act early: Help your child grow and thrive.* Retrieved from https://www.cdc.gov/ncbddd/actearly/index.html

Center for Disease Control and Prevention. (2023-b). *2023 community report on autism.* Retrieved from https://www.cdc.gov/ncbddd/autism/addm-community-report/index.html

Center for Parent Resources and Information. (2023-a). *Categories of disability under part B of IDEA.* Retrieved from https://www.parentcenterhub.org/categories/

Centers for Disease Control and Prevention. (2023-c). *Community report on autism: Autism developmental disabilities monitoring.* Retrieved from https://www.cdc.gov/ncbddd/autism/addm-community-report/index.html

*CEOs are: IN.* (2024). Retrieved from Disability: IN: https://disabilityin.org/ceos-are-in/

Chen, I. (2015). *Wide awake: Why children with autism struggle with sleep.* Retrieved from https://www.spectrumnews.org/features/deep-dive/wide-awake-why-children-with-autism-struggle-with-sleep/

Cherry, K. (2022-a). *The Weschsler adult intelligence scale.* Retrieved from https://www.verywellmind.com/the-wechsler-adult-intelligence-scale

Cherry, K. (2022-b). *Loneliness: Causes and health consequences.* Retrieved from https://www.verywellmind.com/loneliness-causes-effects-and-treatments-

Cherry, K. (2023-a). *Understanding body language and facial expressions.* Retrieved from https://www.verywellmind.com/understand-body-language-and-facial-expressions-4147228

Cherry, K. (2023-b). *Types of nonverbal communication.* Retrieved from https://www.verywellmind.com/types-of-nonverbal-communication-2795397

Cogentica. (2022). *How disability stereotypes are harmful.* Retrieved from https://www.cogentica.com/stereotypes-hurt/

Cohen, S. B. (2018). *Genetic studies intend to help people with autism, not wipe them out.* Retrieved from https://www.newscientist.com/article/2179104-genetic-studies-intend-to-help-people-with-autism-not-wipe-them-out/

Cook, J. (2022). *The Asperkids secret book of social rules: The handbook of (not so obvious) neurotypical social guidelines for autistic teens* (10th ed.). London: Jessica Kingsley Publishers.

Covington, T. (2023). *Traveling with autism: How to handle safety, transitions, and time in transit.* Retrieved from https://www.thezebra.com/resources/driving/traveling-autism/

Cumo, C. M. (2019). *What you need to know about autism.* Santa Barbara, CA: Greenwood Publishers.

Currie, S. (2022). *8 signs and symptoms of autism in adults.* Retrieved from https://meetmonarch.com/health-resources/articles/autism-spectrum-disorder/8-signs-of-autism-in-adults

Davidson Academy. (2021). *Underachievement in gifted students.* Retrieved from https://www.davidsonacademy.unr.edu/blog/underachievement-in-gifted-students/

Davidson Institute. (2022). *Gifted, on the spectrum, or both?: Gifted and twice exceptional.* Retrieved from https://www.davidsongifted.org/gifted-blog/gifted-on-the-spectrum-or-both/

Davis, J. (2010). *Bright, talented, and black: A guide for families of African-American learners.* Goshen, KY: Gifted Unlimited.

Davis, K. (2023). *Unmasking.* Retrieved from https://www.2enews.com/research/unblocking/

deBono, E. (n.d.). *PMI lesson workcard.* Retrieved from https://www.debono.com/de-bono-thinking-lessons-1/1.-PMI-lesson-workcard

*Disability Equality Index.* (2024). Retrieved from Disability: IN: https://disabilityin.org/what-we-do/disability-equality-index/

Dominus, S. (2019). *Open office: What happens when people who have gtrouble fitting into a traditional workplace get one designed just for them? .* Retrieved from https://www.nytimes.com/interactive/2019/02/21/magazine/autism-office-design.html

Dorsey, M. (2023). *Why is routine so important to people with ASD?* Retrieved from https://www.appliedbehavioranalysisedu.org/why-is-routine-so-important-to-people-with-asd/

Drake, K. (2021). *What is the latest research on autism?* Retrieved from https://www.medicalnewstoday.com/articles/what-is-the-latest-research-on-autism

Dweck, C. S. (2016). *Mindset: The new psychology of success: How we can learn to fulfill our potential .* New York, N.Y.: Random House.

Eckerd, M. (2021). *Are autistic people empathic? Is everyone else?* Retrieved from https://www.psychologytoday.com/us/blog/everyday-neurodiversity/202101/are-autistic-people-empathic-is-everyone-else

Elise, K. (2016). *12 famous artists with synesthesia .* Retrieved from https://www.mentalfloss.com/article/88417/12-famous-artists-synesthesia

Epstein, T. S. (2022). *The Montessori philosophy.* Retrieved from https://www.montessori.org/the-montessori-philosophy/

Eustachewich, L. (2019). *Autistic soldiers are joing the IDF through a special Israeli military unit.* Retrieved from https://nypost.com/2019/04/07/autistic-soldiers-are-joining-the-idf-through-a-special-israeli-military-unit/

Feder, J. (2021). *Autism representation in the media and how it impacts real life.* Retrieved from https://www.accessibility.com/blog/autism-representation-in-the-media-and-how-it-impacts-real-life

Feit, K. (2018). *Unit 9900: Autistic teens join the Israeli army.* Retrieved from https://www.hadassah.org/story/unit-9900-autistic-teens-join-the-israeli-army

Flemming, G. (2019). *Learning styles: Holistic or global learning.* Retrieved from https://www.thoughtco.com/holistic-learners

Ford, D. Y. (2011, January). Closing the achievement gap: Gifted education must join the battle. *Gifted Child Today, 34(1),* pp. 31-34.

Furfaro, H. (2020). *Sleep problems in autism, explained.* Retrieved from https://www.spectrumnews.org/news/sleep-problems-autism-explained/

Gennarelli, D. (2022). *Twice exceptional boys: A roadmap to getting it right.* Goshen, KY: Gifted Unlimited.

Gillette, H. (2023). *Why we no longer say high or low functioning for autism.* Retrieved from https://www.healthline.com/health/autism/functioning-labels-autism

Gordon, S. (2022). *What is hyperlexia?* Retrieved from https://www.verywellfamily.com/hyperlexia-signs-diagnosis-and-treatment

Gordon, W. (2020). *What are the different types of learners?* Retrieved from https://www.teachhub.com/teaching-strategies/2020/01/what-are-the-different-types-of-learners/

Grandin, T. (2020). *The way I see it: A personal look at autism* (5 ed.). Arlington, TX: Future Horizons, Inc.

Grossberg, B. (2015). *Asperger's and adulthood: A guide to working, loving, and living with Asperger's syndrome.* Berkeley, CA: Althea Press.

Hanslow, R. (2023). *How to navigate relationships with neurodivergent and chronically ill people.* Retrieved from https://me.mashable.com/sex-dating-relationships/26164/how-to-navigate-relationships-with-neurodivergent-and-chronically-ill-people

Hatfield, S. (2022). *A rising tide lifts all boats: Creating a better work environment for all embracing neurodiversity.* Retrieved from https://www2.deloitte.com/us/en/insights/topics/talent/neurodiversity-in-the-workplace.html

Hayes, M. (2022). *Being twice exceptional.* Philadelphia, PA: Jessica Kingsley Publishers.

Healthline. (2019). *Asperger's treatment: Know your options.* Retrieved from https://www.healthline.com/health/autism/aspergers-treatment

Hebert, T. P. (2022). Supporting the emotional well-being of twice exceptional students using literature. In F. H. Piske, K. H. Collins, & K. B. Arnstein (Eds.), *Critical issues in servicing twice exceptional students* (pp. 75-83). New York, NY: Springer.

Hector, R. L. (2022). *Helping companies and organizations become truly inclusive.* Retrieved from https://www.trulyinclusiveleadership.com/

Heidel, J. A. (2021). *The 8 things autistic people do that your're misreading as a neurotypical.* Retrieved from https://www.thearticulateautistic.com/8-things-autistic-people-do-that-youre-misreading-as-a-neurotypical/

Holland, J. (2023). *What is the self-directed search?* Retrieved from https://self-directed-search.com/what-is-it/

Holland, K. (2021). *Can bipolar disorder and autism co-occur?* Retrieved from https://www.healthline.com/health/bipolar-and-autism

Jackson, L. M. (2022). *Discovering dyscalculia: One family's journey with a math disability.* Lexington, MA: GHF Press.

Jagoo, K. (2021). *Autistic individuals more likely* . Retrieved from https://www.verywellmind.com/autistic-individuals-more-likely-to-self-medicate-for-mental-health-symptoms-5193562

Jameson, T. (2020). *Neurodiversity challenges: Nonvisible, identity and disclosrue.* Retrieved from https://www.linkedin.com/pulse/neurodiversity-challenges-non-visible-identity-jameson-mba-phr/

Jameson, T., O'Malley, S., & McGovern, R. (2020). *NDGifts: Neurodiversity giving individuals full team success.* Retrieved from https://www.ndgiftsmovement.com/

Jolly, J. L., & Robins, J. H. (2022). The Marland Report: A defining moment of gifted education. *Journal for The Education of the Gifted, 45*(1).

Jones, H. (2021). *Types of social cues.* Retrieved from https://www.verywellhealth.com/social-cues-5204407

Jones, J. (2017). *Autism and respect for others.* Retrieved from https://www.autismappleskoolaid.com/autism-respect-others/

Josephson, J., Wolfgang, C., & Mehrenberg, R. (2018). Strategies for supporting students who are twice exceptional . *The Journal of Special Education Apprenticeship, 7*(2).

Kandola, A. (2021). *Levels of autism: Everything you need to know.* Retrieved from https://www.medicalnewstoday.com/articles/325106

Kay, K. (Ed.). (2000). *Uniquely gifted: Identifying and meeting the needs of twice-exceptional students.* Gilsum, NH: Afocus Publishing.

Kelly, O. (2022). *How to recognize signs of OCD in children.* Retrieved from https://www.verywellmind.com/parenting-children-with-ocd

Kessler, C. (2019). *5 tips for helping gifted children make friends.* Retrieved from https://www.sengifted.org/post/kessler-5tips

King, E. W. (2005). Addressing the social and emotional needs of twice exceptional students. *TEACHING Exeptional Children, 38*(1), 16-20.

Klein, B. (2023). *What kind of school is right for a gifted child?* Retrieved from https://www.psychologytoday.com/us/blog/twin-dilemmas/202304/what-kind-of-school-is-right-for-a-gifted-child

Krejcha, K. (2017). *To disclose or not disclose: That is the question.* Retrieved from https://www.spectrumlife.org/blog/to-disclose-or-not-disclose-

Kristenson, S. (2022). *11 benefits of developing a growth mindset in life.* Retrieved from https://www.developgoodhabits.com/benefits-growth-mindset/

Lee, L. (2019). *Meeting the challenges of twice exceptional students.* Retrieved from https://www.edutopia.org/article/meeting-challenge-twice-exceptional-students

Lovecky, D. (2011). *Can you hear the flowers sing? Issues for gifted adults.* Retrieved from https://www.sengifted.org/post/can-you-hear-the-flowers-sing-issues-for-gifted-adults

Lovering, N. (2021). *Autistic and gifted: How to support a twice exceptional child.* Retrieved from https://psychcentral.com/autism/autistic-and-gifted-supporting-the-twice-exceptional-child

Low, K. (2023). *What are the effects of impaired executive functions?* Retrieved from https://www.verywellmind.com/what-are-executive-functions-20463

Lucas, S. (2022). *10 inexpensive ways to help neurodivergent employees succeed*. Retrieved from https://www.inc.com/suzanne-lucas/disabilities-act-employees-inclusivity.html

MacAulay, K. (2022). *Potential causes and risk factors associated with autism spectrum disorder*. Retrieved from https://healthprep.com/articles/conditions/potential-causes-risk-factors-autism-spectrum-disorder/

Make Great Light. (2021). *Flourescent and LED lighting and autism spectrum disorder*. Retrieved from https://www.makegreatlight.com/about-us/blog/fluorescent-led-lighting-autism-spectrum-disorder

Malvik, C. (2020). *4 types of learning styles: How to accomodate a diverse group of students*. Retrieved from https://www.rasmussen.edu/degrees/education/blog/types-of-learning-styles/

Mao, B., Wickland, Pigozzie, & Peterson. (2010). *The third teacher: 79 ways you can use design to transform teaching and learning*. New York, NY: Abrams Publishing.

Margari, L., Giambattista, C., Margari, F., & Trerotoli, P. V. (2021). *Sex differences in autism spectrum disorders: Focus on high functioning children and adolescents*. Retrieved from https://www.frontiersin.org/articles/10.3389/fpsyt.2021.539835/full

Mayo Clinic. (2022). *Resilience: Build sills to endure hardship*. Retrieved from https://www.mayoclinic.org/tests-procedures/resilience-training/in-depth/resilience/art-20046311

Mayo Clinic. (2023-a). *Cyclothymia disorder*. Retrieved from https://www.mayoclinic.org/diseases-conditions/cyclothymia/symptoms-causes

Mayo Clinic. (2023-b). *Mindfulness exercises: See how mindfulness helps you live in the moment*. Retrieved from https://www.mayoclinic.org/healthy-lifestyle/consumer-health/in-depth/mindfulness-exercises/art-20046356

McMurdo, D. (2021). *Heron School for twice- exceptional student*. Retrieved from https://www.moabtimes.com/articles/heron-school-for-twice-exceptional-students/

Mendes, E. A. (2020). *8 behaviors to work on in my Asperger marriage*. Retrieved from https://www.psychologytoday.com/us/blog/the-heart-autism/202004/8-behaviors-work-in-my-asperger-marriage

Meyer, R. N. (2000). *Adult version Australian scale for Asperger's syndrome.* Retrieved from https://www.autismalert.org/uploads/PDF/SCREENING--ASPERGERS--Australian%20Scale%20for%20Aspergers%20in%20Adults%20-%20Draft.pdf

Mulvahill, E. (2022). *How teachers can support twice exceptional students.* Retrieved from https://www.weareteachers.com/twice-exceptional-students/

Myhill, G. (2023). *Understanding neurodiverse relationships.* Retrieved from https://www.aane.org/understanding-neurodiverse-relationships/

Nannery, S., & Nannery, L. (2021). *What to say next: Successful communication in work, life and love with autism spectrum disorder.* New York: Tiller Press.

National Association for Gifted Children. (2019). *Position statement: A definiton of giftedness that guides best practices.* Retrieved from https://nagc.org/page/position-statements

National Association for Gifted Children. (n.d.-a). *Asynchronous development.* Retrieved from https://dev.nagc.org/resources-publications/resources-parents/social-emotional-issues/asynchronous-development

National Association for Gifted Children. (n.d.-b). *Supporting twice exceptional students.* Retrieved from http://dev.nagc.org/supporting-twice-exceptional-students

National Association for Gifted Children. (n.d.-c). *What is giftedness?* Retrieved from https://nagc.org/page/what-is-giftedness

Neff, M. (2023). *Autism and sleep.* Retrieved from https://neurodivergentinsights.com/autism-infographics/autism-and-sleep

Neihart, M. (2011). *The impact of giftedness on psychological well-being.* Retrieved from https://www.sengifted.org/post/the-impact-of-giftedness-on-psychological-well-being

Niehart, M. (2000). Gifted children with Asperger's syndrome. *Gifted Child Quarterly, 44*(4), 222-230.

O'Brien, M., Assouline, S. G., Nicpon, M. F., & Colengelo, N. (2008). *The paradox of giftedness and autism: A packet of information for professionals.* Iowa City: The University of Iowa. Retrieved from http://www.iag-online.org/resources/2e_Site_Resources/ASD/Parents/2eASDmanual.pdf

Olariu, R. (2022). *What are the effects of drinking alcohol for people with autism?* Retrieved from https://spectrumdisorder.com/article/what-are-effects-drinking-alcohol-people-autism

Omer, S. B. (2020). *The discredited doctor hailed by the anti-vacine movement: Riveting biography of Andrew Wakefield is a cautinary lesson in the legacy of hubris.* Retrieved from https://www.nature.com/articles/d41586-020-02989-9

Orloff, J. (2018). *The empath's survival guide: Life strategies for sensative people.* Boulder, CO: Sounds True.

Orvis, K. (2022). *DOD: Safe hangling, storal of 'lethal means' key to suicide prevention.* Retrieved from https://www.defense.gov/News/News-Stories/Article/Article/2998717/dod-safe-handling-storage-of-lethal-means-key-to-suicide-prevention/

Oswald, T. (2020). *Dating on the spectrum: Notes for neurotypical partners.* Retrieved from https://opendoorstherapy.com/dating-on-the-autism-spectrum-notes-for-neurotypical-partners/

Parker, M. (2023). *3 relationship strategies for adults with autism.* Retrieved from https://www.psychologytoday.com/us/blog/the-heart-health-connection/202302/3-relationship-strategies-for-adults-with-autism

Phelps, V. (2022). Motivating gifted adolescents through the power of PIE: Prepardness, innovation, and effort. *Roeper Review, 44*(1), 35-48.

Phelps, V. (2023). The right fit: Finding the best educational program for your gifted child. *Parenting for High Potential, 12*(2), 2-3; 28-31.

Plutte, C., & Dashevsky, A. (2020). *Twice exceptional children: Why making friends is hard and how to support them.* Retrieved from http://growingmindspsych.com/blog/2020/02/13/twice-exceptional-children-why-making-friends-is-hard-and-how-to-support-them/

Prizant, B. M., & Meyer, T. F. (2015). *Uniquely human: A different way of seeing autism.* New York, NY: Simon & Schuster.

Prober, P. (2011). *Counseling gifted adults: A case study*. Retrieved from https://www.sengifted.org/post/counseling-gifted-adults-a-case-study

Prober, P. (2019). *Journey into your rainforest mind: A field guide for gifted adults and teens*. Eugene, OR: Luminare Press.

Pruthi, S. (2023). *Obsessive compulsive disorder (OCD)*. Retrieved from https://www.mayoclinic.org/diseases-conditions/obsessive-compulsive-disorder/symptoms-causes/syc

Psychology Today. (2023 -a). *Synesthesia*. Retrieved from https://www.psychologytoday.com/us/basics/synesthesia

Psychology Today. (2023 -b). *Neurodiversity and the benefits of autism*. Retrieved from https://www.psychologytoday.com/us/basics/autism/neurodiversity-and-the-benefits-autism

Psychology Today. (2023-c). *Growth Mindset*. Retrieved from https://www.psychologytoday.com/us/basics/growth-mindset

Quigley, C. (2023). *6 facts I wish people understood about neurodiversity*. Retrieved from https://www.texthelp.com/resources/blog/6-facts-i-wish-people-understood-about-neurodiversity/

Raising Children Network. (2022). *DSM-5-TR: Austism spectrum disorder diagnosis*. Retrieved from https://raisingchildren.net.au/autism/learning-about-autism/assessment-diagnosis/dsm-5-autism-diagnosis

Rebarbar, E. (2021). *The unexplained link between autism and substance abuse*. Retrieved from https://neuroclastic.com/the-unexplored-link-between-autism-and-substance-abuse/

Reber, D. (2018). *Differently wired*. Retrieved from https://www.ted.com/talks/deborah_reber_differently_wired

Reber, D. (2019). *Differently Wired*. New York, NY: Workman Publishing.

Reber, D., & Hayes, M. (2020). *Dr. Melanie Hayes talks about her Big Minds micro-school and educating 2e children (audio podcast episode 190)*. Retrieved from https://tiltparenting.com/2020/01/07/episode-190-dr-melanie-hayes-talks-about-her-big-minds-micro-school-and-educating-2e-children/

Reber, D., & Hayes, M. (2022). *Dr. Melanie Hayes on living your best life for twice exceptional adults (audio podcast episode #282)*. Retrieved from https://tiltparenting.com/2022/02/22/twice-exceptional-adult/

Reid, S. (2023). *Autism in adults: Recognizing the signs, living with a diagnosis*. Retrieved from https://www.helpguide.org/articles/autism-learning-disabilities/autism-in-adults.htm

Reiners, B. (2022). *How to build an inclusive workpalce environment*. Retrieved from https://builtin.com/diversity-inclusion/inclusion

Reis, S. M., & Renzulli, J. S. (2009). The gifted constitute a single homogenous group and giftedness is a way of being that stay in the person over time and experiences. *Gifted Child Quarterly, 53(4)*, 233-235.

Reis, S. M., & Susan M. Baum, E. B. (2014). An operational definition of twice exceptional learners: Implications and applications. *Gifted Child Quarterly, 58*(3), 217-230.

Reitman, H., Fizzano, p., & Reitman, R. (2014). *Aspertools: The pratical guide for understanding and embracing Asperger's, autism spectrum disorders, and neurodiversity*. Deerfield Beach, FL: Health Communications, Inc.

Renteria, Y. (2023). *Two different brains in love: Conflict resolution in neurodiverse*. Retrieved from https://www.gottman.com/blog/two-different-brains-in-love-conflict-resolution-in-neurodiverse-relationships/

Resnick, A. (2021). *Awareness and allyship: It's a new day for neurodivesity*. Retrieved from https://www.verywellmind.com/a-new-day-for-neurodivergence-5198627

Resnick, A. (2022). *What is neurodivergence and what does it mean to be neurodivergent?* Retrieved from https://www.verywellmind.com/what-is-neurodivergence-and-what-does-it-mean-to-be-neurodivergent-

Rios, C. (2022). *Understanding the different autism spectrum levels*. Retrieved from https://autismdfw.org/understanding-the-different-autism-spectrum-levels/

Rivero, L., & Tivers, E. (2018). *Tips for gifted adults with ADHD*. Retrieved from https://www.psychologytoday.com/us/blog/creative-synthesis/201802/tips-gifted-adults-adhd

Robinson, L., & Smith, M. (2023). *Surviving touch times by building resilience.* Retrieved from https://www.helpguide.org/articles/stress/surviving-tough-times.htm

Robinson, S. K. (2006). *Do schools kill creativity?* Retrieved from https://www.ted.com/talks/sir_ken_robinson_do_schools_kill_creativity

Robinson, S. N. (2023). Doctor of Clinical Psychology and Neuropsychology. (D. Gennarelli, Interviewer)

Rodilla, A. (2022). *What are the Raven Progressive Matrices? The most famous IQ test.* Retrieved from https://www.brain-testing.org/articles-intelligence/raven-progressive-matrices-iq-test

Rogers, K. B. (2002). *Re-forming gifted education: How parents and teachers can match the program to the child.* Goshen, KY: Gifted Unlimited.

Rowell, L. (2023). *Stimming: What it is and why people do it?* Retrieved from https://www.health.com/condition/anxiety/what-is-stimming

Rozsa, M. (2021). *Why autistic people tend to self-medicate at much higher rates.* Retrieved from https://www.salon.com/2021/07/07/new-study-explores-the-link-between-autism-and-substance-abuse/

Rsamussen, C. H. (2023). *Sensory integration in autism spectrum disorders.* Retrieved from https://autism.org/sensory-integration/

Rudy, L. J. (2022). *How speech patterns in autism can affect communication.* Retrieved from https://www.verywellhealth.com/autistic-speech-and-prosody-259883

Saline, S. (2023). *Tips for neurodiverse social communication: Engaging in more enjoyable and effective conversations.* Retrieved from https://drsharonsaline.com/2021/12/08/tips-for-neurodiverse-social-communication-engaging-in-more-enjoyable-and-effective-conversations/

Sanchez, D. (2022). *What is twice exceptional (2e)?* Retrieved from https://www.2eminds.com/twice-exceptional-2e/

Scaturro, C. (2015). *Life as a work in progress.* Retrieved from https://medium.com/personal-growth/life-as-a-work-in-progress-e5e62186186b

Schenkman, L. (2020). *Motor difficulties in autism, explained.* Retrieved from https://www.spectrumnews.org/news/motor-difficulties-in-autism-explained/

Schiff, J. L. (2016). *5 ways to keep employees in the loop.* Retrieved from https://www.cio.com/article/240321/5-ways-to-keep-employees-in-the-loop.html

SENG. (2023). *What is SENG.* Retrieved from https://www.sengifted.org/about

Shore, S. M. (n.d.). *Self-advocacy.* Retrieved from https://www.autism.org/self-advocacy/

Silberman, S. (2015). *Nerotribes: The legacy of autism and the future of neurodiversity.* New York, NY: Avery Publishers.

Silverman, L. (2013). *Giftedness 101.* New York, NY: Springer Publishing.

Silverman, S., Kenworthy, L., & Weinfeld, R. (2014). *School success for kids with high functioning autism.* Waco, TX: Prufrock Press.

Simmons, K. (2018). *The official autism manual 101: Everything you need to know about autism from experts who know and care.* (J. Alderson, Ed.) New York, NY: Skyhorse Publishing.

Sinclair, J. W. (2020-a). *Autism exploitation: How to spot it and make it stop.* Retrieved from https://autisticandunapologetic.com/2020/02/23/autism-exploitation-how-to-spot-it-and-how-to-make-it-stop/

Sinclair, J. W. (2020-b). *Autism and alcohol: The effects of drinking on the spectrum.* Retrieved from https://autisticandunapologetic.com/2020/10/24/autism-alcohol-the-effects-of-drinking-on-the-spectrum/

Sinclair, J. W. (2020-c). *Autism facial expressions: How autistic people express emotions diferently.* Retrieved from https://autisticandunapologetic.com/2020/09/19/autism-facial-expressions-how-autistic-people-express-emotions-differently/

Single Care Team. (2023). *Prescriptoin drug statistics 2023.* Retrieved from https://www.singlecare.com/blog/news/prescription-drug-statistics/

Skolnick, J. F. (2017). *Success for gifted and 2e adults.* Retrieved from https://www.withunderstandingcomescalm.com/success-gifted-2e-adults/

Sruthi, M. (2023). *What are the 4 main types of dyslexia.* Retrieved from https://www.medicinenet.com/what_are_the_4_types_of_dyslexia/article.htm

Stanborough, R. J. (2021). *Autism maksing: To blend or not to blend.* Retrieved from https://www.healthline.com/health/autism/autism-masking

Strategic Psychology. (N.D.). *What is the WAIS-IV?* Retrieved from https://strategicpsychology.com.au/wais/

Summer, J., & Adavadkar, P. (2023). *Autism and sleep.* Retrieved from https://www.sleepfoundation.org/physical-health/autism-and-sleep

Sunderland, M. (2018). *What parents can learn from the story of Gillian Lynne.* Retrieved from https://homeschoolingwithdyslexia.com/gillian-lynne/

Tallo. (2020). *6 companies with neurodiversity recruitment programs.* Retrieved from https://tallo.com/adult-learners/neurodiversity-recruitment/

Taylor, L. (2022). *Communication styles, counseling, and neurodiversity.* Retrieved from https://www.psychologytoday.com/us/blog/the-neurodivergent-therapist/202201/communication-styles-counseling-and-neurodiversity

Tetreault, N. A. (2017). *Brain Fingerprints.* Retrieved from https://www.sengifted.org/post/brain-fingerprints

The Autism Society. (2023). *Autism society: Who we are.* Retrieved from https://autismsociety.org/who-we-are/

The Jonus School. (2022). *5 learning differences: Myths and the facts to set them straight.* Retrieved from https://thejanusschool.org/learning-differences-5-myths/

The Pennsylvania State University. (2013). *Gender stereotyping and women in leadership roles.* Retrieved from https://sites.psu.edu/leadership/2013/07/02/gender-stereotyping-and-women-in-leadership-roles/

The Understood Team. (2023). *The difference between IEP's and 504 plans.* Retrieved from https://www.understood.org/en/articles/the-difference-between-ieps-and-504-plans

The Write Reflection. (2023). *How to talk to a neurodiverse person.* Retrieved from https://www.linkedin.com/pulse/how-talk-neurodiverse-person-the-write-reflection/

Tinsley, M., & Hendrickx, S. (2008). *Asperger syndrome and alcohol: Drinking to cope?* Philadelphia: Jessica Kingsley Publishers.

Tomlinson, C. A. (2017). *How to differentiate instruciton in academically diverse classrooms* (3rd ed.). Alexandria, VA: ASCD.

Trail, B. A. (2006). *15 year review: Parenting twice exceptional children through frustration to success.* Retrieved from https://www. davidsongifted.org/gifted-blog/15-year-review-parenting-twice-exceptional-children-through-frustration-to-success/

Trail, B. A. (2022). *Twice exceptional gifted children: Understanding, teaching and counseling students.* New York, NY: Routlege Publishing.

Troyer, A. K. (2016). *The health benefits of socializing: Four reasons to connect with friends.* Retrieved from https://www.psychologytoday. com/us/blog/living-mild-cognitive-impairment/201606/ the-health-benefits-socializing

Tucker, S. B. (2022). *Embracing neurodiversity.* Retrieved from https:// blog.actionbehavior.com/neurodiversity

Turner, P. (2020). *Can you describe the characteristics of gifted adults?* Retrieved from https://turnerpsychologycalgary.com/giftedness/ characteristics-of-gifted-adults/

Understood. (2023). *ADA accommodations at work: What you need to know.* Retrieved from https://www.understood.org/en/articles/ ada-accommodations-at-work

United States Department of Defense. (2022). *Department of Defense releases the annual report on suicide in the military calendar year 2021.* Retrieved from https://www.defense.gov/News/Releases/ Release/Article/3193806/department-of-defense-releases-the-annual-report-on-suicide-in-the-military-cal/

United States Department of Education. (n.d.). *Every student succeeds act (ESSA).* Retrieved from https://www.ed.gov/ESSA/

United States Department of Education. (N.D.). *IDEA: Individuals with disabilities education act.* Retrieved from https://sites.ed.gov/idea/

United States Department of Labor. (2023-a). *Accommodations.* Retrieved from https://www.dol.gov/agencies/odep/program-areas/employers/ accommodations

United States Department of Labor. (2023-b). *U. S. Department of Labor announces report finding nearly half of accomodatins for disabled workers have not cost.* Retrieved from https://www.dol.gov/ newsroom/releases/odep/odep20230504

United States Equal Employment Opportunity Commission. (2023). Retrieved from https://www.eeoc.gov/

UPMC Children's Community Pediatrics. (N.D.). *Managing stress of the elementary to middle school transition.* Retrieved from https://www.childrenspeds.com/health-resources/school-age/elementary-middle-school-transition

Vance, T. (2018). *Autism and friendship: 30 ways to be a friend to a person on the spectrum.* Retrieved from https://neuroclastic.com/autism-and-friendships-part-2-30-ways-to-be-a-friend-to-a-person-on-the-spectrum/

Wallis, C. (2022). *Autism treatment shifts away from fixing the conditon.* Retrieved from https://www.scientificamerican.com/article/autism-treatment-shifts-away-from-fixing-the-condition/

Warburton, N. (2023). *Do you see a duck or a rabbit: Just what is aspect perception?* Retrieved from https://aeon.co/ideas/do-you-see-a-duck-or-a-rabbit-just-what-is-aspect-perception

Watson, K. (2018). *What is synesthesia?* . Retrieved from https://www.healthline.com/health/synesthesia

Webb, J. T., Amend, E. R., Beljan, P., Webb, N. E., Kuzujanakis, N., Olenchak, F. R., & Goerss, J. (2016). *Misdiagnosis and dual diagnosis of gifted children and adults: ADHD, biploar, OCD, Asperger's, depression, and other disorders.* Goshen, KY: Gifted Unlimited.

Weintraub, K. (2023). *New algorithm detects autism in infants: How might that change care?* . Retrieved from https://www.usatoday.com/story/news/health/2023/02/08/autism-signs-early-life-study/

Wessling, S. (2012). *How other parents add to the challenge of raising gifted kids.* Retrieved from https://sukiwessling.com/2012/07/how-other-parents-add-to-the-challenge-of-raising-gifted-kids/

West, T. (1997). *In the mind's eye.* Amherst, NY: Prometheus.

*Who we are.* (2024). Retrieved from Disability: IN: https://disabilityin.org/who-we-are/about/

Wilson, J. (2014). *What your IQ score doesn't tell you.* Retrieved from https://www.cnn.com/2014/02/19/health/iq-score-meaning/index.html

Winebrenner, S., & Bruelles, D. (2018). *Teaching gifted kids in today's classroom: Strategies and techniques every teacher can use* (4th ed.). Minneapolis, MN: Free Spirit.

Winfrey, O. (2014). *What i know for sure.* New York, NY: Flatiron Books.

Workability Systems. (2020). *Grooved pegboard test.* Retrieved from https://workabilitysystems.com/wp-content/uploads/2021/06/7-Grooved-Pegboard-Test.pdf

World Population Review. (2023). *Drug use by country: 2023.* Retrieved from https://worldpopulationreview.com/country-rankings/drug-use-by-country

Young, E. (2013). *Intelligenc testing: Accurate or extremely biased?* Retrieved from http://www.theneuroethicsblog.com/2013/09/intelligence-testing-accurate-or.html

Zirkel, P. A. (2016). Legal update of gifted education. *Journal of the education of the gifted, 39*(4), 315-337.

# Endnotes

1.. Bauman & Frueh, 2021

2. Ibid

3. Ibid

4. Resnick, 2022

5. Ibid

6. Ibid

7. Ibid

8. American Psychiatric Association, 2013

9. Center for Disease Control and Prevention, 2022 (-a)

10. Cumo, 2019

11. Grandin, 2020

12. Silberman, 2015

13. Ibid

14. Ibid

15. Ibid

16. Currie, 2022

17. Ibid; Also see Google Trends, 2022

18. Grandin, 2020

19. Currie, 2022

20. Webb, Amend, Beljan, Webb, Kuzujanakis, Olenchak, & Goerss, 2016

21. Rudy, 2022

22. Reid, 2022

23. Wood-Sinclair, 2022

24. Jones, 2021

25. Ibid

26. Neihart, 2000

27. Webb, et al., 2016

28. Anderson, 2021; Also see Orloff, 2018

29. Eckerd, 2021

30. Ibid

31. Psychology Today, n.d.

32. Low, 2023

33. Rasmussen, n.d.

34. Ibid

35. Grandin, 2020

36. Rasmussen, n.d.

37. Brain Balance Centers, 2023

38. Schenkman, 2020

39. Rowello, 2020

40. Davis, 2023

41. Ibid

42. Stanborough, 2021

43. Ibid

44. Cage & Whitman, 2019

45. Cage, Di Monaco, & Newell, 2018

46. Bargiela, Steward, & Mandy, 2016

47. Reitman, Fizzano, & Reitman, 2014

48. Reid, 2022

49. Dorsey, 2023

50. Reitman et al., 2014

51. Ibid

52. Furfaro, 2020

53. Ibid; Also see Chen, 2015

54. Furfaro, 2020

55. Ibid

56. Tetreault, 2017

57. Summer & Adavadkar, 2023

58. Cumo, 2019

59. For more information about ASD and gender differences see *Sex differences in autism spectrum disorder: Focus on high functioning children and adolescents*, by Margari, Giambattista, Margari, Ventrua, & Trerotoli (2021)

60. Grandin, 2022

61. Butler, 2017

62. Reid, 2022

63. Rudy, 2022

64. Center for Disease Control and Prevention, 2022 (-b)

65. Center for Disease Control and Prevention, 2022 (-c)

66. Center for Disease Control and Prevention, 2022 (-b)

67. Center for Disease Control and Prevention, 2022 (-d)

68. Center for Disease Control and Prevention, 2022 (-b)

69. Ibid

70. ABA Centers for America, 2021

71. Center for Disease Control and Prevention, 2022 (-b)

72. Center for Disease Control and Prevention, 2022 (-f)

73. Baron-Cohen, 2018

74. Center for Disease Control and Prevention, 2022 (-g)

75. Ibid

76. Ibid

77. MacAulay, 2022

78. Ibid

79. Ibid

80. Baron-Cohen, 2018

81. MacAulay, 2022; Also see the article: *The discredited doctor hailed by the anti-vaccine movement* by Omer (2020)

82. MacAulay, 2022

83. Drake, 2021

84. The Center for Disease Control and Prevention, 2022 (-h)

85. The Center for Disease Control and Prevention, 2022, (-i); See *full 2021 Community Report on Autism* at: https://www. cdc.gov/ncbddd/autism/addm-community-report/documents/ ADDM-Community-Autism-Report-12-2-021_Final-H.pdf

86. The Center for Disease Control and Prevention, 2022 (-i)

87. The Center for Disease Control and Prevention, 2022 (-j)

88. The Center for Disease Control and Prevention, 2022 (-i)

89. The Center for Disease Control and Prevention, 2022 (-k)

90. Gillette, 2023

91. See *Asperger's treatment: Know your options*, 2019

92. See *The autism experience: Understanding autism*, 2022

93. Bel Marra Health, 2015

94. Rios, 2022

95. Ibid

96. Raising Children Network, 2022

97. Ibid

98. Kandola, 2021

99. Ibid

100. Rios, 2022

101. United States Department of Labor, n.d.

102. Ibid

103. Watson, 2018

104. Norton, 2013

105. Ibid

106. Ibid

107. Psychology Today, 2022 (-a)

108. Watson, 2018

109. Elise, 2016

110. Davidson Institute, 2022

111. National Association for Gifted Children, n.d (-c)

112. Lovering, 2021

113. Ibid

114. Amend, Beaver-Gavin, Schular, & Beights, 2008

115. Amend, Beaver-Gavin, Schular, & Beights, 2009

116. Webb, et al., 2016

117. National Association for Gifted Children, n.d. (-a)

118. Webb, et al., 2016

119. Ibid

120. Ibid

121. Ibid

122. Ibid

123. Davidson Institute, 2022

124. Webb, et al., 2016

125. Davidson Institute, 2022

126. Ibid

127. Sanchez, 2022; For more information see *Twice exceptional gifted children: Understanding, teaching, and counseling gifted students*, by Trail (2022); Also see *Supporting twice exceptional students*, by National Association for Gifted Children, n. d (-b)

128. Arky, 2022

129. Assouline, Nicpon, Colengelo, & O'Brien, 2008

130. Cherry, 2022 (-a)

131. Ibid

132. Wilson, 2014

133. Rodilla, 2022

134. Young, 2013

135. Ibid

136. Ibid

137. Young, 2013

138. Ibid

139. Bartmess, 2018

140. Assouline, et al., 2008

141. Ibid

142. Gennarelli, 2022

143. Prober, 2019

144. Lovecky, 2011

145. Eby, 2022

146. Turner, 2020

147. Ibid; Also for more information on gifted adults see *Giftedness 101* by Silverman, 2013

148. Prober, 2011

149. The Pennsylvania State University, 2013

150. My Asperger Child, 2010

151. Endlich, 2020

152. Muinos, 2022

153. Assouline et al., 2008

154. Ibid

155. For more information on misunderstanding people with Asperger's see: https://www.thearticulateautistic.com/8-things-autistic-people-do-that-youre-misreading-as-a-neurotypical/, by Heidel (2021)

156. Cognetica, 2022

157. Soorya, Carpenter, & El-Ghoroury, 2017

158. Arkansas State University, 2016

159. United States Department of Education, n.d.

160. Gennarelli, 2022

161. Ibid

162. Holland, 2021

163. Ibid

164. Ibid

165. Ibid

166. Mayo Clinic, 2023(-b)

167. Webb, et. al., 2016

168. Silverman, Kenworthy, & Weinfeld, 2014

169. For more information on the WAIS-IV, see: https://strategic-psychology.com.au/wais/

170. For more information on the Grooved Pegboard Test see: https://workabilitysystems.com/wp-content/uploads/2021/06/7-Grooved-Pegboard-Test.pdf

171. For information on the adult version of the Australian Scale for Asperger's syndrome see: https://www.autismalert.org/uploads/PDF/SCREENING--ASPERGERS--Australian%20Scale%20for%20Aspergers%20in%20Adults%20-%20Draft.pdf

172. Bartmess, 2018

173. Ibid

174. Webb, et. al., 2016

175. Ibid

176. Ibid

177. Gennarelli, 2022

178. For more information on parenting styles see: https://www.webmd.com/parenting/features/parenting-styles by Brody, 2021

179. Grandin, 2020

180. Ibid

181. Ibid

182. Ibid

183. Jones, 2017

184. Melmed & Marsh, 2020

185. American Academy of Pediatrics, 2019

186. Ibid

187. Weintraub, 2023

188. Ibid

189. Ibid

190. American Academy of Pediatrics, 2019

191. Covington, 2022

192. Epstein, 2022

193. Malvik, 2020

194. Gordon, 2020

195. Ibid

196. Butnik, 2022

197. Braaten, 2023

198. Ibid

199. Gordon, 2022

200. Sruthi, 2022

201. Ansari, 2023; For more information about dyscalculia see Discovering dyscalculia: One family's journey with a math disability by Jackson (2022)

202. Ibid

203. Kelly, 2022

204. Ibid

205. Ibid

206. Ibid

207. Ibid

208. Schenkman, 2020

209. UPMC Children's Community Pediatrics, n.d.

210. Fleming, 2020

211. Davidson Academy, 2021

212. Olariu, 2022

213. Grossberg, 2015

214. Ibid

215. Sinclair, 2020

216. Nannery, 2021

217. Sinclair, 2020

218. Ibid

219. Rebarbar, 2021

220. Ibid

221. Ibid

222. Ibid; For more information see: *Asperger syndrome and alcohol: Drinking to cope* by Tinsley & Hendrickx (2008)

223. SingleCare, 2023

224. Ibid

225. World Population Review, 2023

226. Rozsa, 2021

227. Jagoo, 2021

228. Ibid

229. Ibid

230. Center for Disease Control and Prevention, 2022 (-e)

231. Hatfield, 2022

232. Ibid

233. Who We Are, 2024

234. Disability Equality Index, 2024

235. CEOs are: IN, 2024

236. Feit, 2018; Also see Eustachewich, 2019

237. Ibid

238. Hector, 2022

239. Hatfield, 2022

240. Bauman & Frueh, 2021

241. Ibid

242. Robinson, 2022

243. Holland, 2023

244. Grossberg, 2015

245. Ibid

246. Zavikon, 2021

247. Lee, n.d.

248. Ibid

249. Jameson, 2020

250. Shore, 2023

251.  Gennarelli, 2022

252.  Nannery, et al., 2021

253.  Renteria, 2023

254.  Ibid

255.  Nannery, et al., 2021

256.  Ibid

257.  Parker, 2023

258.  U.S. Department of Defense, 2022

259.  For more information see: *DOD: Safe handling, storage of 'lethal means' key to suicide prevention* by Orvis (2022)

260.  Ibid

261.  Grossberg, 2015

262.  Cherry, 2022 (-b)

263.  Troyer, 2016

264.  Vance, 2018

265.  Parker, 2023

266.  Ibid

267.  Grossberg, 2015

268.  Krejcha, 2017

269.  Vance, 2018

270.  Kessler, 2018

271.  Ibid

272.  Dasjevsly & Plutte, 2020

273.  Ibid

274.  Ibid

275.  Ibid

276.  Oswald, 2020

277.  Mendes, 2020

278.  Oswald, 2020

279.  Renteria, 2023

280.  Hanslow, 2023

281. Ibid

282. Myhill, 2023

283. Ibid

284. Ibid

285. Warburton, 2023; Also see Myhill, 2023

286. Myhill, 2023

287. Hanslow, 2023

288. Ibid

289. Myhill, 2023

290. Renteria, 2023

291. Ibid

292. Evans & Attwood, 2018

293. Renteria, 2023

294. Ibid

295. Hanslowe, 2023

296. Ibid

297. Myhill, 2023

298. Ibid

299. Ibid

300. Mendes, 2020

301. Ibid

302. Winfrey, 2014

303. Skolnick, 2017

304. Rivero, 2018

305. Bailey, 2022

306. Skolnick, 2017

307. Wallis, 2022

308. Ibid

309. Simmons, 2018

310. Psychology Today, 2023 (-b)

311. Ibid

312. Brain Wave Watch, 2022

313. Rivero & Tivers, 2018

314. Ibid

315. Ibid

316. Ibid

317. SENG, 2023

318. Reitman, 2014

319. Mayo Clinic, 2023 (-b)

320. Ibid

321. Ibid

322. Taylor, 2022

323. Better Help, 2023

324. Saline, 2023

325. Cherry, 2023 (-a)

326. Ibid

327. Tucker, 2022

328. Ibid

329. Resnick, 2023

330. Quigley, 2023

331. Ibid

332. Dweck, 2016

333. Psychology Today, 2023

334. Kristenson, 2022

335. Ibid

336. Autism Society of America, 2023

337. Feder, 2021

338. Hayes & Reber, 2022

339. United States Department of Labor, 2023

340. Ibid

341. Hector, 2023

342. Reiners, 2022

343. Hayes, 2022

344. Ibid

345. Quigley, 2023

346. Understood Team, 2023

347. Lucas, 2022

348. Make Great Light, 2021

349. Schiff, 2016

350. Scaturro, 2025

351. Make Great Light, 2021

352. Mayo Clinic, 2023

353. Robinson & Smith, 2023

354. Ibid

355. Ibid

356. Mulvahill, 2022

357. United States Department of Education, n.d.

358. Lee, 2019

359. Ibid

360. Blustain, 2019

361. Neihart, 2000

362. Ibid

363. Klein, 2023

364. Reber, 2019

365. Ibid

366. Gennarelli, 2022

367. Ibid

368. The Jonus School, 2022

369. Gennarelli, 2022

370. Neihart, 2011

371. Reis & Renzulli, 2009

372. Jolly & Robins, 2022

373. See Beljan, 2011; Davis, 2010; Ford, 2011; Webb, et al., 2016

374. Anas, 2022

375. Ibid

376. Grandin, 2020

377. Ibid

378. Bracamonte, 2010

379. Ibid

380. Reber, 2019

381. Reitman, et al., 2014

382. Dweck, 2016

383. King, 2005

384. Reis, Baum, & Burke, 2014

385. Baum & Olenchak, 2002

386. Josephson, Wolfgang, & Mehrenberg, 2018

387. Gennarelli, 2022

388. Information about these educational options and how to implement them can be found in Karen Rogers (2002) book, *Re-Forming Gifted Education: How Parents and Teachers Can Match the Program with the Child*, in Winebrenner and Brulles (2012), *Teaching Gifted Kids in Today's Classroom: Strategies and Techniques Every Teacher Can Use*, 3rd ed., and in Brulles, Brown, and Winebrenner (2016), *Differentiated Lessons for Every Learner: Standards-Based Activities and Extensions for Middle School.*

389. Josephson, et al., 2018

390. Reis, et al., 2014

391. Bracamonte, 2010

392. Adams, 2017

393. See further information about IEP's and 504 Plans by The Understood Team at: https://www.understood.org/en/articles/the-difference-between-ieps-and-504-plans

394. Zirkel, 2016

395. Josephson, et al., 2018

396. Wessling, 2012

397. Josephson, et al., 2018

398. Trail, 2006

399. Gennarelli, 2022

400. Trail, 2006; See also Kay, 2000

401. Gennarelli, 2022

402. Phelps, 2023

403. Ibid

404. Ibid

405. Ibid

406. de Bono, n.d.

407. Maua & OWP/P Architects, 2010

408. Phelps, 2022

409. Reber & Hayes, 2020

410. For more information on differentiation, see *How to Differentiate Instruction in Academically Diverse Classrooms.* (2017, 3rd ed.) by Tomlinson

411. See Bridges Academy at http://losangeles.bridges.edu/approach.html

412. McMurdo, 2021

413. Prizant, 2015

414. Sunderland, 2018; Also see "Do schools kill creativity?" by Robinson, 2006

415. Brown, 2022; Also see: *The mind's eye* by West, 1997

# About the Authors

**John Truitt** was diagnosed as twice-exceptional, gifted with autism spectrum disorder, dyslexia, and other differences, at 45. After a career spent in medical, dental, and medical device start-ups, as owner and Executive Manager, he created *On the Spectrum Foundation.* He is the chief philanthropy officer of this 501 (c) 3 non-profit organization that is dedicated to advocating for 2e and neurodiverse talents through self-discovery and social education. He now speaks professionally and offers life coaching support for 2e adults and teens with ASD and learning differences.

John is a United States citizen and an Australian permanent resident. The latter allows him to live, work, and travel back and forth to Australia. He lives in Durango, Colorado with his wife Ashley and his dog Cassidy. He also teaches twice-exceptional teens at the Heron School in Moab, Utah, and he is starting another business venture that utilizes his strengths and talents.

**Deborah (Deb) Gennarelli** obtained her elementary education degree from East Carolina University. After several years teaching K-5, she trained to become a K-12 gifted intervention specialist, obtaining a master's degree in gifted education from Kent State University.

Deborah has 40 years of experience as an educator working in public and private settings with diverse student populations in three states. Her efforts to be the best teacher possible earned her Teacher of the Year awards in three different school districts. As a gifted intervention specialist, Deborah developed gifted education programs in several districts. These important programs ensured smart students were offered a variety of options to meet their needs in school, including curriculum compacting, mentorships, and acceleration.

Now as a gifted education consultant with her company Smart Strategies LLC, Deborah provides professional development to schools on topics relevant to gifted/2e children and she consults with parents about their needs raising these special students. She also speaks nationally about identification and support of gifted and 2e children.

Deborah's book *Twice Exceptional Boys: A Roadmap to Getting it Right* was published by Gifted Unlimited in 2022.

Deborah lives in Northeast Ohio with her husband Bob. They enjoy spending time with their daughter Nicole, son-in-law Noah, and their delightful grandson Milo.

Printed in the USA
CPSIA information can be obtained
at www.ICGtesting.com
JSHW012151260724
67084JS00003B/4

9 781953 360380